WHAT IS OF FAITH

AS TO

EVERLASTING PUNISHMENT?

WHAT IS OF FAITH

AS TO

EVERLASTING PUNISHMENT?

IN REPLY TO DR. FARRAR'S CHALLENGE

IN HIS 'ETERNAL HOPE,' 1879.

BY THE

REV. E. B. PUSEY, D.D.,

REGIUS PROFESSOR OF HEBREW, CANON OF CHRIST CHURCH.

THIRD EDITION.

WIPF & STOCK · Eugene, Oregon

Wipf and Stock Publishers
199 W 8th Ave, Suite 3
Eugene, OR 97401

What is of Faith as to Everlasting Punishment?, Third Edition
In Reply to Dr. Farrar's Challenge in his 'Eternal Hope,' 1879
By Pusey, E. B.
Softcover ISBN-13: 978-1-6667-3491-1
Hardcover ISBN-13: 978-1-6667-9142-6
eBook ISBN-13: 978-1-6667-9143-3
Publication date 9/14/2021
Previously published by James Parker & Co., 1880

This edition is a scanned facsimile of
the original edition published in 1880.

ADVERTISEMENT TO THE THIRD EDITION.

THE following book, in as far as it is not supplementary to a Sermon (now of old date) on Everlasting Punishment, was concentrated on answering a book of unhappy popularity, Dr. Farrar's 'Eternal Hope.' It did not occur to me to be necessary to state anything as to my own personal belief upon any subject, which had not been ruled to be matter of faith. My one object was to remove, as far as I might be enabled, doubts or perplexities, which that book, I was told, was widely occasioning. It came to me from different quarters, that the young, among whom my lot had been cast as a teacher, were asking, 'What of Dr. Farrar's book?' People, living in the world, who read the book because it was talked about, but had not the information which would enable them to appreciate the arguments used, were asking, 'What of Dr. Farrar's book?' and inferring that, since no one had set himself expressly to answer it, it was unanswerable. It lay on drawing-room tables, as if the subject of the everlasting doom of those who reject God to the end, or of God's awful Attribute of Holiness, were to take their turns with any passing subject of the day. I had not then heard of some in London who expressly alleged that what Dr. Farrar said 'made sin more reasonable.'

Dr. Farrar's belief is happily better than that of his book. In his book unhappily he contented himself with stating that he was not an Universalist, while he did not observe that all the arguments which he used were Universalist, extending even to what he intended to exclude from his consideration, the restoration of Satan. The book, until it is withdrawn, notwithstanding its author's declaration of his personal belief, must remain, as it is, an inconsistent, empassioned pleading for 'Universalism.' It must, as far as it has influence, teach the Universalism which its writer does not believe.

I wished then in the first instance to mitigate the repugnance of intellectual, thoughtful minds, who had been carried away to or encouraged in the disbelief of Hell, by an appeal to first principles of nature or of faith. To this end, I set down those twelve propositions as to man's free-will and the care of Almighty God to save us from losing Himself through its abuse, which Dr. Farrar says that 'with scarcely the smallest verbal alteration I could accept.'

But I see that, having no occasion to speak of myself, I have left room for two misapprehensions as to my own belief.

1. With regard to the number of the lost, I did not mean to lay down anything; but, following one opinion accepted by earnest, devout, Catholics, to insist upon our absolute ignorance about it. I leave all things blindly in His Hand Who became Man, to redeem us from Hell, and Who will come to be our Judge.

But while I have dwelt on our ignorance of what God may do for the soul even in the last hour of its trial, I think that *they* are least likely to be reached by His grace *then*, who have delayed their repentance in view of it. Apart from the possibility that there may be no deathbed, such persons would but too probably have been preparing their souls for final impenitence.

Among the six sins which were accounted of old to be forerunners of the sin against the Holy Ghost, three were, "ᵃ presumption of God's mercy;' 'obstinacy in sin;' and 'impenitence.' The only wish of those who wilfully delay repentance is too probably to escape the pain of repentance here and of hell hereafter.

I should think that those called 'young Arabs' or the victims of man's passions and their own vanity, more likely to be visited by such overflow of the grace of God than our worldly educated rich.

But in dwelling upon these hopes I feel that I must take care not to lessen the sense of the awefulness of the Day of Judgement, which *they* felt, to whom 'the four last things,' Death, Judgement, Heaven, Hell, were subjects of daily meditation. We know that it will be a great reversal of the judgements formed here. Our Judge has said, "ᵇ The last shall be first, and the first last;" "ᶜ Whosoever exalteth himself shall be abased." He has pictured to us the great surprise, which many shall feel, when they find themselves shut out[d]; that many shall suppose that they are His, to whom He shall say, "ᵉ I never knew you: depart from Me, all ye workers of iniquity." He has warned us that they must *strive*[f] here who hope to enter in there, for that the *seeking* in that Day will be too late. He has pictured to us that one and all of those on the left hand will disclaim not having shewn mercy to Him[g] their Judge. How many in our mammon-loving nation think of it? S. Chrysostom says that among so many tens of thousands in Constantinople, you would not find one hundred in the state of salvation[h], and he doubts whether so many. What would he think of our pleasure-loving, mammon-worshipping, poor-forgetting London? Looking on man's side, Massil-

---

ᵃ The other three were, 'despair of salvation;' 'impugning known truth,' 'envy at another's grace.' See the Greek devotions of Bp. Andrews; Litany at the end   Tracts for the Times no. 88. p 80.   ᵇ S. Matt. xx 16.
ᶜ S. Luke xiv. 11.   ᵈ S Matt xxv. 11. S. Luke xiii. 25—27.   ᵉ S. Matt. vii. 23.
ᶠ S. Luke xiii 24   ᵍ S. Matt. xxv. 44.
ʰ οἱ σωζόμενοι S. Chrys. Hom. xxiv. on the Acts n. 4. p. 352

lon, in the dissolute France which was ripening for the French Revolution, after counting among the lost those who did not will to be converted; those who would, but delayed; those who relapsed after every conversion; those who believed that they need no conversion; burst out into the terrible appeal, 'O God, where are Thine elect?' An eloquent French preacher in view of his Sermon, enumerating all which God has done and does for our salvation, burst out into the triumphant appeal, 'O Satan, where are thine elect?' On man's side there is such thick darkness: on God's side all so bright, glowing with His love, except the lightnings of His judgements, which flash through the clouds which hide Him, the temporal judgements annexed to sin as the earnest of the eternal, but often in God's mercy eliciting repentance which may avert them. See we to it, that while we are disputing about the nature of God's judgements, we do not incur them by losing out of sight how, by His mercy, we may escape them."

'If,' says Lacordaire [1], in conclusion of a conference in which he took the more hopeful side, 'if there were only the tenth of the human race, who fell into the snares of hell, would it not be enough to alarm us, and to set each of us, in S. Paul's words, [k] *to work out our own salvation with fear and trembling?*'

'The fear of hell,' it has been often said, 'peoples heaven.' Then, by not preaching the peril of losing God for ever, we should have been the occasion that some should lose it, but that the Church so often in our Lessons repeated to us our Lord's words, and echoed them in the comprehensive Athanasian Creed; had pressed upon us, Lent by Lent, that 'it is a fearful thing to fall into the hands of the living God,' and 'the terrible voice of most just judgement, which shall be pronounced upon' impenitent sinners, 'when it

[1] Conférence 71. end   [k] Phil. ii. 12.

shall be said unto them, Go, ye cursed, into the everlasting fire, which is prepared for the devil and his angels;' had taught us, at least, week by week to pray, 'From Thy wrath and from everlasting damnation, Good Lord, deliver us;' and in the sight of death, put into our mouths the piercing cry, 'O holy and most merciful Saviour, deliver us not into the bitter pains of eternal death.'

Faber says, in his glowing way, '[1] We cannot doubt but that hell has sent into heaven more than half as many souls as it contains itself.' Such sayings would scare us, for not having preached it more, but that one hopes that God's Holy Spirit has repeated our Lord's words and the faith of the Church within to hearts, to whom we have not spoken His truth.

2. The 'everlasting fire,' is, from the very first, with very few notable exceptions, so uniformly spoken of by those who speak of future punishment at all, that I myself believe it literally, although those who do not receive it are free not to receive it. The Church, which has laid down eternity of punishment to be matter of Faith, has not laid down the material character of the punishment.

I would only now add, that for pious minds a simple argument [m] which I did not dwell upon at first, will, I think, overrule all the difficulties which may be raised to the doctrine. Even men who would say, 'I would rather believe S. Matthew wrong than such a doctrine true,' would be shocked at the thought, if, for the name of S. Matthew, there had to be substituted the Name of our Redeemer. And yet if we know anything at all, we know that the doctrine of Everlasting Punishment was taught by Him Who died to save us from it.

CHRIST CHURCH,
   August, 1880.

[1] The Creator and the creature p. 314.
[m] It has been dwelt upon in pp 46—48 ed. 2, and 3.

CONTENTS.

	Page
Dr. Farrar's Appeal.	1
Conversion of a soul by the thought of the hate in hell.	3
Would not Heaven be to Satan the worse hell?	4
Four 'common opinions' as to hell, which Dr. Farrar requires to be repudiated.	5, 6
Extract from a letter of Card. Newman to Professor Plumptre.	6
i. No ground for believing that the majority of mankind are lost.	7
God enlightens all, and judges each, as that light is used.	8
ii. No ground to lay down, who dies wholly out of grace.	12
God parts with none, who do not deliberately and finally reject Him.	14
God's mercies in death unfathomable Ravignan.	16
iii. The belief insisted upon by Dr. Farrar, that the pain of loss, far more than any pain of sense, is the essence of the sufferings of the lost, is already accepted by all.	18
Material fire no matter of faith in East or West.	20, 21
Summary of preceding—Free-will essential to the dignity of man and his free love of God: God's manifold provisions to protect our free-will against our abuse of it.	22
Dr. Farrar rejects Universalism.	25
One only difficulty, Why did God create free-agents?	28
Inconsistency of Universalists, who do not assume the salvation of Satan.	29
Passages of Holy Scripture alleged by Dr. Farrar.	
1) 1 Cor. xv. 20-28.	32
2) Acts iii. 21.	36
3) Rom. xiv. 9.	37
4) 1 Cor. xv. 22.	ib.
i. The words, αἰώνιος, οἱ αἰώνες, always used of eternity in the New Testament.	38—45

	Page
The belief in the eternity of punishment among Christians generally was very mainly rested upon the word αἰώνιος, but our Lord being God and Man, must have known when He used it, how it would be understood.	46
Those who deny eternal punishment, mostly deny other truth.	47
ii. Dr. Farrar's '*palmary argument*,' ' the Jews in our Lord's day understood by Gehenna, a punishment for 12 months; did not believe everlasting punishment, and that our Lord *must* have spoken according to their meaning.'	48
Dr. Farrar wrong, both in the principle and in the fact. Our Lord, if need was, corrected the meaning, attached to words by the Jews.	49
The Jews *did* believe in eternal punishment and called the place, Gehenna.	ib.
1. Book of Judith.	51
2. Book of Enoch.	52—59
3. Fourth book of Esdras. Fragment recovered.	59—60
4. Apocalypse of Baruch.	60—63
5. Psalms of Solomon; final perdition of ungodly.	63—65
6. IVth book of Maccabees. Everlasting fire.	65—68
7. Josephus, uncertainty as to his belief, what was in store for the good; no doubt as to the eternal punishment of the wicked.	68—71
8, 9. Targums. Novel theory as to their date.	71
To place them later, only carries on the evidence.	72
' Second death ' and ' Gehenna ' in Targums.	73—77
Sadducees unendurable to the people.	77 note
Talmud, most of it essentially new.	79
Arbitrariness of R. Akiba's new system.	81
His plans to hold his people together; opposition to Christianity.	84
Ascribes salvation to circumcision.	85
' Gehenna of 12 months ' attributed by Talmud to R. Akiba,	86
And so 86 years after our Lord's Ascension.	87
Two classes only held by R. Akiba to be saved: of Jews, only Apostates lost.	90, 91
Jewish Hell in our third century.	92—95
Talmud *does* teach eternity of punishment. Chief Rabbi Weill.	95
' Eternal punishment of Christians.'	96

	Page
Gehenna, as spoken of by our Lord.	99
Continues to be used as name of the place of the lost among Latins, Greeks, Syrians.	100
And in Coran from Mohammad's Jewish teacher.	ib.
Talmud. None delivered from the lowest hell.	102
Evidence from blasphemy in Talmud.	103, 104
Summary	105
Dr. Farrar's teaching *may* bring out the value of belief in the intermediate state.	106, 107
Our disregard of God's teaching in 1 Cor. iii. not honest.	108
All were believed of old to pass through the fire in the Day of Judgement, wicked only to perish in it.	112—113
Agony of seeing all past sin in the sight of Jesus.	116
Temporary privation of the sight of God has intense pain.	119
Yet the waiting of the intermediate state has unspeakable joy too.	120, 121
Comfort of belief of purifying process after death.	122
Perrone says '(German) Protestants hold it.'	123
Happiness of the preparation of the soul for the beatific Vision of the All Holy God.	124, 125
'The willing agony of God's remedial fire' belongs 'to the vast mass of mankind.' Dr Farrar.	125
Ancient Prayers for the Departed.	125—128

APPENDIX.

i. *On the condemnation of Origen in the 5th General Council.*

Origen denied restoration of Satan.	129
Taught mostly received belief.	130
Held as truth what came from the Apostles.	131
Set down speculations hesitatingly, laid down the faith of the Church, as his rule.	132, 133
Origen's errors blended together; but Universalism was condemned separately.	134, 135
Separate condemnations of Origenism, received by the Church, had the force of a General Council.	136, 137
Origen condemned singly under Mennas; in the fifth Council with Didymus and Evagrius.	138, 139

CONTENTS.   xiii

	Page
Collection of writings of Origen Didymus Evagrius, teaching the 'restitution,' condemned by 5th Council.	140, 141

Witnesses of this.

i. Cyril of Scythopolis.	142, 143
ii. Evagrius. Passages brought before the Council.	144
iii. Victor of Tununum. iv. Maximus of Aquileia.	145
v. Emperor Heraclius in Roman records.	146
vi. Lateran Council A. 649. vii. Sophronius.	147
viii. Imp. Edict in 6th Gen. Council. ix. Leo II.	148
x. Tarasius. xi. 2nd Council of Nice.	149
xii. Gregory ii. Accounts by xiii. Photius, and xiv. Nicephorus, from written documents.	150, 151
Huet's conviction upon the evidence against his previous impressions.	152, 153

ii. Testimony of Martyrs to the belief of Everlasting Punishment.

S. Felicitas and her seven sons.	155, 156
S. Polycarp. S. Biblias. S. Epipodius.	157
SS. Symphorian, Maximus, Dionysia.	158
S. Marcian. S. Claudius.	159
SS. Domnina and Theonilla.	160
S. Victor.	ib.
SS. Tarachus, Probus, Andronicus.	161, 162
S. Crispina. S. Afra.	163, 164
S. Ferreolus. S. Peter Balsamus.	165
S. Julius. S. Patricius.	166
S. Basil of Ancyra. S. Theodoret.	167
S. Sabas. S. Pherbuthe.	168
S. Symeon. S. Miles.	169
SS. Acepsimas, Aithilahas, Joseph.	170

iii. Witnesses to the belief in Eternal Punishment in writers of the early Centuries.

1. S. Ignatius.	173
2. S. Polycarp.	ib.

CONTENTS.

	Page
3. Epistle of the Church of Smyrna.	174
4. Pastor of Hermas.	174—176
Dr. Farrar's claim of the writer as an Universalist.	176 note.
5. The Epistle of Barnabas.	176
6. Ancient Homily (attributed to S. Clement of Rome.)	177
7. S. Justin Martyr, 12 statements.	ib.—178
13th passage, not his, claimed by Dr F.	182 note.
8. S. Irenæus.	182—186
Dr. Farrar claims that he taught 3 opinions, mutually contradictory.	186—187 note.
9. S. Theophilus.	187, 188
10. Tatian.	189
11. Tertullian.	ib.
12. Clement of Alexandria.	190
Dr. Farrar's claim to Clement. He contradicts Universalism.	190, 191 note.
13. Apostolic Constitutions, (probably very ancient)	192
14. Minutius Felix.	193
15. S. Hippolytus.	ib.
16. S. Cyprian.	194
17. The Recognitions of Clement and Clementine Homilies.	196—199
Dr. Farrar upon Clementine Homilies.	197 note.
18. Celsus and Origen.	199
19. Arnobius.	201
20. Lactantius.	ib.
21. Julius Firmicus.	203
22. S. Methodius.	204
23. S. James of Nisibis.	ib.
24. S. Athanasius.	ib.
25. Eusebius.	206
26. Theodore, Bishop of Heraclea, Semi-Arian.	ib.
27. Acacius, disciple of Eusebius of Cæsarea.	207.
28. S. Cyril of Jerusalem.	ib.
29. Lucifer of Cagliari.	208
30. S. Hilary.	ib.
31. S. Zeno.	209
32. S. Cæsarius (brother of S. Greg. Naz.)	210
33. Titus, Bp. of Bozra.	212

CONTENTS.

	Page
34. S. Epiphanius.	212
35. S. Ephraem.	ib.
36. S. Basil.	213
37. S. Gregory Nazianzen, his positive teaching.	215
Passages alleged against his faith.	217
38. S. Gregory of Nyssa. His positive teaching.	219
Could, as an honest man, have no opposite conviction.	220, 221
39. S. Andrew, Bp. of Cæsarea.	222
40. S. Macarius of Egypt.	ib.
41. S. Macarius of Alexandria.	223

42—49. The great fathers of the desert of Scete.

	Page
42. S. Serapion, Bp. of Thmuis.	224
43. Theodorus.	225
44. Paphnutius.	226
45. Daniel, Abbot.	ib.
46. Serenus, Abbot.	227
47. Moyses, Abbot.	ib.
48. Isaac, Abbot.	228
49. Chæremon, Abbot.	229

Diodorus of Tarsus } 'Fathers' of the Nestorians,	229—232
Theodore of Mopsuestia }	
alleged by Dr. Farrar as 'great teachers.'	232
50. Didymus, his positive teaching.	ib.
Inadequacy of the 'traces' adopted by Dr. F. from Neander.	
	232, 233 note.
51. S. Ambrose.	235
Passage alleged by Petavius for his Origenising.	237
52. S. Pacian.	238
53. S. Jerome. His positive teaching.	ib.—239
His supposed doubts as to certain classes.	240—242
54. S. Gaudentius.	242
55. Ruffinus.	243
No ground to suspect evasion with Petavius.	244, 245 note.
56. Tichonius.	245
57. S. Paulinus.	ib.
58. S. Augustine.	ib.
His answer to pleas of different classes, how *they* might escape hell.	248, 249
59. S. Chrysostom. Dr. Farrar's imputation of 'accommodation' *i.e.* that he did not believe what he said.	249, 250

CONTENTS.

	Page
Manifoldness and earnestness of his preaching.	250—266
60. S. Chromatius.	ib.
61. S. Asterius.	267
62. Victor of Antioch The worm of the ungodly a bad conscience.	268
Hesitation as to the fire.	269
63. Pelagius, heretic. (see pp. 135, 241.)	269
64. S. Isidore of Pelusium.	ib.
65. S Cyril of Alexandria.	270
66. S. Maximus of Turin.	271
67. Theodoret.	272
68. Cassian.	273
69. S. Peter Chrysologus.	ib.
70. Sedulius.	ib.
71. S. Proclus.	274
72. Valerian, Bp. of Cimies.	ib.
73. Eusebius Gallicanus.	275
74. Nilus, disciple of S. Chrysostom.	276
75. S. Leo.	ib.
76. Salvian.	278
77. S. Prosper.	280
78. S. James of Sarug.	281
79. Philoxenus of Mabug.	ib.
80. Faustus (Semi-Pelagian).	ib.
81. S. Cæsarius, Archbp. of Arles.	282
82. Julianus Pomerius.	ib.
83. S. Fulgentius.	283
84. S. John Damascene.	284
S. Martin's promise to Satan of the mercy of Christ, if he would repent.	285, 286
Satan's refusal, in like case, in great anger.	286
Do we know that God has cast one soul into hell, of whom He does not know in His absolute knowledge, that a new trial would be useless to it, and that no place would be heaven to it?	287
Characteristics of the above witnesses.	287—289
Diderot and Voltaire.	290

WHAT IS OF FAITH

AS TO

EVERLASTING PUNISHMENT?

I WAS preparing to add to my Sermon on Everlasting Punishment an Appendix on the evidence that the eternity of punishment was held as matter of faith by the Martyrs of the three first centuries, and also by the Fathers generally, and that the denial of this truth had been condemned as heresy by the Fifth General Council, when my attention was drawn to Dr. Farrar's then recent book 'Eternal Hope.' On reading it, I felt that to dwell on these points alone would be useless without removing the impression which Dr. Farrar's empassioned[a] declamation against what he calls 'the current opinions about Hell' is calculated to make. In it also he appeals to those who believe in Hell, 'that if those current opinions are not tenets of faith, they cannot be too honestly or too distinctly repudiated[b].' Me he names, as one of 'those who are such earnest defenders of an endless hell[c].' I *do* fear that the disbelief in it, to which a great impulse has been given

---

[a] 'I speak now no longer with natural passion.' Eternal Hope p. 73.   [b] Ib. Pref. p. lvi. lvii.   [c] Ib. Exc. iii. p. 197.

by writings of late years, must be with great peril to souls. Still more destructive to souls must be the hard thoughts of our God, with which that teaching has been accompanied. No one could write otherwise than earnestly upon a subject so aweful. But my earnest defence alas! has been to preach *one* sermon to the young, among whom God has made me a teacher.

Again he says,

'[d] Here I declare, and call God to witness, that *if the popular doctrine of Hell were true*, I should be ready to resign all hope, not only of a *shortened* but of *any* immortality, if thereby I could save, not *millions* but *one single human soul* from what fear, and superstition, and ignorance, and inveterate hate, and slavish letter-worship, have dreamed and taught of Hell. I call God to witness, that so far from regretting the possible loss of some billions of aeons of bliss by attaching to the word αἰώνιος a sense, in which scores of times it is undeniably found, I would here, and now, and kneeling on my knees, ask Him that I might die as the beasts that perish, and for ever cease to be, rather than that my worst enemy should endure the Hell described by Tertullian, or Minutius Felix, or Jonathan Edwards, or Dr. Pusey, or Mr. Furniss, or Mr. Moody, or Mr. Spurgeon, for one single year.'

This wish is unlike that of S. Paul, who said that for the sake of his brethren he could wish himself separated from the Personal Presence of Christ, Who was His Life, Who lived in him. He spoke of being separated from His *Presence*, not from His

[d] Et. Hope, Exc. iii. p. 202.

love, since he said, '[e] neither death nor life, nor any other creature could separate us from the love of God in Christ Jesus.' He could wish this, if so more might be won to God, might live to God, might be blessed in God, might glorify God. Dr. Farrar (in passionate language which I hope he will retract) says that, *if the 'popular' doctrine of hell were true*, he would forfeit for ever the end, for which he was created and redeemed, the blessed-making vision of his God and His eternal love, if by his intercession and sacrifice of himself he might save one soul, for whom the Precious Death and Intercession of Christ had been unavailing in this life, from that hell which I, he says, described.

For myself, I had feared that I might almost have used too much reserve, in speaking only of what people in those days would, I hoped, most listen to, and to which those to whom I was immediately speaking, with their young fresh hearts would be most alive, the absence of all love. We can scarcely imagine an existence for a single hour with no one to love, no one to love us, with no love from God or man, nothing but hate. I spoke graphically only of the misery of being for ever in the society of such as those must be, whom God would shut out from His Presence for ever. A vivid history has been related which happened a few years ago. "One of the first among living physicians gave us [f] the following narrative:—' A sempstress, careless about religion, was sitting up alone at two or three in the morning, hard

---

[e] Rom. viii. 38, 39.
[f] Author of article in Christian Remembrancer, 'Universalism and Everlasting punishment.' Vol. xlv. p. 446.

at work. The roar of some noisy and dissolute revellers suddenly fell upon her ear. Shocked at their expressions and brutalized mirth, she was struck by the thought, 'What if I had to live with such! What if I were to be condemned to live with them for ever!' This reflection haunted her mind, and she was at length brought to seek Christ."

Yet this is inseparable from the idea of Hell. No one who could love would be there. No one who had anything but that miserable counterfeit of love, self-love, would be there; no one would be there, in whom the natural rudiments of love were not marred and overshadowed by the poison-tree of pride, envy, jealousy, in their empassioned malignity.

But I have often said that I could not but think that to one, such as Satan, full of hatred, envy, jealousy, malignity, the sight of all that unspeakable love in Heaven, in which the blessed are ever bathed, but in which he himself, being what he is, could not share, would be the worst Hell of the two. I believe that he would again cast himself out of it, and that his own worst Hell is, himself. Even on earth those who are what Plato calls '[g]incurable' hate the society of the really good, and intercourse except with those like themselves. '[h]He was made to reprove our

---

[g] 'They who have been guilty of the worst crimes, and are incurable (ἀνίατοι) by reason of their crimes, are made examples; for, as they are incurable, the time has passed, at which they can receive any benefit themselves. But others get good when they behold them for ever enduring the most terrible and painful and fearful sufferings as the penalty of their sins—there they are, hanging up as examples, in the prison-house of the world below, a spectacle and a warning to all unrighteous men who come thither.' Plato, Dialogues, Gorgias Vol. iii. p. 123 ed. Jowett.　　　[h] Wisd. ii. 14, 15.

thoughts; he is grievous unto us even to behold: for his life is not like other men's, his ways are of another fashion.' But here they can vent their hate and spite upon the good. These will *there* be out of their reach. And yet, if they have nothing to do, except to dwell upon themselves, and the misery of having lost the bliss for which they were created; if they have no memories except of the evil, which shut them out from God, and yet through the fixed obstinate malignity of their will, will not repent; with no activity even in nothingnesses, like the absorbing distractions of this world, or its fierce passions: with no love to pour out or to receive (for all love will then be gathered into Heaven) their only vent would be mutual hate. Such must be a torment to themselves. I did not 'describe' even what Dr. Faber[1] called, 'the bright side of Hell.' I spoke of 'hell, with the hell' almost 'left out, the crowning woe, the loss of God.' My object was to fix on the minds of some of the young, against the recent delusions of the day, the one thought of its *eternity*.

As to what Dr. Farrar calls '[j] the common opinions respecting Hell,' he says, 'it is impossible to be mistaken, and I had myself been trained in them,' although 'in these days, they are seldom stated in all their breadth and all their horror.' 'Many of us were scared with it,' he says[k], 'horrified with it, perhaps almost maddened by it in our childhood.'

The four points upon which he dwells are[l], 1) 'the physical torments, the material agonies of eternal

[1] Faber, Spiritual Conferences, (Heaven and Hell) p. 396.
[j] Eternal Hope, Pref. p. lv. [k] Ib. p. 55. [l] Ib. Pref. xxxi. xxxiii.

punishment; 2) the supposition of its necessarily endless duration for all who incur it; 3) the opinion that it is thus incurred by the vast mass of mankind; and 4) that it is a doom passed irreversibly at the moment of death on all who die in a state of sin.'

Of these, the third has no solid foundation whatever; it exists, probably, only in the rigid Calvinistic school, in which Dr. Farrar was educated, and from which his present opinions are a reaction. That school is now happily all-but-extinct, if not altogether extinct, in England. The fourth is probably a misconception. Dr. Farrar means any how, 'a state of' such 'sin' as excludes any 'presence of God's grace, however invisible to man, in the heart[m].' The

[m] The sentence is in a letter of Card. Newman to Prof. Plumptre, published by Prof. P. in the Contemporary May 1878 p. 329. as 'a letter of a R. C. Priest.' The letters are attributed to Card. Newman in Oxenham's Eschatology p. 44. I reprint the main parts of the first letter, for its characteristic clearness and value; .. 'It seems to me that you do not deny eternal punishment; but you aim at withdrawing from so aweful a doom vast multitudes who have popularly been considered to fall under it, and to substitute for it in their case a purgatorial punishment, extending (as in the case of the antediluvians) through long ages; at the same time avoiding the word 'purgatory,' on account of its associations.

'There is nothing, I think, in the view incompatible with the faith of Catholics.

'What we cannot accept (any more than the mass of Protestants and of divines of the Ancient Church) is one of your incidental statements, that man's probation for his eternal destiny, as well as his purification, continue after this life.

' Nor does this doctrine seem necessary for your main point; for Catholics are able to hold purgatory without accepting it, merely by holding that there are innumerable degrees of grace and sanctity among the saved, and that those who go to purgatory, however many die one and all with the presence of God's grace and the earnest of

that '*the vast mass of mankind are lost.*' 7

first is a point, not declared to be essential to the belief in Hell. I will venture to say what I have to say upon them in a different order.

i. Dr. Farrar's third point, that, in the belief of those who believe everlasting punishment, 'it is incurred by the vast mass of mankind' seems to have dwelt most upon his mind (to argue from his almost uniform mention of it[n] when he speaks of eternal punishment). It is further aggravated by

eternal life, however invisible to man, already in their hearts,—an assumption not greater than yours; for it is quite as great an assumption to believe, as you do, in the *future happiness* of those who 'die and make no sign,' as to believe, as I may do, in the present *faith and repentance* of those who die and make no sign.'

'[n] That this doom awaits the *vast majority* of mankind.' Eternal Hope Pref. p. xxii. 'the belief, that the unhappy race of God's children in His great family of man are *all-but-universally* condemned to endless torturings &c' Ib. p. xxxiv. 'the *common view* that it would have been better for *most* of our race to have been unborn.' Ib. p. xlvii. "I was of course immediately faced by the question, 'How can life be regarded as worth living *by the majority of mankind*, if, as is taught by the current religious teaching, *they* are *doomed* to everlasting damnation?'" Ib. p. lv. 'the evil complacency with which some cheerfully accept the belief that they are living and moving in the midst of *millions doomed irreversibly to everlasting perdition*' Ib. p. 65. 'have turned God's Gospel of plenteous redemption into an anathema of *all-but-universal perdition.*' Ib. p. 67. 'an endless hell for *most* of the human race.' p. 71. note. 'supposing, as thousands of Theologians have taught for thousands of years, *the vast majority* are in the next world for ever lost.' p. 91. 'those who turn the Gospel of salvation *for most men* into a threat of doom.' p. 128. 'in *all-but-universal* perpetuity of sin.' p. 155. 'the crude dogmatism which we hear so frequently of the endlessness of material torments for *the majority of mankind.*' p. 179. 'the post-Reformation dogma of *an all-but-universal*, unmitigated and irreversible doom to endless torments at the moment of death.' Cont. Rev June 1878 p 576. The Rev H. N. Oxenham in

8 *God the Holy Ghost teaches all men knowledge.*

his engrafting into it the heresy of Calvin, that 'º the majority of mankind are doomed to hell by an absolute predestination.'

Most of us, happily, in our youth heard nothing of all this, or of the Calvinistic dogma of 'reprobation,' except to hear it rejected as something horrible.

In regard to the heathen, apart from Theology, the three simple words of the Psalmist 'ᴾ teacheth man knowledge,' tell us of an universal teaching of mankind, the whole race of man individually, man by man, by the Spirit of God. God the Holy Ghost (it is matter of faith) visits and has visited every soul of man whom God has made, and those who heard His voice and obeyed it, as far as they knew, belonged to Christ, and were saved for His merits, Whom, had they known, they would have obeyed and loved.

He Himself enlightens them, as S. John says, ᑫ "In

his Catholic Eschatology (p. 22.) says, ' I am not myself acquainted with a single Universalist writer who does not argue as though the doctrine he is assailing involved the damnation of the great majority of mankind.' He instances Sir. J. Stephen, Mr. S. Cox, Prof. Mayor, Mr. Jukes, and one (not Dean Stanley) who wrote as *Anglicanus*. On these grounds Mr. Mill Sen. rejected Christianity. Mill's Autobiography p. 41. Three Essays on religion p. 114, 115.) Having been educated in the Creed of Scotch Presbyterianism, the doctrine of everlasting punishment came to him in the Calvinistic form. Mr. Theodore Parker, who revolted from it to Unitarianism, had also been educated as a Calvinist. º Et. Hope p. 68.

ᴾ Ps. xciv. 10. למד is used of an actual teaching of knowledge, not of mere teaching through correction, Ps. xxv. 4 ; li. 15 ; cxix. 12, 26, 60, 66, 68, 108, 124, 135, 171 ; cxxxii. 12 ; of man to God—in irony Job xxi. 22 ; ידע is used of the knowledge of God made known through creation Ps. xix. 3 ; of the knowledge of God, primarily Pr. i. 7, 22, 29 ; Is. v. 13 ; taught by God, Ps. cxix. 66.
ᑫ S. John i. 4.

The Word enlightens all born into the world. 9

Him was Life, and the Life was the Light of men;" of all *men* that Life was, is, and ever will be the Light; 'the Life of God in the soul of men.' 'The Light of mankind has been, is, and ever will be, the Manifestation of the Life within them of the Living and Life-giving Word.' And again "[r] He was the true Light who lighteneth every man that cometh into the world.[s]" But that light has shone and shines very unequally among those, on whom the light of the Gospel has not shone. We are then wholly ignorant of the rule, by which they will be judged. What would be heavy sin in us, may be none in them; we cannot tell how far the exposure of infants may be a sin in China, unless God by His secret voice appeal to any individual parent against the hereditary custom, or cannibalism in a nation of can-

[r] S. John i. 9. Wisdom i. 7, 'The Spirit of the Lord hath filled the world,' is further quoted by later Theologians. See de Lugo de fide xii. 3. Suarez de fide xii. 6. quoted by Oxenham Cath. Eschat. p. 26. note.

[s] The idiom of the later Jews, כל באי עולם ' all who come into the world,' is decisive for this rendering Lightfoot ad loc. quotes 'Doth not the sun arise upon all who come into the world? Hieros. Sanh. f. 26. 3; all who come into the world cannot create one fly. Ib. f. 25. 4; In the beginning of the year, all who come into the world pass before the face of God. Rosh hashanah c. i. hal. i.' This outweighs the grammatical fact that $\pi\hat{a}s$ with the participle, in S. John, generally has the article. (S. John iii. 8, 15, 16, 20; iv. 13; vi. 40, 45; viii. 34; xi. 26; xii. 46; xv. 2; xvi. 2; xviii. 4, 37; xix. 12; 1 S. John ii. 23, 29; iii. 3, 4, 6 (bis), 9, 10, 15; iv. 7; v. 1 (bis), 4, 10; 2 S. John 9.) All the cases are nominatives, except S. John xviii. 6. and subjects of an universal affirmative. In S. John xv. 2 init. there is no article.

The rendering, "The true light, which lighteneth every man, was coming into the world," leaves the same sense, though less marked. But the Word was not then '*coming* into the world.' It was come.

nibals. But since we are not God, and He has not bestowed on us His prerogative of searching the hearts, we have absolutely no ground, upon which to form a judgement; nor do Christians form any.

With the actual heathen far out of reach of the Gospel, must be counted a large portion of the poor, which the Church has lost in large cities, as London and Paris, on whose souls the light of the Gospel never shone. London is alas! in all probability one of the largest heathen cities in the world, and very many of its inhabitants will be judged, we must suppose, by the same law as the heathen in China and Japan. "God will," in the great Day, S. Paul says[t], "judge the secrets of men by Jesus Christ according to my Gospel." The very terms forbid *our* judging, since they are the *secrets* of the heart which God will judge.

Although Holy Scripture holds out no idea, that mere change of place will effect a change of soul, that those who would not have God *to the very last*, will be less obstinate, because they pass out of this world, it says nothing about the proportion of the saved or the lost. Vocations are lost every day. Many high places in heaven still stand vacant: many who began well fail of the promise which they once gave: there are every where stunted souls, souls which have not corresponded to the grace of God. "Many are called, but few are chosen." There is alas! abundance and superabundance of room for a saddening picture of the waste of God's grace, without coming near the question which our Lord refused to answer, "Are there few that shall be saved?"

[t] Rom. ii. 16.

Infants, not members of Xt, have natural happiness. 11

He gave us a warning about ourselves. He told us nothing about the proportion of the lost to the saved.

A horrible saying of the hard Calvin as to non-elect infants, which probably no other could have uttered, does duty in the writings of Universalists, like the one description of Tertullian [u] which he probably uttered to scare the heathen. It is now the universal belief, that, although children who had not been made members of Christ are not admitted to that bliss which Christ purchased for us, the Beatific Vision of God, yet since they lost it not by fault of their own, they do not feel any loss, but lead lives of natural happiness; a happiness, which has one element wanting to that of adults still in the flesh, that they, never, in thought word or deed, knew of actual sin against God Who made them.

ii. Dr. Farrar's assumption that 'the popular belief of Hell' is, that the vast mass of mankind falls into it, seems to me to depend upon another assumption, which occurs in his third point, that the vast mass of mankind 'die in a state of *sin*.' He assumes that the vast majority of us all are at the time of death not only '[x] still imperfect and unworthy,' but 'not yet in a state of grace;' and so, unless there

[u] He is alleged as a specimen of the Church, whereas his harshness drove him out of the Church, by Gibbon, Decline and Fall T. ii. c. 16.; by Dean Perowne on Ps. 109 Pref.; after him by Mr. Lowe on the same Psalm; by Lecky hostilely, as 'a striking illustration of the effect of the belief in eternal punishment' (Hist. of Rationalism i. p. 342); by Alger (Doct. of future state p. 513) as one of 'hundreds nay thousands of the most accredited Christian writers, who shewed the same fiendish spirit.' (quoted by Oxenham l. c, p 94 note). Tertullian is one of three, of wonderful gifts, of whose own salvation the Church has had misgivings.   [x] Et. H. Pr. p. xxviii.

12 *No ground to lay down*, who *dies out of grace.*

be, in the words of the Lutheran Martensen, 'a realm of progressive developement, in which souls are prepared and matured for the final judgement,' the vast majority of mankind would be lost.

The argument implies that we know a great deal of souls, which are "[y] the secret things of the Lord our God." How do we or can we *know*, what souls do not die in a state of grace? Take the worst case almost that can be imagined, a soul dying immediately upon the commission of some deadly sin. Take the case of one falling in a duel, but repenting, for the love of God, after he had been mortally wounded (such a history has been recorded and believed); or that (which made much impression) of an unbeliever, who had lately been inculcating unbelief, and who rose from an adulteress' bed, to fall back and die in the arms of the adulteress: or of one who committed suicide and repented, when the means employed had begun to work their effect. Extreme cases we must leave to the mercy of Him Who died for them. They have been before their Judge. No one can say that Ahab,—educated in the foul idolatries of his father Omri, but who "sold himself to work wickedness," "whom Jezebel his wife stirred up," and who died in a battle, against which God had warned him and he neglected the warning and maltreated the prophet who warned him in the Name of God,—did not repent when, "stayed up in his chariot till even," he felt the judgement of God in that mortal wound. He had, three years before, humbled himself before God, and God had rewarded his self-humiliation by a temporal reprieve of the sentence upon him and

[y] Deut. xxix. 29.

his house. We may hope that Absalom, parricide as he was in intention, repented, when hanging between heaven and earth by the hair which had been his pride, before Joab's servants slew him. We readily believe that the disobedient prophet repented, after the false prophet, his seducer, had pronounced his temporal sentence from God, ere the lion met him [z]. Solomon, after his early promise and God's abundant gifts, fell away in a premature old age, the result probably of his sensuality. An interval was left, after God's temporal judgements began. He died probably at fifty-eight. If, as has been commonly thought, he wrote Ecclesiastes in that interval, he too probably repented and was saved [a]. Herod was

[z] S. Augustine speaks undoubtingly of his having suffered temporal punishment only. De cura pro mort. c. vii. n. 9. Short Treatises pp. 526, 527. Oxf. Tr.

[a] S. Hilary (Tract. in Ps. lii. § 12) S. Ambrose (Apolog. altera c. iii. n. 13-16.) S. Cyril (Cat. ii. 13) S. Jerome (Ep. ad Salvinam, T. i. 500 Vall. Lib. 13 in Ezek. T. v. 526) speak unhesitatingly of his repentance. S. Jerome says that 'the Hebrews' of his time 'say that the book is Solomon's, repenting for the offence he had given to God in the matter of the women whom he took to himself, relying, as he did, too much on his wisdom and riches.' Comm. in Eccles. c. i. T. iii. 392. Vall. On the other hand, S. Augustine uses in one place the strong words ' was rejected by,' in Ps. 127. init. T. iv. p. 17. Oxf. Tr.; in another he insists negatively on no repentance of his being recorded, or any indulgence of God, c. Faust. xxii. 87. T. viii. p. 415. The above are from J. Keble, ' on the character and history of Solomon.' Occasional Papers, pp. 423—431. S. Chrysostom in one place contrasts David's recovery from his fall, with the absence of any such account of Solomon; ' but the son shewed nothing of the sort.' (Hom. xxiii. in 2 Cor. p. 270. Oxf. Tr.) In another he says, that he rose from the dark abyss, and uttered those great words, meet for heaven, ' vanity of vanities, all is vanity.' cont. eos qui subintrod. habent, n. 12. T. i. pp. 246, 247.

stricken, because he accepted the blasphemous praise of the multitude for a speech which no doubt was eloquent. We know not that his pride was not healthfully humbled, when he felt the hand of God in the loathsome disease, of which he died. God has recorded to us the outward end of Ananias, which struck awe into others. We *know* not, whether it was an agony of remorse and repentance by which he died and so was saved, though the temporal judgement of God was irreversible. It is possible. There is a remarkable instance recorded of one who, being penitent, died in the agony of penitence, lest his soul should not be saved. Nebuchadnezzar[b] repented, while outwardly he was a maniac, and God tells us that He accepted his repentance[c]. If Antiochus Epiphanes, picture as he is of *the* Antichrist, made sincerely the profession attributed to him by the author of the 2nd book of the Maccabees, '[d] it is meet to become subject to God;' and was sincere in his promise to make reparation for his ill-deeds, 'leaving off his great pride, and coming to the knowledge of himself by the scourge of God, his pain increasing every moment and unable to abide his own smell'—if he did all this, and sincerely, his miserable death was to him the saving of his soul.

The Church, it has been beautifully said, 'has its long lists of saints; it has not inserted *one* name in any catalogue of the damned.'

God, in His Providence, seems just now to have set before our eyes His unwillingness to part with a soul, in the sequel of a crime, which fixed people's

---

[b] See Daniel the Prophet p. 434—436.
[c] Dan. v. 21, 22.   [d] 2 Macc. ix. 11—18, 28.

minds through the horrors of the attempts to conceal it. A humbler penitence would have been happier to hear of. Yet God won at last. One of His creatures closed a long course of sin and crime through murder, committed to conceal manslaughter perpetrated under the influence of drink. The unhappy criminal seemed to herself in the power of Satan, before she committed it; when committed, she struggled on in desperate impenitence, adding sin to sin to conceal it and to escape its consequence. She abandoned one false-witness for another, but found no belief. God shut her up to repentance by absolute hoplessness as to this life. Escape might have led to final impenitence. His just judgement, "whoso sheddeth man's blood, by man shall his blood be shed," which cut off all avenue to human mercy, threw wide open the portals of mercy for eternity; "Whoso cometh unto Me, I will in no wise cast out." "ᵉ O the depth of the riches both of the wisdom and knowledge of God! How unsearchable are His judgements; and His ways past finding out!"

The only drawback in this case was the unmitigated confidence of security, such as the most innocent might have.

The proverbial, "'He died and made no sign,' had it been other than a poetic fiction, might have been significant of awe-stricken penitence in sight of its sins and of approaching judgement, as well, as the poet makes it, of despair.

When people were, in my early youth, discussing

ᵉ Rom. xi. 33.
ᶠ Cardinal Beaufort's death in Henry VIth, Act iii. St. 3. Quoted in Dr. F. Et. Hope p. 105.

the use of the words 'as our hope is, this our brother doth' an evangelical Clergyman who had the cure of a very large parish [g] told me, that he had never said this without having some measure of hope. And he had not then thought of what God might do for the soul in those last moments, even when it could hold communication with none but Him.

It is very miserable to think of those very late conversions, by which a person turns from sin to God, when the very power of sinning has left him. Miserable is a half-wrecked soul; miserable is the waste of grace, of the love of Jesus, of the degree of bliss which might have been the portion of that soul. But in speaking of hell, the only question is, as to those who are saved from it. What God does for the soul, when the eye is turned up in death and shrouded, the frame stiffened, every limb motionless, every power of expression gone, is one of the secrets of the Divine compassion.

'We take good heed,' says an accredited writer [h], 'never to affirm positively the reprobation of any one in particular, whatever may be his religion, country, period, nay, his conduct. In the soul, at the last moment of its passage on the threshold of eternity, there occur doubtless Divine mysteries of justice, but above all of mercy and of love; 'mercy triumpheth over justice.' We abstain from sounding indiscreetly the Divine counsels, but we know indubitably that on each occasion they are worthy of God and of His infinite goodness as well as of His justice.'

Perhaps He does the more, because the soul is not

[g] Wolverhampton [h] P. Ravignan Confér. 36, t ii. p. 521.

tempted to waste or parade or profane His prodigality of mercy. It has been said with wondrous beauty, "[1] I have no profession of faith to make about them [those without], except that God is infinitely merciful to every soul; that no one ever has been, or ever can be lost by surprise or trapped in his ignorance; and as to those who may be lost, I confidently believe that our Heavenly Father threw His arms round each created spirit, and looked it full in the face with bright eyes of love, in the darkness of its mortal life, and that of its own deliberate will it would not have Him.'

But the whole of Dr. Farrar's declamation against the belief that the eternal condition of the soul, as saved or lost, is fixed at death, rests on his own assumption, that he *knows* that the vast majority die in a state, shutting out the grace of God.

The instinct of mankind is in conformity with the teaching of Holy Scripture, that we shall be judged "for the things done in the body, whether they be good or bad." Our Lord declares it distinctly in His account of His own judgement at the Great Day. How souls shall, in the long intermediate state, be prepared for the vision and fruition of God, we can plainly know nothing, unless God reveal it. A further *probation*, after this life, is clearly a mere human imagination. 'Universalism' itself does not require it. It is only a human theory, devised to make 'universalism' plausible. A continuation of the discipline of the soul, a preparation for the Beatific Vision, a developement of faculties as yet undeveloped here, continued influences from God maturing the soul, a

[1] Faber, 'The Creator and the creature.' B. 3. ii. end.

purifying it from the stains of sin, of this or the like there is no question. The one question, which Dr. Farrar and others have taken upon themselves to decide, is, that souls, which to the last have shut out the grace of God, may have a fresh probation in the world to come; in a word, that this life is not our trial-time. However, of this hereafter. Here I would only say, that Dr. Farrar's demand of a new probation for those who have failed here, as necessary to vindicate the love of God, turns on the presumption, that *we* know, what God alone *can* know, who have so failed; and that He, the Searcher of hearts, will account any to have failed in this life, whom He does not know to be finally irrecoverable.

iii. On the first point, 'the endless tortures,' Dr. Farrar has himself stipulated, in one respect, for what is the mind of the Church everywhere:—'ᴊ hold that, as the very word 'damnation' once implied, the 'pain of loss,' i. e. the loss, it may be for ever, of the Beatific Vision, is, far more than any pain of sense or physical torture, the essence of the sufferings of the lost'—I can hardly imagine any religious mind, which had taken time to think, thinking otherwise.

With regard to the corporeal sufferings, it may suffice to say, that neither the Church nor any portion of it has so laid down any doctrine in regard to them, as to make the acceptance of them an integral part of the doctrine itself.

Fire is the most excruciating suffering, of which we have any experience here. The flesh shrinks from the slightest touch of it. Since then S. Paul has

ᴊ Pref. p. xxxv.

The Church has not defined that the fire is material. 19

said of the Day of Judgement, "^k knowing the terror of the Lord, we persuade men," I dare not myself lessen any terror, to which our Lord's words may give rise. The dread of hell peoples heaven: perhaps millions have been scared back from sin by the dread of it. They 'turned back,' as S. Augustine so often says, 'from God displeased to God appeased.' Their terror at the aweful Holiness of God, with which nothing defiled could dwell, turned them back in penitence and self-abhorrence to seek Him in His love.

He himself had felt it. He says to God, '[1] Thy right hand was continually ready to pluck me out of the mire, and to wash me throughly, and I knew it not; nor did any thing call me back from a yet deeper gulf of carnal pleasures, but the fear of death, and of Thy judgement to come; which, amid all my changes, never departed from my breast.'

What those sufferings will be for those who, to the last, obstinately shut out the love of God, will not depend upon our opinion of them here. Holy Scripture warns us of them and of their intensity; it does not define their quality. To use the words of a writer who speaks the mind of the large Roman Communion; '[m] This alone is matter of faith, that there is a hell;' i. e. that there are punishments laid up for the ungodly, and that these will be eternal, i. e. without end. All the rest, as to the place or nature of the punishment, are not matter of faith. For as Pétau says judiciously, after Vasquez, 'By no decree of the Church nor in any Synod has it been defined, viz. either that the fire is corporeal, or

[k] 2 Cor. v. 11. [1] S. Aug. Conf. B. vi. 16. p. 105. Oxf. Tr.
[m] Perrone de Deo Creatore P. iii. c. vi. art. 3. n. 729.

that there is a place under the earth, where the dæmons and the lost are tormented.'

Fathers of highest esteem have held the immaterial character of the eternal punishment, and their sayings have not been condemned, like those of Origen.

S. Jerome says [n],

'The worm which will never die and the fire which never will be quenched is by very many (plerisque) understood of the conscience of sinners, which tortures them when under punishment, why, through their own fault and sin, they missed the good of the elect.'

And S. Ambrose [o],

'There is no gnashing of corporeal teeth, nor any perpetual *fire* of *corporeal* flames, nor is the worm *corporeal*.—The fire is that which the sadness over transgressions generates, because the sins pierce with compunction the mind and sense of the irrational soul of the guilty, and eat out the, as it were, bowels of conscience; which sins are generated like worms out of each, as it were from the body of the sinner. The Lord declared this by Isaiah; "And they shall see the carcases of the men who have transgressed against Me, and their worm shall not die, and their fire shall not be quenched." The gnashing of teeth also indicates the feeling of one indignant because each repents too late, is too late wroth with himself, groans over himself too late, that he offended with such obstinate wickedness.'

S. Augustine speaks of it, as undecided;

'[p] There will therefore continue without end that eternal death of the damned, that is, alienation from

[n] in Is. lxvi. fin.   [o] in S. Luc. c. vii. nn. 205, 206.
[p] Enchirid. n. 29. Short Treatises p. 153. Oxf. Tr.

the life of God, and itself will be common to all, whatever men according to their human feelings may imagine concerning variety of punishments, or concerning relief or intermission of pains; as the eternal life of the Saints will remain in common the life of all, in whatever distinction of honours they harmoniously shine.'

In the Greek Communion, S. John Damascene, who, although late, stands for them as the summary of their great fathers, wrote;

'q We shall rise again then, our souls again united to the bodies, which have become incorruptible and put off corruption, and shall be placed before the aweful judgement of Christ; and the devil and his demons and his man, i. e. Anti-Christ, and the ungodly and sinners shall be delivered to the everlasting fire, not material fire like ours, but such as God knoweth. But they who have done good shall shine forth as the sun with the Angels to life everlasting with our Lord Jesus Christ, ever seeing Him and seen by Him, and enjoying with Him unceasing joy.'

The agreement of Theophylact is the more remarkable, because he carries on the belief, that the punishments are spiritual, so late (A.D. 1077) and that he, to such an extent, though not exclusively[r], represents S. Chrysostom.

'[s] The worm and the fire, which punish sinners, is the conscience of each, and the memory of the foul deeds committed in this life, which prey upon him like a worm, and scorch him like fire.'

But now before entering into the proofs of the

[q] de Fide L. iv. fin.　　　　[r] See Benedictine Preface.
[s] on S. Mark c. ix.

eternity of punishment to those who *will* incur it, let me sum up in one what has been said ;

1. Without free-will, man would be inferior to the lower animals, which have a sort of limited freedom of choice.

2. Absolute free-will implies the power of choosing amiss and, having chosen amiss, to persevere in choosing amiss. It would be self-contradictory, that Almighty God should create a free agent capable of loving Him, without being capable also of rejecting His love.

3. The higher and more complete and pervading the freewill is, the more completely an evil choice will pervade and disorder the whole being.

4. But without free-will we could not freely love God. Freedom is a condition of love.

5. In eternity those who behold Him will know what the bliss is, eternally to love Him. But then that bliss involves the intolerable misery of losing Him through our own evil choice. To lose God and be alienated from Him is in itself Hell, or the vestibule of Hell.

6. But that His creatures may not lose Him, God, when He created all His rational creatures with free-will, created them also in grace, so that they had the full power to choose aright, and could not choose amiss, except by resisting the drawing of God to love Him.

7. The only hindrance to man's salvation is, in any case, the obstinate misuse of that free-will, with which God endowed him, in order that he might freely love Him.

8. God wills that all should be saved, if they *will*

it, and to this end gave His Son to die for them, and the Holy Ghost to teach them.

9. The merits of Jesus reach to every soul who wills to be saved, whether in this life they knew Him or knew Him not.

10. God the Holy Ghost visits every soul which God has created, and each soul will be judged as it responded or did not respond to the degree of light which He bestowed on it, not by our maxims, but by the wisdom and love of Almighty God.

11. We know absolutely nothing of the proportion of the saved to the lost or who will be lost; but this we *do* know, that none will be lost, who do not obstinately to the end and in the end refuse God. None will be lost, whom God *can* save, without destroying in them His own gift of free-will.

12. With regard to the *nature* of the sufferings, nothing is matter of faith. No one doubts that the very special suffering will be the loss of God (pœna damni): that, being what they are, they know that they were made by God for Himself, and yet, through their own obstinate will, will not have Him. As to 'pains of sense,' the Church has no where laid down as a matter of faith, the material character of the worm and the fire, or that they denote more than the gnawing of remorse. Although then it would be very rash to lay down dogmatically, that the 'fire' is *not* to be understood literally, as it has been understood almost universally by Christians, yet no one has a right to urge those representations, from which the imagination so shrinks, as a ground for refusing to believe in hell, since he is left free not to believe them.

iv. It is otherwise as to the remaining demand of

Dr. Farrar, that we should give up the belief in the eternity of punishment for all who incur it. For this would be to give up part of that Faith which our Lord gave, as a protection to all those who suffer for Him sooner than give up Himself.

"[t] I say unto you My friends, Be not afraid of them that kill the body, and after that have no more that they can do. But I will forewarn you whom ye shall fear: Fear Him, which after He hath killed hath power to cast into hell; yea, I say unto you, Fear Him." This fear of being for ever separated from Christ in hell strengthened the weakness of the flesh in Christian martyrs, as we see from the sayings of some of them [u]; this roused some who, for the extremity of suffering, had once denied Him, to endure fearlessly all torments for Him [v]: the dread of the eternal fire made that which consumed the flesh to be like Elijah's chariot of fire, which bore him above all of earth: this fire expelled the evil passions of the flesh [w]: this article of their faith the unlettered barbarians [x] knew of, as belonging to the primitive Creed, as much as the words of our Lord in the Athanasian. '[w] The fear of hell brought them to the crown of the kingdom.' This we dare not take away, lest we be contradicting our Lord.

But now perhaps that those unfounded fears have been removed, 1) that the lost are the greater part of the human race, and 2) that all are lost whom

[t] S. Luke xii. 4, 5. See also S. Matt. x. 28.
[u] See below, Belief of the early martyrs.
[v] See the account of the recovery of Biblias who had apostatized, Eus. H. E. v. 7. ibid. [w] S. Chrys. on the Statues Hom. xv. n. 2.
[x] S. Irenæus adv. hær. iii. 4.

man's eyes cannot see to be in a state of grace, some who have gone thus far, may be ready to consider more patiently the irrelevance of the alleged proofs of Universalism or the disproof of the Faith of the Church, which Dr. Farrar uses and enforces, but which he does not adopt.

Dr. Farrar says that the statements, that he '[y]denied the existence of hell' or 'denounced the doctrine of eternal punishment,' '[z]are merely ignorant perversions of what' he 'tried to teach.' He himself rejects[z], 1) '*Universalism*,' 'the opinion that all men will be ultimately saved;' 2) *Annihilationism*, or 'the opinion that, after a retributive punishment, the wicked will be destroyed.' He says, '[a]I dare not lay down any dogma of Universalism: partly because it is not clearly revealed to us, and partly because it is impossible for us to estimate the hardening effect of obstinate persistence in evil, and the power of the human will to resist the law and reject the love of God.'

Dr. Farrar '[b] sets aside the question of the salvability of devils, as beyond our range.' This is inconsistent; for if everlasting fire is to be not penal fire, which lasts for ever, but an Æonian fire created to purify those who fall into it, then it was [as we shall see] expressly created for the devil and his angels.

He says moreover repeatedly, '[c] I am not an universalist;' '[d] I cannot preach the certainty of Universalism;' '[y] I have never denied, nay, in despite of yearning hope, I have expressly admitted the possibility of even endless misery for those who abide in the determined impenitence of final and willing sin.'

[y] Pref. to 9th thousand p. xiii. [z] Pref. p. xxix. [a] Ib. p. xxiv.
[b] Eternal Hope p. 158 note. [c] p. 86 note. [d] Ib. p 84.

No Theologian, nay, no Christian believes or ever believed that any will fall into hell, except through 'determined and final impenitence.'

It is difficult for another to understand the difference between a 'dogma of Universalism' which the author 'dares not lay down,' and 'a hope' which is also 'ᵉa doctrine;' 'ᶠa truth,' 'ᵍ *truths*, which have been displaced by groundless *opinions*, and which are *necessary* for the purity, almost for the very existence of that faith, which is the one sole hope of the suffering world;' 'ʰa doctrine which alone can stem the spread of infidelity;' essential to thinking 'ⁱnoble thoughts of God.'

It is difficult also to attach any definite idea to the words which Dr. Farrar has selected to characterise his belief, 'Eternal Hope.' Hope, we know, as a virtue and grace, when this fleeting scene is over, will be swallowed up in fruition, as faith shall be in the vision of our God. 'Eternal hope,' must be a hope which never receives its accomplishment; ever longing; ever stretching on; never attaining: an 'Æonian' hope, which *we*, not the lost, are to hold about their 'Æonian' punishment: that, however long they may hold out against the love of God, they may give way at last. In the sermon ʲ it is a hope for the 'poor in spirit;' the mourners, 'even if death overtake them, before the final victory is won;' though they 'may have to be purified in that Gehenna of Æonian fire beyond the grave.' In the defence of the doctrine it dwindles down into 'ᵏthe doctrine (that is) that, even if in the short space of

ᵉ Eternal Hope Pref. p. xvi.   ᶠ Ib. p. xx.   ᵍ Ib. p. lxiii.   ʰ Ib. p. lxv.
ⁱ Et. H. p. 116.   ʲ Ib. p. 88.   ᵏ Dr. F. Contemp. Rev. T. 32. p. 571.

human life the soul have not yet been weaned from sin, there may be for *some*, at any rate, a hope of recovery, a possibility of amendment, if not after the last judgement, at least in some disembodied condition beyond the grave.'

But no Christian has denied, few, I should think, would doubt that, to those who had struggled to the last, God would give repentance in the hour of death, whatever they might have to suffer in the delay of the sight of God, for which they will then know that they were made, or in the long undistracted memory of their own vileness and ingratitude toward Him Who loved them and gave Himself for them. But any how a change in the soul, which should be short of the change between rejecting God and accepting Him, before the Day of Judgement, might be believed by any one who yet believed in the everlasting loss of those who finally rejected Him. This is not 'Eternal hope,' nor 'a purifying in the Gehenna of Æonian fire.'

Dr. Farrar never mentions the future punishment of the wicked without adding to it some of the untrue 'accretions' which he blends with it; but, in his representations, its eternity is as much an 'accretion' as they. Yet 'ending' and 'non-ending' are contradictories, which admit of no intermediate qualification. If man is admitted to be immortal, and punishment is not to be endless, there is no other conclusion but that he should be restored. I am thankful that Dr. Farrar is not an universalist. There is no end of human inconsistencies. But I fear that his book will teach Universalism, since he denounces so energetically the only faith which can resist it.

But Dr. Farrar, in rejecting Universalism, virtually gives up all arguments, which Universalists draw from texts of Holy Scripture or from à priori reasoning.

1. The only difficulty in reason is the creation of free-agents, whose perfection and bliss it should be to love God and be the objects of His love. God cannot cease to be That Which He Is, the supreme Good in Himself, and of all His rational creation. His love cannot cease to be essential to their bliss, though they reject it. The difficulty, insoluble in this life, is, why Almighty God created beings with a free choice, and exposed Himself to His creatures' choice, knowing that some who would not choose Him, must be unutterably miserable through their loss of Him. In this world we can but marvel at the condescending goodness of God, that He should so prize the free love of His creatures (and of our poor selves among them), that He shonld put Himself at their choice, that they might, by the enabling assistance of His Grace, eternally love Him, and be for ever filled with His love and be one with Him, notwithstanding the inevitable misery to those, who, through their own obstinately evil choice, would not have Him.

The question of reason, why did God create *one* who, He knew, would be miserable through his free endless hate of Him, holds equally, if there were none but Satan. The old Universalists saw consistently, that any theory of universal restoration is inconsistent, which does not include the restoration of Satan.

2. Equally, as to the texts cited in behalf of what

is called 'restitution.' The stress, which is laid upon the word 'all,' is absolutely annihilated, unless it includes 'Satan and his angels.' Nay, in that 'other Gospel,' which Dr. Farrar rejects, but which Satan is trying to induce men to substitute for the 'everlasting Gospel' of Christ, he and his angels, not we, are the special objects of the love of God. In the true Gospel, it has been dwelt upon, that our Lord says that He will say to those whom He shall place on His Right Hand, "Come, ye blessed of My Father, inherit the kingdom prepared for you from the foundation of the world." The righteous are saved, because the Father has blessed them for His dearly Beloved Son's sake, Whom He gave, that "whosoever should believe in Him should not perish, but have everlasting life." Our Lord dwells upon the truth, that the kingdom is the gift of God, and teaches us that it is so.

[1] But to those on the left hand He does not say, " Ye cursed of My Father;" for, not *He* laid the curse upon them, but their own works; and He says, " into the everlasting fire,"—not, prepared for them, but—" prepared for the devil and his angels." 'I, He saith, 'prepared the kingdom for you: but the fire no more for you, but for the devil and his angels; but since ye cast yourselves therein, impute it to yourselves.'

But, according to this adulterated gospel, the 'everlasting fire' is not everlasting but temporary :— it is to be a purifying fire, '[k] a Gehenna of Æonian fire beyond the grave,' by which sinners, who, even in the last moment of this life, *would* resist all the

[1] S. Chrys. on S. Matt. xxv. Hom. lxxix. 2. p. 1050. Oxf. Tr.

pleadings of His grace and offers of forgiveness, are *by a new probation* to be won. In the express meaning of our Lord's words that fire was not primarily 'prepared' for them, but, 'for the devil and his angels.' The devils, were, according to this interpretation, the primary objects of His love.

The other texts, alleged in encouragement of the hope that all the wicked will be ultimately restored, may be arranged under the following classes;

i) Passages, which declare that Christ died for all.

Of this blessed truth no Christian doubts, unless as far as there be still rigid disciples of Calvin. The Church hath ever taught it; it teaches it everywhere. "[m] God sent not His Son into the world to condemn the world, but that the world through Him might be saved." "[n] He is the propitation for our sins and not for ours only, but for the whole world." "[o] He gave Himself a ransom for all, to be testified in due time." "[p] We have seen and do testify that the Father hath sent the Son to be the Saviour of the world." "[q] He tasted death for every man." "[r] The grace of God hath appeared, which is saving unto all men." Such was the purpose of the Infinite mercy of God. All was complete on His part. But that same Scripture is full of aweful warning, that we take heed lest we forfeit it for ourselves through the "deceitfulness of sin." "I," our Lord says[s], "if I be lifted up from the earth, will draw all men unto Me." The Cross has a mighty attraction. The love of Him Who died for us on it, has, through all the

[m] S. John iii. 17.   [n] 1 S. John ii. 2.   [o] 1 Tim. ii. 6.
[p] 1 S. John iv. 14. [q] Heb. ii. 9.   [r] Tit. ii. 11.   [s] S. John xii. 32.

God wills all to be saved, but not against their will. 31

ages since that Precious Death, drawn laden souls to it. But the magnet of His love has not drawn us like stocks and stones, without and against our wills. The will must surrender itself at last; else it will reject even Almighty Infinite Love.

This condition is even mentioned in some of the texts alleged. "[t]Who willeth all men to be saved, and to come to the knowledge of the truth." "[u]Who is the Saviour of all men, specially of those who believe." Yet there have been at all times those who turned away from the truth and who would not believe. "[v]How often," our Lord appealed to those who heard Him, "would I have gathered you together, as a hen gathereth her chickens under her wings, and ye would not." "[w]God willeth not that *any* should perish;" "but," he adds, "that all should come to repentance; before the Day of the Lord shall come as a thief in the night," "[x]looking for and hasting unto the coming of the Day of God, wherein the heavens, being on fire, shall be dissolved, and the elements shall melt with fervent heat." He says by the Prophet Ezekiel, "[y]I have no pleasure in the death of the wicked, but that the wicked turn from his way and live; turn ye, turn ye, from your evil ways:" but he adds the mournful appeal, "Why *will* ye die, O house of Israel?" They could then incur that death, if they *would* not turn.

He willeth that we should be saved, but He willeth not to do violence to our will, which He holds sacred, as the finite image of His own Infinite Will, free, after the likeness of His own Almighty Will,

[t] 1 Tim. ii. 4.   [u] Ib. iv. 10.   [v] S. Matt. xxiii. 37.
[w] 2 S. Pet. iii. 9.   [x] Ib. 12.   [y] Ezek. xviii. 23.

"Who doth whatsoever pleaseth Him." If He were to force our wills, He would make us lower than the beasts that perish; for they too have a limited will. He will mightily influence, constrain by His love, plead, put good thoughts into our souls, knock at the closed door, repeat His pleadings again and again; but still there is that sad, "Ye would not," before which Omnipotent love was obliged by the conditions of our nature which He had given us, to turn away. Man has still the power to refuse even the overwhelming, sweet, attractive, all-but-compulsory power of the love of God. He says, that He 'willeth all men to be saved,' but He does not say that He will force those who will not come.

ii) In other passages, the context and the idiom are alike neglected.

1. S. Paul, in his glowing picture of the triumph of our Lord for us His people, bursts forth, "*z* Now is Christ risen from the dead, and become the first-fruits of them that slept. For since by man came death, by man came also the resurrection of the dead. For as in Adam all die, even so in Christ shall all be made alive. But every man in his own order: Christ the first-fruits; afterward, they that are Christ's at His Coming. Then cometh the end, when He shall have delivered up the kingdom to God, even the Father; when He shall have put down all rule and all authority and power. For He must reign, till He hath put all enemies under His feet. The last enemy that shall be destroyed is death. For He hath put all things under His feet. But when He saith, all

z 1 Cor. xv. 20—28.

things are put under Him, it is manifest that He is excepted, which did put all things under Him. And when all things shall be subdued unto Him, then shall the Son also Himself be subject unto Him that put all things under Him, that God may be all in all."

It is S. Paul's summary of the proofs of the Resurrection of Christ. He refuted those who denied the resurrection of the body by establishing the Resurrection of Christ, without which our whole faith in Christ were empty. The proof of the Resurrection of Christ lay in the testimony of all those who had seen Him alive after He had risen from the dead. S. Paul closes it with his own. On the Resurrection and Ascension, began His mediatorial kingdom, as God-Man, given to Him by the Father; at His Coming to judge the world, His 'appearing,' the mediatorial kingdom will have had its perfection: there will then be no more sin in any of us, His subjects, for which to intercede; no enemies, from whom to defend His own; no imperfection, which to perfect, that God may be 'all in all.' The time then, when God shall be 'all in all,' is not after countless ages, but at the Coming of Christ.

But also the being 'all in all' is language, which God uses in Holy Scripture in a very definite meaning. S. Paul uses the same words of God's present gifts to us in this life, inchoate here, to be perfected hereafter. To be 'all,' 'every thing, to a person,' is a common way of speaking, as among the Greeks and Latins[a], so among us also. We have the further full

[a] See a very large collection of passages from Greek and Latin writers in Wetstein on 1 Cor. xv. 28. pp. 167, 168.

expression, which Dr. Farrar too uses in this same book, of being 'all in all to another[b].' It means, that the one being, who is spoken of, is to the other, 'instead of all.' He, to whom he is 'all,' needs nothing else to fill any office or fill up any void. But to be 'all *in* all' is a fruit of the Incarnation. It is already begun in us, who are Christians. S. Paul counts it as our privilege. In contrast with all outward things, upon which Jew or Greek boasted themselves, there is, he says, one thing to the Christian, to be '*in* Christ.' All those outward distinctions were nothing worth; '[c] circumcision or uncircumcision; Barbarian, Scythian, bond or free.' One thing only stands instead of all, to be *in* Christ. If you have only Him, you will obtain the same as those who have them. '[d] But Christ,' he saith, 'is all and *in* all,' i. e. Christ will be all things to you, both dignity and race; and He, One and the Same, *in* you all. S. Paul says not only 'all in all' but 'Christ is all things *and* in all.' He is 'all things, and *in* all' His members, as God is "all in all," by indwelling in us.

S. Paul says in the same Epistle to the Corinthians, that God[e] worked *all things in all*, i.e. in all those Christians, of whom he was speaking.

Since then this is a received idiom, that "Christ is all things *in* all," who are members of Him; that "God worketh all things *in* all" those Christians, of whom the Apostle had just spoken, it would be plainly unnatural and contrary to the idiom, to interpret

---

[b] 'Ask happy lovers, when they know the joy of being all in all to each other.' Eternal Hope p. 34.

[c] Col. iii. 11.   [d] S Chrys. ad loc.   [e] 1 Cor. xii. 6.

the saying, 'that God may be all *in* all,' of any others than those just spoken of, 'those who are Christ's at His Coming;' and to make it include all those to whom, He has told us, at His coming, He shall say, 'Depart from Me;' as also Satan and his angels.

The words then can have no bearing upon any post-æonian restoration. It has been, from of old, the ground-work of Universalism, but it has only been made to yield a support to it by taking 'all in all' as a mere phrase, apart from its meaning in Holy Scripture, or even from its popular use. As interpreted by the Universalists, God would not be 'all things in all,' unless He indwelt Satan too in the fulness of His Spirit and Presence, as, although not as much as, that created being, who is nearest to Himself. Satan too, in *this* explanation, must be the dwelling-place of the Trinity.

2. S. Peter, in his second preaching of the Resurrection of Christ, told the Jews, that "'the heavens must receive Jesus," 'until' a time at the end of this world. This time is, according to different renderings of the word, either absolutely 'the restoration of all things,' or 'until the times of the completion of all things which God spake by the mouth of His holy prophets which have been since the world began.' This last seems to me the natural construction of the words in themselves, and, according to this construction which has been adopted by very old and competent authority [g], the words would have no bearing what-

---

[f] Acts iii. 21.

[g] They are so taken by Didymus, and an anonymous Greek Scholiast in the Catena on the Acts, ed. Cramer. Hesychius interprets the word, 'fulfilment.' S. Irenæus has 'dispositionis' (or-

ever upon the subject, for which they are currently quoted.

But if the phrase is to be rendered 'until the times of the restitution' or 'restoration of all things,' as our Lord says of Elias, he "[h] shall first come and restore all things," then the whole idiom must be taken in that same sense, of that great restoration which Elijah was to effect, at the end of this visible state of things, before our Lord's second Coming, when " [i] he shall turn the heart of the fathers to the children, and the heart of the children to their fathers, lest I come and smite the earth with a curse." Clearly also since S. Peter says, that the heavens must receive Jesus Christ 'until the time of the restoration of all things,' the time must be that, of which the angels spake to the Apostles, "this same Jesus, which is taken up from you into heaven, shall so come in like manner as ye have seen Him go into heaven." It must be, until He come to be our Judge, not until the Æonian periods, of which Universalists speak.

dering) iii. 12. 3. Theophylact has, 'all things must be restored and come to an end;' and as a summary of the meaning, 'The prophets said that many things should happen which have not yet been fulfilled, but are yet coming and shall come to pass till the end. For Christ, being taken up into heaven, remains there till the end of the world, to come thence with power, when all things which the prophets foretold shall have been completed, ἀποκαταστάντων.' ad loc. Tertullian has, 'tempore exhibitionis omnium quæ locutus est Deus.' De resurr. carnis c. 23. p. 396. Rig. The Vulg. and Vers. ant. have 'in tempore restitutionis omnium quæ locutus est Deus.' The Peshito has, 'to the fulfilment of the time of all those things which God spake.' The literal Heracleota has, 'unto the time of the restitution of all the things which God hath spoken ' &c.

[h] S Matt. xvii. 11.   [i] Mal. iv. 6.

3. Again, when S. Paul says that "*ᵏ Christ both died and rose and revived, that He might be Lord both of the dead and the living,*" he must be speaking of those two classes, of whom he had spoken just before, those who "¹ live unto the Lord" and those who "die unto the Lord," and who, 'whether they live or die, are the Lord's,' not of those to whom He shall say, " I never knew you; depart from Me, all ye workers of iniquity."

4. So when he says, "ᵐ As in Adam all die, even so in Christ shall *all* be made alive," he must be speaking of those, of whom he had just spoken, "ⁿ which are fallen asleep in Christ;" those who by spiritual birth belong to Christ, as by their natural birth they belonged to Adam; "they who are Christ's," as he says again; not those of whom he says in another place, "ᵒ If any man hath not the Spirit of Christ, he is none of His."

5. S. Paul appeals to those who "ᵖ despise the riches of the goodness and forbearance and longsuffering of God; not knowing that the goodness of God leadeth thee to repentance, but after thy hardness and impenitent heart treasurest unto thyself wrath in the day of wrath and revelation of the righteous judgement of God; Who will render to every man according to his deeds: to them who by patient continuance in well-doing seek for glory and honour and immortality, eternal life: but unto them that are contentious, and do not obey the truth, but obey unrighteousness, indignation and wrath, tribulation and anguish, upon every soul of man that doeth evil."

ᵏ Rom. xiv. 9.   ˡ Ib. 8.   ᵐ 1 Cor. xv. 22.
ⁿ Ib. 18.   ᵒ Rom. viii. 9.   ᵖ Ib. ii. 4—9.

What encouragement Dr. Farrar can think that these words give to those who *do* treasure to themselves wrath, I cannot imagine.

There are yet two criticisms to be noticed; 1. the denial that αἰώνιος means everlasting, 'because it is used,' Dr. Farrar says [q], 'over and over again, of things transitory,' 2. that our Lord, in speaking of Gehenna, must have used the word in the sense in which Dr. Farrar thinks that the Talmudists use it, and in which he assumes that the Jews used it in our Lord's time, and must have understood Him.

1. On the use of the word αἰώνιος in classical Greek, I have appended to the sermon on Everlasting Punishment a note written for me, in view of my Sermon, by the best Greek Oxford Scholar of his day, my friend, the Rev. J. Riddell [r]. It appears from this, that the word was used strictly of eternity, an eternal existence, such as shall be, when time shall be no more [s]. In the New Testament it occurs seventy-one times: of eternal life [t], forty-four times; of Almighty God, His Spirit and His glory [u], three times; of the kingdom of Christ [x], His Redemption [y], the Blood of His covenant [z], His Gospel [a], salvation [b], our habitation in heaven [c];

[q] Et. Hope, Exc. iii. p. 199.   [r] Fellow of Balliol.   [s] Rev. x. 6.
[t] S. Matt. xix. 16, 29; xxv. 46; S. Mark x. 17, 30; S. Luke x. 25; xviii. 18, 30; S. John, uniformly, twenty three times, iii. 15, 16, 36; iv. 14, 36; v. 24, 39; vi. 27, 40, 47, 54, 68; x. 28; xii. 25, 50; xvii. 2, 3. 1 S. John i. 2; ii. 25; iii. 15; v. 11, 13, 20. Acts xiii. 46, 48; S Paul, Rom. ii. 7; v. 21; vi. 22, 23; Gal. vi. 8; 1 Tim. i. 16; vi. 12, 19; Tit. i. 2; iii. 7; S. Jude 21; the habitations of the righteous, S. Luke xvi. 9; 2 Cor. v. 1.
[u] Rom. xvi. 26   Heb ix. 14.   1 Tim. vi. 16   [x] 2 S. Pet i. 11.
[y] Heb. ix. 12.   [z] Ib xiii. 20.   [a] Rev. xiv. 6.   [b] Heb. v. 9.
[c] S Luke xvi. 9.   2 Cor. v. 1.

of the glory laid up for us[d], thrice; our inheritance[e], consolation[f], of a sharer of eternal life[g]; of eternal fire[h], thrice; of punishment, judgement, destruction[i], four times[j].

Of the future then it is no where used in the New Testament, except of eternal life or punishment.

There is indeed one aweful exception, according to a probable reading in one passage, noticed by Dr. Farrar: although that reading is not certain enough to allow us certainly to claim our Lord's authority. If this reading were certain, it would involve that our Lord spoke in one place not of 'judgement,' but of 'sin' beyond the grave, saying, '[k] is in danger of

[d] 2 Cor. iv. 17, 18.   2 Tim. ii. 16.   1 S. Pet. v. 10.
[e] Heb. ix. 15.   [f] 2 Thess. ii. 16.   [g] Philem. 15.
[h] S. Matt. xviii. 8; xxv. 41.   S. Jude 7.
[i] S. Matt. xxv. 46.   S Mark iii 29.   2 Thess i. 9.   Heb. vi. 2.
[j] Dr. Farrar says (Et. H. p. 202.) 'Cæsarius Dial. 3. even observes that the Origenist argument on the terminability of torment was derived from the use of the very word.   Huet Origen. Opp. pp. 231, 233 Paris.'

The argument, quoted by Cæsarius, must be confused, for no Greek could have so argued. The words are, 'Not as some fabler thought, the chastisement of sinners shall have an end, because the Lord called the fire of punishment αἰώνιον only, and not αἰώνιον αἰώνων.' Cæsar. Dial. iii. Interr. 139. in Gall. Bibl. Patr. vi. 99. The statement being anonymous, although Origen was probably meant by 'the fabler,' no one is responsible for such impossible Greek.

[k] S. Mark iii. 29. 'is in danger of eternal sin.' 'Such is the true reading, ἁμαρτήματος אBL.; ἁμαρτίας C.D not κρίσεως.' Et. Hope p. 112. note. There is, any how, nothing of 'a *doom* to everlasting sin,' of which Dr. Farrar speaks.

The preponderance of authority seems to be in favour of ἁμαρτήματος, although there are weighty authorities for κρίσεως.

For ἁμαρτήματος are אBLΔ. 28. 33. 2pe (a S. Petersburg MS. collated by M. Muralt.)

For ἁμαρτίας (apparently, C.1ma manu) D. 13. 69. 346. S. Ath.

everlasting sin.' If these words be His, they speak of an 'everlasting sin,' a sin bound up (so to speak) with the existence of the sinner[1], since he is not freed from it; or, to use the language of universalists, as æonian as the fire.

The same idea of absolute eternity lies in the three remaining passages, in words spoken after the manner of men, "eternal times." We cannot speak of the '[m]everlasting Now' of eternity, save in language borrowed from time. When the Psalmist says, "[n]from everlasting to everlasting, Thou art God," the language is necessarily inadequate, because 'from' implies a beginning, but God is without beginning. Another expression, "[o]Thy throne is from everlasting," lit. 'from then,' is perhaps most exempt from the idea of time; i. e. look back as far as you will, go back and back and back beyond all those æons, of which men speak, then too and 'from then' was God. Still the word 'from' implies time, and time is God's creation. He is not *from* it, but it from Him.

With these agree S. Cypr. (ii) S. Aug. Ital. (except Cod. Brix. 6th cent.) Vulg. (except Tol. MS.) Copt. Goth.

For κρίσεως are A E F G H K M S U V Γ Π Pesh , Syr-Heracl., Ital. in Cod. Brix., Vulg. in Tol. MS.

On the one side are the Itala, indicating the existence of the reading in the 2nd cent.; א (Cod. Sinait.) BC. Copt. Goth. of the ivth; On the other the Peshito of the 2nd cent. [My son has verified the present reading in one MS. of the vth, another of the vth or vith cent.], and others; A of the vth cent. with the mass of uncial MSS. and Syr. Heracl. at the end of the vth.

[1] Even Origen speaks of sins 'in ipsis ita animabus infixa ut nequeant aboleri, in Lev. Hom. 8. n. 5. Opp. ii. 231. ed. de la Rue.

[m] 'An everlasting Now of misery.' Southey, Thalaba.

[n] Ps. xc. 2.   [o] Ib. xciii. 2.

But whatever God has done, or does, or shall do, lay ever in the depths of His Immutable Mind. He knew in all eternity that He would create man, engraced, but endowed with free-will, and capable of falling from Him. He knew that He should restore, redeem him, and at what cost. This was the eternal purpose, which He ever had before creation, in the silence of His own ever-present eternity. It lay as much there, when He had not yet created any being, when nothing existed save Himself, Father Son and Holy Ghost, as when He revealed it.

When then S. Paul says, 'P The secret of man's redemption through Jesus Christ had been kept in silence in eternal times,' he is speaking of an absolute eternity, as eternal as Almighty God Himself. So he speaks again "ᑫ of the mystery which was *hid from the ages,* ἀπὸ τῶν αἰώνων, *in* God, Who created all things by Christ Jesus, that *now* might be made known to the principalities and powers in heavenly places through the Church the manifold wisdom of God according to the purpose of the ages (τῶν αἰώνων) which [purpose] He hath wrought in Christ Jesus our Lord." S. Paul places us altogether (so to speak) in the Being of God. It is before creation, not known until then 'to the principalities and powers in heavenly places;' the purpose of God in the ages past, but before time was; for it was before creation, and time is a portion of God's creation.

When then, again, he says that God "ʳsaved us and called us with a holy calling, not according to our works, but according to His own purpose and grace, which was given us in Christ Jesus before eter-

P Rom. xvi. 25.   q Eph. iii. 9-11.   r 2 Tim. i. 9, 10.

nal times, but has now been made manifest through the appearance of Christ Jesus;" he must mean that God gave it to us in purpose from all eternity, as he says elsewhere, that He [s]chose us in Christ "*before the foundation of the world,*" not *from* its foundation, but before it. '[t] For although before the creation of the world there was neither motion nor any time, yet in that immense space of eternity, as Jerome says here, ' we must believe that there was an eternity of ages, in which the Father ever was with the Son and Holy Spirit; and, so to say, all Eternity is one time of God, yea, innumerable times, since He Himself is Infinite, Who, before times, transcends all time.' The years of our world are not yet full six thousand, and how many eternities, how many times, how many origins of ages must we suppose that there have been, in which Angels, Thrones, Dominions and other Powers served God, and without changes and measures of times existed at the command of God!'

'And indeed you can hardly understand otherwise what we read in David, "[u] I thought of the days of old and the eternal years," nor could you understand otherwise what Micah says, "[v] And His goings forth have been from the beginning, from the days of eternity." For if, as the fathers affirm with wonderful consent [x], the prophet speaks of the everlasting Birth of the Divine Word, what days of eternity can he mean save Eternity itself? Paul then writes in the

[s] Eph. i. 4. πρὸ καταβολῆς κόσμου.   [t] Justiniani on Tit. i. 2.
   [u] Ps. lxxvii. 5.   [v] Micah v. 2.
   [x] Justiniani quotes S. Jerome on Mic. v. Euseb. Dem. Ev. vii. 2. S. Chrys. Quod Christus sit Deus, and on Ps. xliv [xlv] 6. S. Cyril de Trin. L. ii. v. fin. and Hom. 4 cont. Nest. Theodoret.

'Ages of ages' used uniformly of eternity. 43

present place, that eternal life was promised "[y] before the times of ages."'

And on another place[y] he says, "what the force of the word 'promised' is, Augustine explains in this way: '[z] How did God promise, since He promised to men, who as yet were not before eternal times? except that in His own Eternity and in His own Word, Co-Eternal with Himself, that was already fixed by predestination, which was to be in its own time?'"

I cannot then but think that the paraphrase of our translation is verbally inaccurate, when it substitutes in one place, 'since the world began,' for 'before eternal times;' for the word is not 'since,' but 'before.' The other paraphrase, 'before the world began,' although inadequate, is so far correct. But then S. Paul (in a place, which Dr. F. employs for the contrary, as though it were self-evident,) uses the word 'eternal' in the two successive verses in the self-same sense; in the first [a] he is speaking of the eternal purpose of God; in the second [b], of God Himself, the Eternal.

The same uniformity of usage, although not the same contrast, occurs in the substantive word αἰών. The same words 'for ever and ever' (lit. 'for the ages of the ages') are used in the ascription of glory to God[c], to the Lord [d] [Jesus], to Jesus[e]; to God the Father and the Lamb[f], of the endless life of Jesus[g], of the reign of Christ[h], of the sufferings of the lost[i], of the devil[k], of the reign of the saints[l].

[y] 2 Tim. i. 10.   [z] De civ. Dei xii. 16.   [a] Rom. xvi. 25.   [b] Ib. 26.
[c] Phil iv. 20. 1 Tim. i. 17. 1 Pet. iv. 11. v. 11. Rev. vii. 12; x. 6.
       [d] 2 Tim. iv. 18.   [e] Heb. xiii. 21. Rev. i. 6.
[f] Rev. v. 13.   [g] Ib. i. 18, iv. 9, 10, xv. 7. In Eph. iii. 21, the singular is used τοῦ αἰῶνος τῶν αἰώνων.   [h] Rev. xi. 15.
    [i] Ib. xiv. 11, xix. 3.   [k] Ib. xx. 10.   [l] Ib xxii. 5.

They who deny that any of the words used of future punishment in Holy Scripture express eternity, would do well to consider, whether there is any way, in which Almighty God *could* have expressed it, which they would have accepted, as meaning it.

S. Augustine sums up the argument as to the meaning of the word, drawn from the parallelism, in a way, the weight of which has of late not been felt.

'[m]What a thing it is, to account eternal punishment to be a fire of long duration, and eternal life to be without end, since Christ comprised both in that very same place, in one and the same sentence, saying, "These shall go into eternal punishment, but the righteous into life eternal!" If both are eternal, either both must be understood to be lasting with an end, or both perpetual without end. For like is related to like; on the one side, eternal punishment; on the other, eternal life. But to say in one and the same sentence, life eternal shall be without end, punishment eternal shall have an end, were too absurd: whence, since the eternal life of the saints shall be without end, punishment eternal too shall doubtless have no end to those whose it shall be.'

The argument is not merely from language. It has a moral and religious aspect. Any ordinary writer, who drew a contrast between two things, would, if he wished to be understood, use the self-same word in the self-same sense. He would avoid ambiguity. If he did not, we should count him ignorant of language, or, if it were intentional, dishonest. I asked, '[n] In what matter of this world would you trust one who, in any matter of this world, should use

[m] de Civ. Dei xxi. 23.   [n] Serm. on Everlasting Punishment p. 24.

the self-same word in two distinct senses in the self-same sentence, without giving any hint that he was so doing? In none. Find any case in which you would trust a man, who did so in the things of men, and then ascribe it to your God in the things of God. I could not trust man. I could not believe it of my God.'

Dr. Farrar calls it '°a battered and aged argument:' he says that 'it is of all arguments on the question the most absolutely and hopelessly futile :' he bids us 'not think, that it will weigh the 1000th part of a scruple with those, who [as they think] have again and again furnished the proof, why *they* regard it as absolutely inconclusive.' I doubt it not in the least. Never did any argument weigh any thing against a foregone conclusion. Arguments are never of any use, except as predisposing for the grace of God. Arguments were of use but to few on Mars' Hill, or to one only, 'whose heart the Lord opened,' 'by the river's side,' or for the conversion of the world. They were counted foolishness. But 'p the foolishness of God is wiser than men.' S. Augustine, as his teaching was, often reminded his hearers, 'the Teacher is within.' Dr. Farrar is not surprised that the '°glaring commonplaceness of the argument should render it a stronghold of some who are content with the obvious and the superficial.' The Gospel is for those who are 'content with the obvious,' —the poor. During three centuries of martyrdom the simple received our Lord's words in their simple sense. He did not use 'q emotional appeals.' He,

o Cont. Rev. June 1878 p. 581.   p 1 Cor. i. 25.

q 'That hard exaggerated and damnatory literalism, that unreasonable insistence on admitted metaphors and emotional appeals.' Dr. Farrar Cont. Rev. l. c p. 573.

the Truth, taught, He tells us, what He had received from the Father, "ʳI have given unto them the words which Thou gavest Me; and they have received them."

The argument, however, from the word αἰώνιος does not rest simply upon its use in the New Testament. People are apt to take up their Bible as a book indeed of authority to themselves, but upon which they are free to put any meaning, which they can justify to themselves, or which *they* think most accordant to the attributes of God. They comment upon it, as a book, which has come somehow into their hands, and which they are to explain, with all the advantages, which modern criticism or enlightenment (as they deem it) enables them to put upon single words. It does not occur to them, that the teaching in our Lord's words is not of to-day or yesterday, but from Him Who came to save mankind from their sins and from the fruits of their sins, and at the same time to "ˢreveal the wrath from heaven against all ungodliness and unrighteousness of men," from which He came to save them. What did He teach as to the doom of those who obstinately to and in the end refuse His grace?

No one has yet been found to doubt that the mass of Christians have from the first believed the future punishment of the lost to be everlasting. We see it, even apart from Holy Scripture, in those close upon the times of Jesus; it was the faith of the martyrs; it was recognised as the faith of Christians by the heathen. Oneᵗ who searched for human causes of the first marvellous propagation of the Gospel, count-

ʳ S. John xvii. 8.   ˢ Rom i 18.   ᵗ Gibbon.

ed this belief as one of his five causes; that the Christians believed it so energetically, as to be able to impress their belief on the heathen also. No one doubts that the millions upon millions of Christians, century after century, have believed it. It is owned to have been from the first the faith of the Creeds. From Whose words did all before the Origenists learn their belief in Hell? Upon Whose words do all who now believe it, rest their belief? In Whose words have all who have believed it expressed their belief? Whose words have all who disbelieved it had to explain away? The very disputes about the word αἰώνιος shew, from Whom they learned it;

> 'Christ on Himself, considerate Master, took
> The utterance of that doctrine's fearful sound:
> The Fount of Love His servants sends to tell
> Love's deeds; Himself reveals the sinner's Hell.'

Men strangely do not reflect that the denial of this doctrine involves the terrible blasphemy, that He, the Truth, so taught, that His disciples, *on the authority of His words*, believed what these hold not to be true; that He did, in fact, not foresee the effect of His own words: He Who knew all things, Who was God as well as Man, 'Who can neither deceive nor be deceived.'

Had our Blessed Lord been a mere human teacher, this would have involved no inconsistency. It presents no difficulty to the Socinian, or those who (as many Universalists) really deny the Incarnation, or that our Lord was very God[u]. But Dr. Farrar and

---

[u] A thoughtful writer in the Christian Remembrancer, April 1863 (and so previous to Dr. Farrar's book), said, 'Subject to the correction of more profound and laborious students, we avow that, in our

48 *Jesus, being God, knew how His words wd be understood.*

many who have followed him fully believe this truth. Our Lord in His Human mind, illumined by the Godhead with which It was united, must have seen how the words, in which He conveyed His revelation would be understood. Had Universalists been right, He, the Divine Teacher, would have used misleading words, which did (God forbid!) mislead the millions upon millions of His disciples who dutifully took them in their obvious meaning.

2. But beyond the argument from the 'æonian,' that the punishment of the lost *need* not be thought to be eternal, Dr. Farrar has another, which he calls his 'palmary argument,' from our Lord's use of the word Gehenna; that our Lord can*not* have meant to teach that the sufferings of unrepented sin would be eternal.

We must, he says, understand by 'hell' what our Lord meant by Gehenna, and, as used by our Lord, Gehenna did *not* mean endless torment. 'ᵛ In spite of unfair depreciation, I venture to say that, hastily as my book was produced, no modern writer has furnished a fuller contribution from Jewish testimonies to the decision of this important question; and if the position cannot be shaken, how strongly does it tell in favour of Eternal Hope!'

'ʷ It surely cannot be denied, that our Blessed Lord, speaking as 'a Jew to Jews among Jews,' must have used the words of His day in the sense wherein

---

own examination of this matter, *we have not been able to discover a single impugner of the dogma of eternal punishment who is consistent in his denial, and at the same time orthodox.*'

ᵛ Contemporary Review June 1878 p. 585.
ʷ Eternal Hope p. 81, note.

these words would have been understood by His hearers."

Dr. Farrar is mistaken, both in the principle which he lays down, and as to the facts, bearing upon it.

His principle is that, if our Lord used any religious term, already in use among the Jews, He must have used it in the self-same sense, meaning exactly what they meant. But, although, in God's mercy, He took our flesh of the seed of Abraham, He came amongst us to make a new revelation. Then, although He used their language, to engraft His teaching upon their past belief, He had, when need was, to stamp that language anew. This, every one owns that He did as to the terms, 'the kingdom of God,' 'the Messiah,' 'the being born again,' and many others. If then the meaning of a word, already in use among the Jews, is clear from the context of our Lord's words, the question, in what sense the Jews at any time used it among themselves, may be matter of interest in regard to *their* history; it has no bearing upon the revelation made by our Lord.

In regard to the facts, Dr. Farrar dismisses summarily or overlooks the evidence that the Jews believed in eternal punishment before or at the time of the Coming of our Lord, and called the place of that punishment Gehenna. So that His use of the word Gehenna would, according to Dr. Farrar's argument, be one of the proofs (if proof were needed) that He *did* mean to teach the everlastingness of punishment beyond the grave.

In works before or soon after the time of our Lord, Gehenna is described or named in Jewish Apocryphal books; the book of Enoch, the ivth book of Esdras, the Apocalypse of Baruch, and the Targum of Jonathan.

Belief in the eternity of future punishment is contained in the Book of Judith, in the 4th book of Maccabees, in the so-called Psalms of Solomon: the second death is mentioned in the Targums of Onkelos and Jonathan: Josephus attests the belief of the Pharisees and the Essenes in the eternity of punishment.

The later Jewish authorities which Dr. Farrar quotes, all come from the disciples of those who had rejected our Lord. The chief were employed in maintaining their ground against the Gospel of Him, Whom their fathers had crucified. They were not representatives of the ancient teaching. Their temple destroyed, themselves banished from their holy city, they had to build up a new righteousness, apart from hope in the Messiah and from sacrifice. Some gave up the hope of a Messiah altogether[x]; some looked only for one who should free them from their earthly masters, and restore their national greatness. Over against Christianity and to hinder conversions to Jesus, they fenced in their people from straying by dependence upon their privileges as descendants of Abraham, or of those with whom God made a covenant at Mount Sinai.

It will be most convenient, first to consider the evidence that the Jews, before or about the time of our Lord, did believe the punishment of the lost to

[x] 'Grass will grow on thy chin, Akiba, before the Messiah will appear.' Saying of Jochanan b. Torta. See Jewish authorities in Graetz iv. 150.

Book of Judith.

be everlasting; and then the evidences that the Talmudical writers and their modern followers believed that the penalties were everlasting for those who incurred them, excepting only 'the sinners of their own people' who did not apostatise, i.e. become Christians, and a class, whom they called 'the righteous of the nations of the earth.'

1. THE BOOK OF JUDITH. It would be out of place to enter here into any of the controversies about the book itself. It is enough to state that in these days, in which everything is disputed, no one places it later than the 2nd century before our Lord[y]. It is therefore an evidence of the belief of the Jews at the time of His Coming. In the remarkable hymn in the mouth of Judith, at its close, she says, '[z] Wo to the nations who rise up against my race! The Almighty Lord will take vengeance on them in the Day of Judgement, putting fire and worms into their flesh, and they shall weep in sensible torment for ever.'

The Vulgate has a different reading [a]; 'He will

[y] Ewald, on inadequate grounds, places it B.C. 130. Fritzsche says, 'Firmly as I am convinced that the book was written in the 2nd century before Christ, scarcely somewhat earlier and still less somewhat later, still I can find no indication of any more definite time. Obviously the author was a Jew of Palestine. The Greek translation will have been made not long after the book was written.' Exeg. Handb. z. d. Apocr. i. 2. p. 130. Jahn also places it at the time of the Maccabees. Einl. i. n. 246. No one regards Volkmar, who after his fashion, places it after our Lord, viz. in the Parthian war of Trajan (d. 4te buch Ezra p. 6. Theol. Jahrb. 1856, 7) since it is quoted before that time by S. Clement Ep. i.

[z] Judith xvi. 17.   [a] ΚΑΥΣΟΝΤΑΙ for ΚΛΑΥΣΟΝΤΑΙ the difference being only that the LXX text has ΛΛ for Λ.

put fire into their flesh, that they should be burned and feel for ever.'

The Syriac agrees in the main with this, 'And He will give their flesh to the fire and the worms, and they shall feel the burning for their iniquity for ever.'

This is the earliest explanation of the words of Isaiah. Although not received into the Jewish canon, the book must have had some authority with the Jews of that time, in that the translation of it was received into the Septuagint. 'The Day of Judgement' must be the one Great Day, in which the Lord shall judge [b]. The temporal judgement on Holofernes and the Assyrians was past; there is, of course, no eternity in any temporal judgement; nor could the worms who preyed on the corpses, or the fire kindled to consume them, be everlasting. It speaks of God's final judgement on the wicked and prepared for our Lord's solemn sanction of the language [c], "where their worm dieth not and their fire is not quenched."

2. THE BOOK OF ENOCH. The priority of the Book of Enoch to our era has been questioned only by

[b] In Ecclesiasticus vii. 17. the language of Isaiah lxvi. 12 is used of the punishment of the ungodly. 'The vengeance of the ungodly is fire and worms.' Fritzsche says of this place, 'The main idea is that of the acutest most piercing suffering: to strengthen which, the suffering is spoken of as eternal. This last is nothing but historical exaggeration. For to take it literally, altogether contradicts the mode of thought of the Hebrew mind at that time.' ad loc. Yet Fritzsche had himself placed the book about the time of the book of Enoch, which is full of the doctrine of eternal punishment. Nor plainly could it strengthen the idea, unless it were meant to be understood as literally true. [c] S. Mark ix. 44, 46, 48.

Book of Enoch.   53

one writer [d], whom even destructive critics suppose to have been unconsciously actuated by anxiety to lower the date of our Scriptures.

Of Jewish writers it is quoted, very frequently in the Testament of the twelve Patriarchs[e], as also in the Zohar[f]. Among Christians, Tertullian alone regards it as of authority, and he, as his way was, wishing to make out a case, but owning that it was not in the Jewish Canon[g]. Others[h] quoted it largely, as containing truth, as far as they cited it. Very many, S. Jerome said[i], rejected the epistle of S. Jude, for quoting it, being an Apocryphal book.

The writer, in an earnest preface in the name of Enoch, announces judgement to come, and the different lots of the righteous and the wicked. In this occur the words, quoted by S. Jude. After saying how all God's creation obeyed Him, except the wicked, he addresses the ungodly, '[j] Ye have not

[d] Volkmar. See some notice of the Book of Enoch in Daniel the Prophet, pp. 386—394.

[e] See in Fabric. cod. Pseudep. Vet. T. pp. 160 sqq.

[f] See Wolf Bibl. Heb. T. i. sub tit.

[g] " I know that the writing of Enoch, which assigns this order to Angels, is not received by some, because it is not received into the Jewish canon." He sums up, "by us nothing is to be rejected which pertaineth to us. And we read that all scripture, suited to edification, is divinely-inspired &c. de cult. fem. i. 2. He quotes it also Ib. ii. 10. de Idol. c. 4.

[h] S. Justin, in Apol. 2. S. Iren. iv. 30. Clem. Alex. Ecl. Proph. pp. 801, 808. Pædag. iii. 2, and in substance Strom. v. p. 550; perhaps Celsus; Origen de Princ. i. 3. iv. ult., in Num. 34; Hom. 28. in Joann. T. viii.; Anatol. Alex. (on the beginning of the year) ap. Eus. H.E. viii. ult. S. Hil. on Ps. cxxxii. 3. See at length in Fabric. l. c.

[i] Catal. Scriptt. Eccl. c. 4.   [j] c. 5. p. 2 Dillmann.

persevered nor fulfilled the law of the Lord, but have transgressed it and with proud blaspheming words out of your impure mouth have insulted His Greatness. Ye hard-hearted, ye shall find no peace: and therefore ye will curse your days, and the years of your life shall perish: great will be the everlasting damnation, and ye will find no pardon.'

In the book itself, which is loosely connected with this preface, he first describes the punishment of the angels, whose fall he supposes to be related in Gen. vi. 2—4.

'[k] And again, the Lord said to Rufael, [1] Bind Azâzêl hand and foot and lay him in the darkness: make an opening in the waste which is in Dudâêl and lay him therein—and cover him with darkness, that he remain there for ever, and cover his face that he see not the light. And on the great day of judgement he is to be cast into the burning.'

And to Michael God said '[1] When all their sons [of these fallen angels] shall have slain each other, and they shall have seen the destruction of their loves, bind them fast under the hills of the earth for seventy generations till the day of their judgement and their full end, till the last judgement be held for all eternity: in those days shall they be carried away to the fiery abyss: in torment and in prison shall they be shut up for all eternity.'

Elsewhere he describes two other places of punishment, both of fire; the one for '[m] stars which had transgressed the command of the Most High God, and they are burned here, until 10,000 worlds, the

[k] Ib. c. 10. n. 5, 6. p. 5.   [1] Ib. n. 12.
[m] Ib. c. 21 nn 1—6. p 12.

number of the days of their guilt, be accomplished,' the other still more terrible, [n] where was a great fire, into which great pillars of fire fell, surrounded by an abyss. Of this he is told, 'This place is the prison of the angels, and here are they held imprisoned to all eternity.'

The abode of the lost the writer describes so minutely, that the editor of the book[o] considers it beyond question, that he means the valley of Hinnom. '[p]I saw a holy mountain [Zion] and beneath and East of it a water which flows towards the South [Siloah], and I saw towards the East another mountain of like height[q] [Mount of Olives] and between them both, a valley deep but not broad, [the valley of Jehoshaphat] in which was another water [Kedron]; to the West of this, another mountain [Mount of Evil Counsel] lower than it and not high, and beneath it between them both, was a valley [Gehinnom].'

n Ib. 7—10.

o Dillmann, note on 26, 15, p. 131. p c. 26. p. 15.

q 'The highest top of Mount Zion is 2530 Paris feet [2678 Eng.], of the Mount of Olives 2556 Paris feet [2725½ Eng.].' Schubert Reise ii. 521. Ib. 'In the explanation of these localities in c. 27, Gehinnom alone is spoken of further.—But that the valley of Hinnom is to be this place of punishment near Jerusalem, comes partly from the historical import of this valley, as Jer. vii. 31. xix. 5. xxxii. 35, then from Josiah's act, (2 Kings xxiii. 10.) then from Jeremiah's curse, Jer. vii. 32, 33. xix. 6 sqq. (our author calls it 'an accursed valley' v. 1.) partly from the nature of the soil. For (according to the Talmud, Erubin f. 19 a) smoke came up there, which indicated subterranean fire. Lastly, that fire will be the instrument of punishment in this Gehenna, is a conception framed upon Is. lxvi. 24, 15, 16. Gen. xix. 24. Ps. xi. 6. and so many other places of the O.T. The entire conception is, that God through His creative power, through which He once made the earth divide to receive the

56   *Answer to Dr. F's 'palmary argument.'*

Enoch is supposed to ask the Angel [r], 'whereto is this blessed land, quite filled with trees, and this accursed valley in the midst?' '[s]Uriel answered me, This accursed valley is for those who are accursed to eternity: here must all those be collected, who speak with their mouth unseemly speeches towards God and speak insolently of His glory: here they are collected, and here is the place of their punishment; and, in the last time, here shall the spectacle of a righteous judgement upon them be given before the righteous to eternity for evermore.'

The two places of punishment, the one for the angels, the other for the lost among men are distinguished at the close of the work.

'[t] And the judgement passed first on the stars, and they were judged and found guilty and went to the place of damnation: and they were cast into a deep place full of fire, flaming, and of pillars of fire: and those seventy shepherds were judged and found guilty and also cast into that fiery deep: and I saw then, how another like deep was opened in the midst of the earth, full of fire, and they brought thither those blinded sheep; and they were all judged and found guilty and were cast into that fiery deep and they burned: but that deep was to the right of that house.'

The eternity of the punishment is mentioned in the following chapter;

'[u] And they [who will not be converted] shall be

company of Korah (Num. xvi. 30.), will hereafter, in the Judgement of the Messiah in the valley of Hinnom, beneath which the fire already burns, cleave the earth and cast the damned into the pool of fire.' Dillmann Notes p. 132.   [r] c. 27. n. 1. p. 15.
    [s] Ib. n. 2.   [t] c. 90. n. 24-26.   [u] c. 91. 9.

cast into the damnation of fire, and shall perish in anger and in the mighty damnation which lasts to eternity.'

The finality of the judgement is pictured in one place vividly, though not according to our belief; in two passages, the lost ask of the angel of punishment respite, that they might ask mercy of God.

'ʷ In those days shall the mighty kings who possess the earth beg from the punishing Angel, to whom they were delivered, to give them a little rest.' They say, 'ˣ And now we long for a little rest, but find none: we are driven away, and obtain it not: light has disappeared before us, and darkness is our abode for ever and ever.'

In the other, the mighty offer all they have, in vain it seems, because they cease not from sin.

'ʸ And there I saw a deep valley, whose mouth was open, and all who dwell in the continent and in the sea and in the islands shall bring thither gifts and presents and tribute, but that deep valley will not be full; and they commit transgression with their hands, and they, sinners, devour iniquitously all wherein they labour, so they, the sinners, will perish before the Presence of the Lord of spirits, and will be chased away unceasingly from the surface of His earth for all eternity. For I saw the angels of punishment, how they went and prepared all instruments for Satan. And I asked the Angel of Peace who went with me, For whom do they prepare these instruments? And he said to me, They prepare them for the kings and the mighty of this earth, that they may be destroyed with them.—ᶻ And I looked

ʷ c. 63.   ˣ Ib. 6.   ʸ c. 53.   ᶻ c. 54.

up and turned to another region of the earth and I saw there a deep valley with burning fire: and they brought the kings and mighty ones and placed them in that deep valley, and there I saw how they made instruments for them, iron chains of unimaginable weight: and I asked the Angel of Peace who was with me, For whom are these chains prepared? he said to me, For the hosts of Azâzêl, to take them and lay them in the lowest hell—as the Lord of spirits hath commanded. Michael and Gabriel, Rufael and Fanuel will bind them on that great Day and cast them into the furnace of flaming fire, that the Lord of spirits may take vengeance on them for their unrighteousness, that they became subject to Satan and led those who dwell on the earth astray.'

It is needless to multiply passages, since one main object of the book is to encourage the righteous to persevere amid the heaviness of the times, in thought of the everlasting retribution to good and bad.

'[a] Woe to you, ye sinners, when ye die in your sins, and those like you say of you, Blessed are ye sinners; ye have seen all your days, and now have ye died in happiness and wealth, and have seen no affliction and no massacre in your life: in glory have ye died and judgement was not executed upon you in your life. Know ye well that your souls will be brought down into the kingdom of the dead and will be in evil case and your trouble will be great; and into darkness and chains and the burning flame will your spirit enter in the great Judgement, and the great Judgement will be for all generations unto eternity. Woe to you, for ye have no

[a] c 103 n. 5—8.

peace.' To the righteous it is said, '[b] Hope ye and give not up your hope; for ye shall have great joy like the Angels of heaven; since this is before you, ye will not have to hide yourselves on the day of the great Judgement, and shall not be found to be sinners, and the everlasting damnation shall be far from you for all generations of the world.'

3. FOURTH BOOK OF ESDRAS[c]. No one doubts that this book of Esdras is of Jewish origin. It has been very popular in the East, having been translated into Æthiopic, Syriac, Armenian, Arabic. The portion immediately concerning this question has only been lately discovered in Latin, although it existed in the four Eastern versions and is quoted as Ezra's and Scripture by S. Ambrose [d].

The fragment, so long lost to us in the West, begins, '[e] A lake of torment shall appear, and over against it a place of rest: and the oven of Gehenna

---

[b] n. 104. 4, 5.

[c] ' Learned men are now mostly well agreed that it was written towards the end of the first century.' 'The old Latin translation is of a better stamp than that of the other sacred books, and the translator, who in my opinion lived in the 3rd century, seems but seldom to have misunderstood the Greek.' Fritzsche Libri Apocryphi V. T. Praef. p. xxvii. The *translator* then, according to Fritzsche, lived at the time when Vogel, in the superficial criticism of the last century (1795), would have it, that the passage was added by a Christian. Hilgenfeld followed him, yet not so as to affect the argument, since he conceded the genuineness of the first 16 verses which contain the mention of Gehenna. Die Propheten Ezra and Daniel p. 30 sq. 'Both used very weak arguments.' Fritzsche l. c.

[d] de bono mortis cc. 10, 11.

[e] Bensley, Missing Fragment of the ivth book of Ezra, vii. 36 pp. 55, 56. Ceriani, translation from the Syriac, Monn. Sacra et Prof. T. i. fasc 2. p. 108.

shall be shewn, and over against it a paradise of delight; and then shall the Highest say to the risen nations, See and understand Him Whom ye denied, or Whom ye did not serve, or Whose observances ye despised: behold on this side and that; here is pleasure and rest; and there, fire and torments.' And further on, '*f*in regard to death......if one be of those who have despised and not kept the way of the Most High, or who despised His law and who hated those who fear Him, their souls shall not enter the habitations [garners]; but shall wander about thenceforth in torments, ever grieving and sad; first, because they despised the law of the Most High; secondly, because they cannot be converted to good, that they may live; thirdly, because they see the reward laid up for those who have believed the testimony of the Most High; fourthly, they consider the torment laid up for themselves at the last; fifthly, seeing that the habitations [garners] of others are guarded by Angels in great stillness; sixthly, seeing how they shall pass therefrom to torment; seventhly, which is the greatest of all, because they shall waste away in confusion and be consumed in shame and wither in fear, seeing the glory of the Most High, before Whom while they lived they sinned, and before Whom they shall begin, in the last times to be judged.' One ground of the rest of the righteous is that '*g*they shall see the complication in which the souls of the impious wander, and the punishment which awaits them.'

4. THE APOCALYPSE OF BARUCH was written probably shortly after the ivth book of Ezra, and soon

---

f Bensley p. 63. Ceriani p. 209.   *g* Bens p. 67. Cer. p. 110.

after the destruction of Jerusalem. It says, '[h] When the time of the coming of the Messiah shall be fulfilled, and He shall return in glory, then all those who fell asleep in hope of Him shall rise again; and it shall be in that time, the garners, in which the number of the souls of the righteous was guarded, shall be opened, and they shall go forth, and the multitude of souls shall appear together in one company, of one mind; and the former shall rejoice and the last shall not be saddened. For it knows that the time is come, of which it is said, that it shall be the end of times. But the souls of the ungodly, when they shall see all these things, shall the more pine away. For they know that their punishment is come and their perdition arrived.'

He addresses the symbolic cedar[1] which remained from the wood of wickedness. 'Go thou then also, O cedar, after the wood which went away before thee, and become dust with it, and let your mould be mingled: and lie ye now down in anguish, and rest in torment, until thy last time shall come, in which thou shalt again return and be yet more tormented.' He says, further,

'[j] For there is a time which shall not pass away, and an hour shall come, which shall abide to eternity, and a new world which shall not turn to corruption those who have penetrated into its beginning and shall not have pity on those who shall go to punishment.—To these, the righteous, shall be given the world to come, but the domicile of the rest, who are many, shall be in the fire.'

[h] Apoc. Baruch in Monn. Sacr. et Prof. T. i. fasc. 2 p. 80 ed. Ceriani.
[1] c. 36. p. 82.   [j] c. 44. pp. 83, 84.

Baruch himself complains, '^k What shall be said to the first Eve who obeyed the serpent; for this whole multitude is gone to torment, and those whom the fire devours are countless?'

Of the resurrection, he says, '^l after that appointed day shall have passed away, then will the look of those who are condemned be changed, and the glory of those who shall have been justified. They who despised My law, and stopped their ears that they might not hear wisdom, nor receive understanding— shall first see [the glory of the righteous], and afterwards go to be tormented.'

'To Moses,' he says, among other things were revealed '^m the end of ages and the beginning of the Day of Judgement and the mouth of Gehenna and the state of vengeance and the region of faith and the place of hope and the likeness of torment to come.' Of Manasses he says, that 'in this world he was called ungodly, and at the end his dwelling was in the fire[n].'

To Baruch God said, '^o Go and teach the people as much as thou canst, that they may learn, so that they should not die in the last time, but learn that they may live in the last times.' He himself closes his letter, '^p Prepare ye your souls, that, when ye have ended your voyage and disembarked, ye may rest, and not be condemned, for the Most High will bring all these things. *There* will be no more place of repentance, nor bound to times, nor length to hours, nor change of way, nor place for petition,

^k n. 48. p. 85.   ^l no. 51. p. 86.
^m ib. n. 59. p. 89.   ⁿ n. 64. p 91.
^o n. 76. p. 94.   ^p n. 85. p. 98.

n sending of entreaties, nor obtaining knowledge, nor giving of charity, nor place for repentance of soul or deprecations for offences, nor entreaties of parents nor orison of prophets, nor help of the righteous; but *there* will be sentence to the destruction (corruptionem) of the way of fire, and the path which leadeth to the hot coals: wherefore there is one law through one, one period (sæculum) and an end to all those who are in it. Then will He give life to those whom He shall find, and shall be propitious to them, and shall at the same time destroy those who shall be defiled in sins.'

5. The exact date of the so-called PSALMS OF SOLOMON is still matter of debate, between the time of Antiochus Epiphanes and that of Pompey. But any how they are allowed to be Jewish, and before our Lord. The mention of the life to come occurs but incidentally in the contrast of the future lot of the righteous and the wicked. Like language occurs in the Psalms, which the writer had in his mind. The Psalmist too knew of the different lot of the righteous and the wicked; that 'q the way of the ungodly shall perish;' that 'r the end of the upright is peace, the end of the wicked shall be cut off;' that 's the workers of wickedness do flourish, to be destroyed for ever.'

The Psalms of Solomon express, perhaps in more marked antithesis, the final abode of the righteous and the wicked; and that, as the result of a day of judgement of God. The lot of the righteous is life; that of the wicked, Hades, darkness and perdition.

q Ps. i. 6.   r Ib. xxxvii. 37, 38.   s Ib. xcii. 7.

64 *Answer to Dr. F's 'palmary argument.'*

The third of these Psalms is a marked contrast of the conduct of the righteous and the wicked in the trials of life. The righteous stumbles and looketh to God, does not add to sin, but expiates sins of ignorance by fasting, and God cleanseth him. 't The sinner also stumbled, and curseth his life, the day of his birth and the birth-pangs: he added sins upon sins to his life: he fell, for evil is his fall and he shall not rise again; the perdition [u] of the sinner shall be for ever. And he shall not be remembered, when He [God] visiteth the righteous. This is the portion of the sinners for ever. But they which fear the Lord shall rise again unto everlasting life, and their life is in the light of the Lord and shall no more fail.'

The same contrast occurs in the 14th and 15th of these Psalms. ' [v] The wicked remembered not God, that the ways of men are ever known before Him, and He knoweth the store-houses of the heart, before they are done. Wherefore their inheritance is Hades and darkness and perdition; and they shall not be found in the day of the mercy of the righteous. But the holy ones of the Lord shall inherit life in rejoicing.'

In the 15th; 'He who doeth these things [the righteous] shall not be moved for ever by evil: the flame of fire and wrath of the unrighteous shall not touch him, when it goeth forth against sinners from the presence of the Lord, to destroy the whole substance of the ungodly.—For they shall flee, as though

---

[t] Ps. Sal. iii. 11—16 Fabric. cod. pseudep. V. T. p. 27. Fritzsch. Libb. Apocr. App. pp. 569—589.

[u] $\dot{\eta}$ $\dot{a}\pi\omega\lambda\epsilon\iota a$ [v] xiv. 4-7. pp. 583, 584.

famine pursued them, from the holy ones; it shall follow upon the sinners and take hold on them, and they who commit transgression shall not escape the judgement of the Lord; they shall be holden as by expert enemies [w]. For the token of perdition is on their brow. And the inheritance of the sinners is perdition and darkness, and their transgressions shall pursue them even to Hades beneath. Their inheritance shall not be found by their children. For the transgressions shall utterly desolate the houses of sinners, and the sinners shall *perish for ever in the day of the Lord's Doom.* When God shall visit the earth in His judgement, to requite sinners for evermore [x]. But they that fear the Lord shall be compassionated in it, and shall live in the compassion of their God [y].'

In another Psalm the sinner is said to be guilty of his soul in perdition.

'[z] He that doeth righteousness treasureth to himself life with the Lord, and he that doeth unrighteous things, himself is guilty of his soul in perdition.'

'[a] For the Lord will spare His holy ones and will wipe out their transgressions in correction; for the life of the righteous is for ever. But the sinners shall be borne away ($ἀρθήσονται$) unto perdition, and their memorial shall no more be found.'

6. THE FOURTH BOOK OF MACCABEES. The book is attributed to Josephus, as a certain fact, by Eusebius [b], S. Jerome [c], and Philostorgius [d], as well as by

[w] πολεμίων ἐμπείρων [x] ἀποδοῦναι ἁμαρτωλοῖς εἰς τὸν αἰῶνα χρόνον
[y] xv. 6—end. pp. 583, 584. [z] ix. 9. p. 580.
[a] xiii. 9, 10. p. 583. [b] H. E. iii. 10, 6.
[c] Catal. scriptt. Eccles. c. 13. and adv. Pelag. ii. 6.
[d] Hist. Eccl. Epit. I. 1

other later writers, probably following these. Moderns who think it to be by another, on account of variations from Josephus, still place it before the destruction of Jerusalem [e].

The book seems to have been very popular among Christian converts for its lesson of unconquerable endurance amidst sufferings, such as martyrs alone knew.

In the second book of Maccabees the threatenings to the persecutor are more vague, '[f] thou hast not yet escaped the judgement of Almighty God ;' '[g] think not thou, that takest in hand to fight against God, that thou shalt escape unpunished.' But this might be anticipation of the temporal punishment which the writer subsequently relates. One only of the brothers, while he expresses distinctly his own hope of a resurrection, says to the tyrant, '[h] for to thee there shall be no resurrection *to life*.' It seems as if he had in his mind the words of Daniel, "[i] Many of them that sleep in the dust of the earth shall awake ; some to everlasting life, some to shame and everlasting contempt." He does not deny the resurrection of the tyrant, but his resurrection *to life*.

In the Fourth book the brethren, one after the other, retort upon the persecutor, that by his savagery to them he was preparing for himself eternal torment. This is only the one half of the occasions, in which the Christian martyrs refer to the everlasting torments. This they seem to have inherited. The other half, their awe for themselves, occurs among the Christian martyrs only. This

---

[e] Grimm zu d. Apocr. ii. 293.
[f] 2 Macc. vii. 35.   [g] Ib. 19.   [h] Ib. 14.   [i] Dan. xii. 2.

belonged to reality, and could not form part of an ideal picture, like that in the Fourth book of the Maccabees. At first they speak as one, 'ʲTry then, tyrant; and if thou shalt put our lives to death for godliness, think not that by torturing thou wilt injure us. For we, through this suffering and endurance, shall bear off the prize of virtue and shall be with God, for Whom also we suffer; but thou, for thine arbitrary foul slaughter of us, shalt endure everlasting torment ᵏ, by the judgement of God.' 'ˡWe,' said the third brother, when about to die, 'we, most blood-defiled tyrant, suffer these things for discipline and virtue to Godward; but thou for impiety and blood-guiltiness shalt endure indissoluble torments.' The fourth, when invited with soft words not to share the madness of his brethren, said, 'ᵐBy the blessed death of my brethren and the everlasting perdition of the tyrant, and the eternal life of the godly, I will not deny my noble brotherhood.'

The youngest addressed the tyrant, 'ⁿImpious tyrant, of all wicked the most ungodly, art thou not ashamed, having received from God good things and the kingdom, to slay His servants and to torture those who practise piety? In requital of which, Divine judgement stores thee up for a more vehement and everlasting fire; and tortures will not let thee go for all eternity º.'

The writer himself, in his own person, says of the seven, that they exhorted each other; 'ᵖLet us with our whole hearts consecrate our souls to God Who gave them, and lend our bodies to the keeping of the

ʲ 4 Macc. ix. 7—9.   ᵏ Fritzche removes διὰ πύρος.   ˡ Ib. x. 10.
ᵐ Ib. 15.   ⁿ Ib xii 11, 12.   º εἰς ὅλον τὸν αἰῶνα.   ᵖ Ib xiii. 13, 14.

law. Let us not fear him who seemeth to slay [q]; for there is a great strife for the soul and peril in eternal torment laid up for them who transgress the command of God!'

7. JOSEPHUS. The writings of Josephus are an apology for his people to their Roman masters. This object is most prominent in his books against Apion. But it runs throughout. It leads him occasionally to suppress what the Romans would ridicule, or what would be disparaging to the Jews. The Romans ridiculed the institution of the sabbath, as the Jews observed it. He mentions it but slightly, and while giving an account of the manna, passes over the mention of the special miracle which relates to it. He omits the idolatry, into which they fell even at Mount Sinai, and in this one case even distorts the history [r]. But when he is not under this bias, his account is reliable and relied upon. He attempts to make doctrine look more reasonable to the Romans by comparisons with Heathenism, as in comparing the shewbread to a ceremony at Delphi, or the rewards or punishments after death with the Elysian fields or Tartarus.

But he does not falsify the doctrines themselves.

It belongs then probably to this same spirit of avoiding what might offend the Romans, that he uses a vague term as to the doctrine of the resurrection of the body, at which the philosophers of Mars' hill mocked, and which the heathen generally ridiculed.

[q] Fritzche removes τὸ σῶμα.
[r] These, and one or two others are alleged by Dr. Wotton, Misc. Disc. Pref. pp. xxxiii-xlv.

Josephus.

He says that the Pharisees held that every soul is immortal, but that the soul of the good only passed into another body, but that of the evil is punished with everlasting vengeance.' In one way, the body which we hope to receive is 'other,' though not 'another,' in that it will be a spiritual body.

Even if Josephus had meant to ascribe to the Pharisees a belief in a transmigration of the soul, there would have been no reason to think him wrong. The question of the disciples, "[s] Did this man sin or his parents, that he was born blind?" implies some such belief (as S. Cyril of Alexandria also thinks). Of the earlier Jewish writers, the Cabbalists ascribe the Bahir, in which it is taught, to R. Nechonia b. Hakkana. R. Ishak Luria (end of 3rd cent.) is quoted as teaching it. A later writer says, that "[t] it is an article of faith to our whole congregation and no one denies and rejects it, except R. Saadia Haggaon [xth cent.] and the Badrashi [u] as may be seen

---

[s] S. John ix. 2. The saying in Wisdom viii. 2. 'rather, being good, I came into a body undefiled,' although strictly true of the soul of our Lord alone, may, I suppose, be interpreted relatively and undogmatically, of a soul with good natural dispositions. It does not necessarily imply præexistence of the soul, only what is commonly received, Creationism in contrast with Traducianism.

[t] Manasseh b. Israel, Nishmath Chaim, Maamar 4. c. 6. f. 152. 2. in Eisenm. ii 23. He says 'It is known to all my people that the book Zohar and all the books of the Cabbalists hold firmly this doctrine.' He quotes R. Levi b. Chabib [beg. of 16th cent.], 'There is another very great multitude of the wise of Israel who believe it, and have written upon it, that it is true belief and one of the foundations of the law, to remove the objection of evil befalling the righteous, and we ought all to hold this faith without doubting.'

[u] 'The *Badrashi*, (Dr. Neubauer informs me,) is Yedaiah happenini, of *Béziers;* the letter אגרת ההתנצלות, quoted by Manasseh b.

in the letter of defence to R. Salomo b. Adrath,' about 1304.

Josephus, although he speaks vaguely as to the body which the righteous receive after death, speaks, not vaguely [x] but, very distinctly as to the belief of the eternal punishment of the wicked.

The passages of Josephus are,

"[y] The Pharisees have a faith, that souls have a deathless force, and that beneath the earth there are punishments and rewards to those who cultivated vice or virtue in life; and on the one is inflicted a perpetual imprisonment, while the other have permission again to live."

"[z] (The Essenes) separate off for the bad souls a certain dark and cold cave, full of unintermitting punishments. And the Greeks seem to me, according to the same conception, to assign the islands of the blessed to the valiant, whom they call heroes and demigods; but to the souls of the evil, the place of the ungodly in Ades, where also they fable that some are punished, the Sisyphi and Tantali and Ixions and Tityi. First they establish that souls are eternal; then (they hope) that this will be an incitement to virtue and deterrer from vice. For that the good will become better in life, in hope of honour even after death; and that the impetus of the bad

---

Israel, was written about 1304 and often reprinted.' He is the author of the בחינת עולם. See Wolf B. H. T. i. n. 677.

[x] Dr. F., with his wonted impetuosity, says, " I have not referred to the *vague* testimony of Josephus, because I regard him as an utterly untrustworthy witness, and because what he says is contradicted on this, as on a multitude of other subjects, by overwhelming and untainted testimony." Et. H. Exc. v. pp. 213, 214.

[y] Jos. Ant. 18. 1, 3.   [z] Id. B. J. ii. 8, 11.

will be impeded by fear, when they expect that, even if undetected in this life, they would after their dissolution endure immortal punishment."

"ᵃ The Pharisees, who are accounted to expound the laws accurately and to be the first sect, refer every thing to fate and God; (they hold) that the doing good or no depends for the most part upon men, but that fate also helps each; that every soul is imperishable, but that the souls of the good alone go into another body, but that those of the bad are punished with everlasting vengeance."

8, 9. THE TARGUMS. Absolutely nothing turns on the dates of the two great Targums. The representative of the new theory ᵇ as to their date admires the 'rare unity' infused into the version ascribed to Onkelos, and attributes it to 'those who collected the different fragments with their variants, and reduced them into one:' that on the Prophets, ascribed to Jonathan B. Uzziel, he says, 'certainly is the work, not of one or of two but of twenty, of fifty and more Meturgemanim, Haggadists, and Halachists. The edition, however, we repeat it advisedly, has the undeniable stamp of one master-mind, and its individual workings; its manner and peculiarity are indelibly impressed upon the whole labour from the first page to the last.'

Our elder criticism, which would have held the unity of character in each version to be an additional proof of the tradition of the unity of authorship, was, I think, sounder. One who could read Onkelos, ob-

ᵃ Jos. B. J. ii. 8. 14.
ᵇ Deutzsch in Smith Bibl. Dict. iii. 1644, 1645.

72 *Answer to Dr. F.'s 'palmary argument.'*

serve his marvellous unity and yet think the version to have been merely cemented out of different fragments by one master mind (or still worse of more minds), seems to me the slave of his theory. It is a criticism, which matches the well-known paradox of the P. Hardouin.

However, the later date assigned to the Targums by those modern critics would but prolong the period, during which the belief expressed in them was held by the Jews. For they were altogether inaccessible to Christians, who did not understand their language, and did not know of them. Those interested in lowering their date, in order to deprive us of contemporary evidence of our belief among the Jews, are confronted by the difficulty, 'How came the Jews in those same Targums to sanction an interpretation which agrees with our belief in the Messiah, not with their expectations? how came they to substitute 'Messiah' for 'Shiloh' in Jacob's prophecy for Judah [c]; or, after Balaam's prophecy of the Star which should arise out of Jacob had been falsely attributed by Rabbi Akiba to Barcochab, to ascribe it for the first time to the Messiah [d]?' Again it seems to me inexplicable how any one, at the date assigned by these writers to the Targum on the prophets, should unhesitatingly explain Micah v. 2, of the birth of the Messiah at Bethlehem, or paraphrase, 'O tower of Ader [a mile from Bethlehem] Ophlah of

---

[c] Gen xlix. 10. 'until the king Messiah comes, whose is the kingdom.' Targ. Onk. and Hieros. 'until the time that the king Messiah comes, the little one of his sons.' Targ. Jon.

[d] Deutzsch p. 1649 notices the fact of the citations by Onkelos, but attempts no explanation.

the daughter of Zion, unto thee shall it come the first dominion,' by 'But Thou, Messiah of Israel, who wast hidden for the sins of Israel, to Thee shall the kingdom come,' when no one of the race of Israel remained in the city of Bethlehem [e].

However, nothing turns upon it. For Dr. Deutzsch himself ascribed the final collection of the Targum of Onkelos to some time about the end of the 3rd or beginning of the 4th century [f]; the Targum on the Prophets he ascribes to 'some time, though not long after Onkelos or about the middle of the 4th century.' But, terrible as had been the ruin of the Jewish people in this interval, there is in these versions no trace of any alteration of belief in regard to future punishment. The passages are of the simplest sort; they merely introduce the mention of the 'second death' or the name Gehenna into their paraphrases of Holy Scripture; just as, in so many prophecies, the interpretation consists in the simple introduction of the word 'Messiah.'

1. Onkelos expands the words 'Let Reuben live and not die' into 'Let Reuben live in life eternal and not die the second death.' A later Targum on Deut. xxxiii. 6. has, '[g] Let Reuben live in this world and not die by the second death, whereby the wicked die in the world to come.' Jonathan sometimes puts the simple phrase: he expands Is. xxii. 14. 'This iniquity shall not be forgiven you till ye die' by adding 'the second death.' Kimchi [h] explains his

[e] On the fable of the hiding of the Messiah see Dr. Pusey on Micah v. 2 p. 333. Martini Pug. fid. p. 279. It is alluded to by Trypho in S. Just. dial. c. 8.   [f] Deutzsch l. c. p. 1644.

[g] Yerushalmi ib. Targ. Jon. omits 'second.'   [h] ad loc.

meaning; "Jonathan interprets 'death' here of the second death, by which he means the death of the soul in the world to come." Jonathan again paraphrases Is. lxv. 5, 6, 'Their wrath is as smoke before Me, their vengeance is in Gehenna, wherein the fire burneth every day; Lo, it is written before Me, I will not give them lengthening in life, but I will repay them vengeance for their guilt, and will give their bodies to the second death;' and again, '¹the Lord shall make you die the second death.' In another place, he adds 'ᵏthey shall die the second death, and shall not live in the world to come.'

This is the sense in which the word occurs 4 times in the Apocalypse with the same variations. "He that overcometh shall not be hurt of the second death" (Rev. ii. 11.); "On such the second death hath no power" (ib. xx. 6.); "And death and hell were cast into the lake of fire. This is the second death." (ib. 14.) "But the fearful and unbelieving &c &c. and all liars shall have their part in the lake which burneth with fire and brimstone; which is the second death." (ib. xxi. 8.)

In a later Targum the equivalent expression is used; 'The death by which the wicked shall die in the world to come.'

'¹And for all this, forbid that we should lift up our eyes unto them [the women of Midian] or gaze on one of them, that we might not be guilty in one of them, and might not die by the death which the wicked die in the world to come, and this might be remembered for us in the day of the great judgement, to atone for our souls before the Lord.'

¹ Is. lxv. 15.   ᵏ On Jer li. 39.   ˡ Jon. on Num. xxxi. 50.

2. Jonathan himself elsewhere inserts the word Gehenna as the name of the place of 'everlasting burnings' after the great Judgement Day.

'ᵐThe guilty are broken in Zion; fear hath taken hold of sinners who steal their ways. They say, Who of us shall dwell in Zion, wherein is the brightness of His Presence, as a consuming fire? Who of us shall dwell in Jerusalem, where the wicked shall be judged, to be delivered to Gehenna, the everlasting burnings?'

3. In the immediate context, the vision of God is contrasted with the lot of those going down to Gehenna.

'ⁿThine eyes shall see the glory of the Shechinah of the King of ages in His beauty; thou shalt consider and behold those descending to the land of Gehenna.'

4. The casting of the wicked into Gehenna is contrasted with the gathering of His own people.

'ᵒThou art revealed to collect the dispersed of Thy people; yea, Thou art ready to bring nigh Thy captivity to be revealed in Thy might to thrust all the wicked into Gehenna.'

5. In the immediate context, he contrasts those delivered to Gehenna, as the penalty of habitual transgression of God's Law, with the lot of the doers of the law who shall be raised again.

'ᵖThou art He Who quickenest the dead, and Thou raisest again the bones of their dead bodies. They shall live and praise before Thee, all those who lay in the dust, because Thy dew is a dew of light to the doers of Thy law; and the wicked to whom Thou

ᵐ Jon. on Is. xxxiii. 14.   ⁿ Ib. v. 17.
ᵒ Id. on Is. xxvi. 15.   ᵖ Ib. v. 19.

hast given might and they transgressed Thy law, Thou wilt deliver to Gehenna.'

6. In the Targum on the Psalms the destruction of the wicked in the smoke of Gehenna is compared to the lambs first fattened, then slain.

'q For the wicked shall perish and the enemies of the Lord, as the glory of lambs, which are first fattened and then slain; so the wicked shall fall and be consumed in the smoke of Gehenna.'

7. The exemption of Israel from Gehenna is stated by the later Jonathan on Exodus.

'r And thou shalt place a veil for the door of the court for the merits of the mothers of the world, which is spread at the gate of Gehenna, lest the souls of the children of the people of Israel should enter there;' as

8. in the Targum on Ruth, Ruth is congratulated that, by becoming a proselyte, she would be saved from the judgement of Gehenna.

's The Lord will requite thee with a good requital in this world for thy good deed, and be thy perfect reward in the world which cometh, from JHVH the God of Israel, that thou hast come to be a proselyte and to hide thyself under the shadow of the majesty of His glory, and through this righteousness thou shalt be saved from the judgement of Gehenna, that thy portion be with Sarah and Rebecca and Rachel and Leah.'

9. The Targum on the Psalms speaks of the wicked evil man being chased by the angel of death and cast down to Gehenna, in contrast with arising to life eternal.

q Targ. on Ps. xxxvii. 20.   r Jon. on Exod xl 8.   s Targ. on Ruth ii. 12.

'ᵗLet there fall upon them coals from heaven; into the fire of Gehenna let them cast them as burning coals, that they rise not again to life eternal. A man who smootheth a calumnious tongue cannot be directed in the land of the living; the violent evil man the angel of death shall chase, and cast him down into Gehenna.'

10. That on Ecclesiastes speaks of sinners cut off from the holy Place, where the righteous dwell, who went to be burned in Gehenna.

'ᵘ And in truth I have seen sinners, who were buried and consumed out of the earth from the holy place where the righteous dwell, who went to be burned in Gehenna, and were forgotten from among the inhabitants of the city; and as they did, it was done unto them.'

Various as the authorities are, and varied as are the precise terms which they use, writing also in part in different languages, the belief which they concurrently express is uniform and unmistakeable. One only exception there was of persons among the wealthyᵛ who did not believe in the life to come, the Sadducees: but whoever did believe in it, believed in the eternity of the weal and woe, which God would allot to the righteous or the wicked.

ᵗ on Ps. cxl. 12.   ᵘ Targ. on Eccl. viii. 10.
ᵛ 'The Sadducees only persuaded the rich, but had no followers among the people; the Pharisees had the multitude as their allies.' Jos. Ant. 13. 10. 6. He speaks of the power of the Pharisees Ib. 15. 5. [The Sadducees] 'do nothing, so to speak, of any moment; for if they should come to any office, they, of necessity and against their will, go over to what the Pharisees say, since otherwise they would not be endurable to the people.' Ib. 18. 1. 4.

The question here is solely, what was the belief at the time when our Lord taught. Dr. Farrar lays down, that the Talmud does contain evidence which overrules all besides. He assumes that, as a whole, it is *the* witness as to the religious belief in our Lord's time; and that one statement in it, which limits the belief in the duration of future punishment in Gehenna to 12 months [for the Jews,] necessarily rules what our Lord meant by the word.

The argument is inconsistent with Dr. Farrar's previous argument about the word αἰώνιος; for punishment during 11, or at most 12 months could not, by any abuse of language, be called 'everlasting.'

But in regard to the Talmud itself, the most recent opinion among the advanced Jewish school (i. e. those who believe most in Talmudism and least in Holy Scripture as a whole) is, that the Mishna and the Talmud were not committed to writing until the middle of the vith cent. '[w]The correction of the old widely-spread error, as if Mishna and Talmud were committed to writing as soon as they were collected and brought into one, belongs to Luzzato. He proved acutely and completely, that contrariwise Mishna and Talmud were, afterwards as before, preserved only orally; until, in the Saburean period in the time of R. Gisa and Simona (550) 50 years before the rise of Mohammad they were written (comp. Kerem Chemed A. 1838. p. 62 sq).' But further,

1. The specific statement as to the duration of punishment in Gehenna was, according to the Talmud itself, the doctrine of one who lived some 80 years after our Lord's Ascension.

[w] Graetz Gesch. d. Juden iv note 35 p. 494.

2. That saying did not relate to mankind in general, but to the Jews only.

3. It was not the exclusive belief among the Jews, even after it became popular among them.

Talmudism was an essentially new system, consequent upon the destruction of the temple and of the whole system of worship, whereof the temple was the centre. The sacrifices, wherein the Jew had seen the tokens of acceptance and forgiveness of sins through shedding of Blood, and had looked on to a Redeemer, were gone; gone was all their central worship, which spread its roots through their whole faith; gone was all connection with the past. It was an utter prostration. Prayer, even at a distance from Jerusalem, had still been connected with the morning and evening sacrifice. 'The pious zealots thought that they might not taste meat or wine, since they could no more be offered on the altar.'

Every thing had to be built up anew. The one teacher, who clung most scrupulously to the past, R. Eliezer b. Hyrcanos [died about 116, 17] failed, even through his stiff and exclusive adherence to that past. He had diligently mastered all which had been transmitted heretofore. His teacher, R. Jochanan, called him, '[x] a well-cemented cistern, which did not let a drop through.' He would answer no question, for which he could not allege authority. His usual answer to such questions was, 'I know not, for I have not received it.' What he had received, he treasured diligently. It was a sore memory of his death-bed, that having been placed under the ban by Gamaliel ii. (who was himself deposed for his severity), and so cut

[x] Graetz iv. 45.

off from intercourse with others, he had had no means of imparting it. His spirit revived with the opportunity of imparting some of it; he died with some of it on his lips. But he had no school, and *most* of his knowledge perished with him. The author of the system which displaced his, said in a funeral oration over him, '^y By his death the book of doctrine is buried.' A funeral oration is, of course, not to be taken to the letter. Old traditions still existed, and were quoted.

The system of R. Akiba, who displaced his, was an enlargement of that of his teacher R. Nachum of Gimso. Both were essentially new. They were traditions which they transmitted, not what they had received. So far from being evidences of what was taught in the time of our Lord, they were evidences of what was originated, some 70 or 80 years after His Ascension.

'^zThe peculiar mode of teaching of R. Nachum consisted in this, that he derived the oral teaching out of the sacred text, on the ground of certain particles, which the lawgiver, in framing the laws, had purposely employed as hints. According to him such particles were not only to serve to the syntax of the sentence, but were rather set down as indications of expansions or limitations of the law as given.'

'^a What this school had merely thrown out and left imperfect, R. Akiba raised into a developed system, and made therewith a turning-point in Jewish history.'

'^b R. Akiba laid down, as the fundamental principle of his system, his conviction that the verbal

^y R Akiba, Sanhedr. 68. b. 101. b. Yerushalmi Sabbat ii. p. 5. b. Sota end, in Graetz iv. 49.   ^z Ib. p. 22.   ^a Ib. p. 54.   ^b Ib p. 55.

meaning of the Law, specially in its legal [practical] portion is quite different from that of any other writing. Human language, besides words absolutely necessary, employs certain terms, figures of speech, repetitions, embellishments, in one word a certain Form, which is nearly superfluous in regard to the meaning, and was only intended for euphony and taste. Contrariwise, in the language of the Law, nothing is Form. All in it is Essence: there is nothing superfluous, no word, no syllable, not even a letter: every peculiarity of expression, every conjunction, every mark, is to be regarded as some higher reference, as a hint, as a deeper indication. In this respect R. Akiba went far beyond his teacher, Nachum of Gimso, who had only discovered indications in some particles of Scripture. R. Akiba found them in every element of the sentence, which does not strictly belong to the meaning. R. Akiba accordingly added a number of rules of interpretation and inference to those of Hillel and Nachum, which furnished starting-points quite new for the traditional law. If an inference was discovered through the right use of the rules, then, according to his system, this inference would become the premiss of a new inference, and so on ad infinitum. In this proceeding R. Akiba shrank from no results. His pupil Nehemiah of Emmaus had a difficulty about the interpretation of a particle, 'Thou shalt reverence the Lord thy God' [the interpretation of *eth* 'with' would make it] '*with* thy God,' since this would lead to the inference that one might give Divine reverence to another Being besides God, which, amid the attacks of Christianity on the absolute [unipersonal] unity of God, did not seem so harmless. Nehemiah was, on account of this difficulty, about to give up this mode of teaching. R. Akiba set aside the objection, saying, 'In this sentence too the law would suggest, that besides God, we ought to reverence His Holy Word, the Thora.'

'[c] R. Akiba, with his system, had broken a new path, opened new points of view. The traditional material, of which some said, that it hung upon a hair, and had no ground in the Scripture, received thereby a basis; practical controversies were thereby in part ended. R. Akiba's contemporaries were astonished, dazzled, carried away with a system, which, new as it was, seemed at the same time to be old. R. Tarphon or Tryphon, who, before, was superior to R. Akiba, said respectfully to him, 'Who parts from thee, parts from his eternal life; what tradition forgets, that thou through thy interpretation restorest.' R. Joshua, who was before his teacher, said thereof in amazement, 'Would one could remove the cataracts from the eyes of R. Jochanan b. Sakkai that he might see, how idle his fear was, that a rule would have to be given up, because it had no ground in the text of Scripture! Lo, R. Akiba has found a support for it.' It was confessed that the law would have been forgotten, or at least neglected, if R. Akiba had not given it a support. It was said with an exaggerating enthusiasm, 'many legal definitions, unknown to Moses, had dawned on R. Akiba.' This system R. Akiba carried so far, as to infer from a single letter [d], that a priest's married daughter, if guilty of adultery, was to be burned alive.

[c] Ib. p. 56. [d] R. Ismael, who wished to modify this system, asked him, ' Will you then for this letter inflict death by fire ? ' Ib. p. 61.

'ᵉ People shrank not from owning, that on certain points they had hitherto been in error or doubt, until R. Akiba had hit upon what was right through his peculiar method. The old Mishna (Mishna rishona) was often directly set aside by the younger (M. acharona or Mishna of R. Akiba), and this latter taken as the rule. The youths who were eager to learn and had more interest in acute developements and comparisons, than in dry transmission of matters of memory, flocked round him. Myths make his hearers 12,000 or even twice 12,000; a modest account limits them to 300.'

The popularity of the system is shewn by its adoption in the Greek Translation of Aquila, himself a disciple of R. Akibaᶠ, which was meant to displace the too Christian translation of the LXX. which, being præ-Christian, was, although Jewish, free from prejudice against Christianity.

The 'tradition of R. Akiba' was known to S. Epiphanius ᵍ.

After the extirpating measures, by which Hadrian sought to repress any like revolt to that, which R. Akiba is said to have planned and made Bar Cochab its head, R. Meir, the favourite disciple of R. Akiba, carried on his plan. 'ʰ He completed his collection; what in R. Akiba's Mishna was insulated or fragmentary was made a whole and rounded. But this arrangement, did not make any claim to be an exclusive rule, any more than that of any of his colleagues; every teacher of the law, who had a circle

ᵉ Ib. p. 58.   ᶠ Ib. p. 114.
ᵍ δευτέρα δὲ [παράδοσις] τοῦ καλουμένου Ραββιακίβα. S. Epiph. c. Hær. xxxiii. 9.   ʰ Graetz ib. p. 195.

of disciples, delivered the accumulated material, in what form he liked and thought suitable.'

The enthusiasm, with which this phantastic theory was adopted and propagated, shews the need which was felt of some system, by which to replace what had been lost to them, and as a dam against the rising waters of the Gospel. It bears its novelty stamped upon it. Where it resembles the Gospel, it was probably borrowed from it, with which its authors were well acquainted: in other respects it was intended as a fence against it.

R. Akiba himself was the first memorable fulfilment of our Lord's prophecy, "[1] I am come in My Father's Name and ye receive Me not: if another shall come in his own name, him ye will receive."

R. Akiba knew from prophecy that the time, in which the Messiah was to come, was, any how, near its close; so filled was he with the thought of his near coming, that whatever seemed disastrous to others, to him seemed a token of the approaching deliverance[j]. His travels far and wide, mentioned in Jewish authorities[k], are supposed to have been a preparation for the wide rebellion which involved such horrible bloodshed. He saluted Barcochab as the Messiah; 'Kosiba is arisen as a star in Jacob.'

Barcochab, forbearing to all besides, "[l] commanded the Christians to be carried off to severe punishment,

[1] S. John v. 43.

[j] e. g. his joy when he saw a fox coming out of the holy of holies. See my comm. on Micah p. 316.

[k] Rosh ha-shanah 26. a. Yebamot 121. a. 122. a. Baba Kama 113. a. Sifri on Num. v. 8, in Graetz iv. 148

[l] S. Justin's Apol. i. 31. The Apology dates only nine years alter than the death of Barcochab.

unless they would deny Jesus the Christ and blaspheme Him.'

Akiba himself says, 'ᵐ no one who reads foreign books shall have part in the world to come.' By foreign books, he probably meant Christian.

Our Lord had warned His people of both temporal and eternal consequences of their rejection of Himself Who came to save them. The temporal consequences fell upon them, in the destruction of their city and temple by Titus. Akiba was persuaded with a desperate fanaticism, that they would be reversed by the Messiah whom he still so tenaciously expected, who should rebuild the temple, free them from the Roman yoke, and make Jerusalem the Empress of the world. The temporal visitation under Adrian was more terrible than that under Titus.

Our Lord had warned them of their eternal loss. "He that believeth not in Me is condemned already, because he hath not believed in the Only-begotten Son of God." Akiba said that they were saved already by the covenant of circumcision; that Hell had no power over the circumcised, or over those with whom God made a covenant at Sinai; that to them it was but a purgatory for 12 months at most. Practically a son was not allowed to pray for his father during the twelfth month, lest he should bring evil report on him, as having been a

[m] 'All Israel has a portion in the world to come. And these Israelites have no portion in the world to come; he who saith there is no quickening of the dead, there is no law from heaven, and an Epicurus; R. Akiba says, he also who readeth foreign books, and who muttereth Exod. xv. 26. over a wound' Sanhedr. c. 11 Mishna iv. p. 159. Surenh. With the exception of the last class they are regarded as apostates.

bad liver; since the punishment of even bad livers was supposed to cease at the end of the twelfth.

Sometimes it is clear from the contrast that this purgatory is said of the wicked *in Israel*—'[n] The judgement of the wicked in Gehenna is 12 months, and after that the righteous come and say, 'Lord of the world, these are the men, who came early and late to the house of assembly, and read the "Hear, O Israel," and prayed and did the rest of the commandments.' Forthwith God saith, 'if it be so, go and heal them.' Forthwith the righteous go and stand on the dust of the wicked and pray for mercy upon them, and God maketh them stand upon their feet from their dust, from beneath the soles of the feet of the righteous, and bringeth them to the life of the world to come. Wherefore it is said, "[o] And ye shall tread down the wicked, for they shall be dust under the soles of your feet."'

Rabbi Akiba's ground for making Gehenna to the Jews a Purgatory of 12 months is after his usual fashion; '[p] he too (R. Akiba) was in the habit of saying, five things lasted for 12 months; the judgement of the generation of the Deluge 12 months; the judgement of Job 12 months; the judgement of the Egyptians 12 months; the judgement of Gog and Magog in the time to come 12 months; the judgement of the wicked in Gehenna 12 months; as it is said, "[q] And from one new moon to another."'

The passage has R. Akiba's characteristic fancifulness, stringing together things with a certain like-

---

[n] Yalkut Shim'oni f. 88. 3. Eis. ii. 355.   [o] Mal. iv. 3.
[p] Edyoth c. 2 n. 10. Mishna Surenhus. T. iv. p. 335.
[q] Is. lxvi. 23.

ness upon a text, which gives no support to what he builds upon it. The flood moreover prevailed upon the earth 190 days [r]; of the length of Job's suffering there is no term assigned; nor of the plagues of Egypt; nor of the destruction of Gog and Magog; only that the burial of the corpses was to last 7 months [s].

Nor is there any visible connection between the period of 12 months, and the text "from one new moon to another." But this was R. Akiba's way of founding his new system.

What *is* of moment is, that this period of 12 months of purgatory for the Jew was invented by R. Akiba alone, and received on his authority, 86 years after the Ascension of our Lord, and so has no bearing upon His teaching.

Another passage of his (if it is his) seems to be founded on the Christian belief that our Lord preached to the spirits kept in ward and took with Him to Heaven all who had waited for His Coming. Rabbi Akiba seems to mean that God would do as much through the Messiah whom *he* expected, as Christians believed that Jesus had done; nay, that his Messiah would do as much for the *wicked* in Israel, although they repented not in the time of repentance.

The passage [t] which Dr. Farrar calls 'magnificent,' turns upon a play upon the words in Isaiah, "They who keep the truth," for which he substitutes, 'They who keep the Amens.' 'God,' he says, 'has a key of Gehenna, according to that saying, "Open ye the

[r] Gen. vii. 17, 24.   [s] Ezek. xxxix.12, 14.
[t] Othioth R. Akiba p. 15, 4, 16, 1, quoted by Eisenm. ii. 361, 362.

gates, and let a righteous nation keeping emunim," 'rather, keeping amanim, i. e. which saith Amen,' "enter in." For on account of the Amen which the wicked answer out of the midst of Gehenna, they are delivered from Gehenna. The Holy and Blessed One will sit in the Garden of Eden and preach, and all the righteous sitting before Him, and all the inhabitants of Heaven standing on their feet. On the Right Hand of God will be the sun with the planets; and the moon and all the stars on the left; and the Holy and Blessed One explaineth to them the meaning of the new law which He is about to give them by the hand of the Messiah. And when He arriveth at the Aggadah, Zerubbabel son of Shealtiel standeth on his feet and saith, '[u]Be the Name of God magnified and sanctified,' and his voice goeth from the one end of the world to the other, and all the inhabitants of the world answer, Amen. And the wicked too of Israel and the righteous of the nations of the world who are left in Gehenna answer and say Amen out of the midst of Gehenna, until the whole world is shaken, and their voice is heard in the Presence of the Holy and Blessed One; and He asketh concerning them, and saith, 'What is the voice of great tumult which I hear?' The ministering angels answer and say before Him, 'Lord of the world, These are the wicked of Israel and the righteous of the nations of the world who are left in Gehenna, who answer Amen from the midst of Gehenna.' Forthwith the

[u] A fable is told of the same R. Akiba, how he rescued a soul from Gehenna by teaching his son to say, 'Bless the Blessed Lord for ever and ever.' Nishmath Chaiim from R. Tanchuma Midrash Parasha Toledoth Noah in Eisenm. ii 357—359.

compassions of the Holy and Blessed One are moved exceedingly for them, and He saith, 'What more shall I do to them in addition to this former judgement? The evil nature is the cause thereof.' At that time the Holy and Blessed One taketh the keys of Gehenna and giveth them to Michael and Gabriel, as is said, 'Open the gates and let the righteous nation which keepeth emunim enter in.' Forthwith Michael and Gabriel go and open the forty thousand [v] gates of Gehenna and bring them up out of the midst of Gehenna. Which sheweth' [how?] 'that each Gehenna is 300 long and 300 broad, and 1000 farsa's [x] thick and 1000 farsa's deep, and every wicked man who falleth therein cannot arise out of it. What do Michael and Gabriel at that time? They lay hold of the hand of each one of them, as a man raiseth up his fellow and bringeth him up with a rope out of the midst of the pit. And it is said, 'And He brought him up out of the horrible pit, and out of the miry clay.' And Gabriel and Michael stand over them in that same hour, and wash them and anoint them and heal them from the wounds of hell and clothe

[v] In the Yalkut Shim'oni, where is the same account of the deliverance of the 'wicked Israelites and the righteous nations of the world,' the gates are said to be 8,000 (On Is. f. 46. 1. n. 296. in Eisenm. ii. 333.). In the Midrash hanne'elam f. 48. 1. 2. quoted in the lesser Yalkut Reubeni, they are 50 (Eisenm. ib.). In the Coran Sur. 15, Pirke R. Elieser c. 43, and the modern Emek hammelech f. 144. 2. Nishmath chaiim f. 39. (from the Zohar) there are 7 only (Ib. 334). The Talmud (Erubin f. 19. 1) mentions 3 only, as also the Megalleh amukkoth f. 78. 2. Reshith Chochma f. 47. 1. Eisenm. Ib.

[x] 'The modern farsakh varies. It is estimated at from $3\frac{1}{2}$ to 4 miles or from 30 to 35 furlongs.' Rawlinson on Herod. iii. 53 T. iii. p. 260.

them in good garments and hold them by the hand and bring them before the Face of the Holy and Blessed One in the presence of all the righteous etc. etc.

Those who are supposed to be brought out of Gehenna are twice marked to have been of two classes, 'the wicked of Israel' and 'the righteous of the nations of the world.' It may be that Maimonides[y] is right in his larger interpretation, 'that this last class are not proselytes from the Gentiles, but is equivalent to those, of whom S. Peter says, that "in every nation he that feareth God and worketh righteousness is accepted with Him." Still they are only these two classes; of the *un*righteous nothing is said; but since they are not brought out, R. Akiba must have supposed them to be left. The passage then, instead of contradicting, implies the belief in everlasting punishment for all the *un*righteous heathen, all those, of whom S. Paul speaks in his terrible description in the 1st chapter of the Romans.

Not knowing of a Redeemer, he limits the saved to two classes, those saved by the outward covenant of circumcision, whether such were circumcised in

[y] "Whoever accepteth the 7 precepts [of Noah,] and is careful to do them, he is one of the ' pious of the people of the world ' and has a portion in the world to come ; and he who receiveth them and doeth them because the Blessed One commandeth them in the Law; and he who shall receive and do them because God commanded them in the law, and made it known to us by the hand of Moses our Master that the children of Noah were beforetime commanded to do them : but if he doth them on account of the weight of reason, he is not *ger toshab*, a stranger entitled to dwell in the land, and not of 'the pious of the people of this world ' and not of their wise." Maimon Yad chasaka B. 4. f. 290. 2, quoted by Eisenm. ii. 235.

heart or no, and those Gentiles who, having not the law, are a law unto themselves. For sinners, who were not circumcised, they know of no remedy. Specifically there are declared to have no portion in the world to come, [z] not the men of Sodom only, but the generation of the deluge, of the dispersion, that which perished in the wilderness, the company of Corah; three kings, Jeroboam, Ahab, and Manasses, (though this was questioned as to Manasses) and four private individuals, Balaam, Doeg, Ahitophel, Gehazi.

These were the maxims impressed on the Jewish mind during the first centuries after Christ came: 1) that God was bound by His own promise that no circumcised person should be cast into hell: 2) that if any circumcised person were cast into hell, he must in some way be made uncircumcised; 3) that no Jew was allowed to remain in hell above twelve months.

R. Meir, the disciple of R. Akiba [a], said, '[b] Circumcision is acceptable, for God sware to Abraham that no circumcised person should go to Gehenna; for it was said, '[c] In that day God made a covenant with Abraham &c.' And who goes down thither? What is written after this? "[d] The Kenites and the Kenizzites and the Kadmonites." And so Ezekiel says, "[e] go down and be thou laid with the uncircumcised &c." But the heretics and the apostates and the transgressors of Israel who have denied God, he

[z] Sanhedr. ii. 2. 3. Surenhus. Mishna iv. p. 263.
[a] Wolf B.H. pp. 850, 851.
[b] quoted in Midrash Tillim f. 7. c.2 in Eisenm. ii. 339.
[c] Gen. xv. 18   [d] ib. 19.   [e] Ezek. xxxii. 19.

draweth down to them a foreskin, and they fall into Gehenna, as is said, "'he hath put forth his hand against those which be at peace with him, he defiled his covenant.'" No Israelite then, according to him, is lost, except one who denies God, i.e. ceases to be an Israelite, apostatizing.

Resh Lakish (a disciple of R. Jochanan [g] in our 2nd or 3rd cent.) is quoted as saying that "[h] the fire of Gehenna has no power over the sinners of Israel;" R. Eliezer, that "[i] the fire of hell has no power over the pupils of the wise."

R. Joshua ben Levi, one of the latest Mishnical Doctors, who was fabled to have been carried alive to Paradise, gives an account of the hell, the belief in which, and the exemption of the worst Jews from it, was inculcated on his contemporaries:

"[j] We measured the first house in the dwelling of Gehenna: I found it 100 miles long and 50 miles broad; and there were many pits, and lions of fire standing there, and when men fell therein, the lions devour them, and after the fire has eaten them, they arise anew, and they cast them into the fire of each house in the first dwelling. And I measured the second house in the second dwelling and I found in it as in the first; and I asked as to the first house, and they say, In the first house there are ten nations, and with them is Absalom; and one nation says to another, If we rebelled, in that we did not re-

[f] Ps. lv. 20.   [g] Wolf Bibl. Heb. ii. 881, 882, 874, 875.
[h] Erubin f. 19. 1. Chagiga f. 27. 1. in Eisenm. ii. 343.   See Yalkut chadash Ib.   [i] Chagiga l.c. Ib.
[j] quoted from Moses b. Nachman, Torath haadam, by Eisenmenger, ii. 340, 341.

ceive the law, what have ye done wrong? And these answer, We have rebelled like you. And they say to Absalom, If thou hast not received (the Law), thy fathers have received: why art thou stricken thus? He saith to them, Because I despised my father. And an Angel cometh and scourgeth each one with whips of fire: and he who scourgeth them is Kushiel: and he saith, Cast them; and they cast them, and they are consumed in the fire: and they bring others, and he scourgeth them and casteth them into the fire; and so each, man by man, until all the ungodly are completed. And after this they bring Absalom to be scourged, and a voice cometh from heaven [Bath-kol] and saith, Scourge him not and burn him not, because he is of the sons of My beloved, who said at Sinai, 'We will hearken and be obedient.' After they have ceased to scourge and burn the wicked, they come out of the fire, as if they had not been burned, and they scourge them again, and thus they do to them seven times in the day and three times by night; and Absalom is kept from all these things, because he is the son of David. And in the second dwelling there are ten nations, and they judge them in the like manner, and Doeg is among them; and he who scourgeth them is Lahatiel: and Doeg is delivered from all these, because he is of the sons of those who said at Sinai, 'We will be obedient and hearken.' And in the third house there are ten nations; and they judge them in like way; and he who scourgeth them is Shaftiel; and Korah and his company are kept from all these things, because they had said, 'We will be obedient and hearken.' And the fourth house is like, and in it are ten nations;

and Jeroboam is with them : and he who scourgeth them is Maccathiel; and Jeroboam is freed from all these things, because he studied the law. and he is of the sons of Israel who said at Sinai, 'We will be obedient and hearken.' And the fifth house is judged in the like way : and Ahab is with them: and he who scourgeth them is Chutriel: and Ahab is preserved from all these things, because he is of the sons of Israel who said at Sinai, 'We will be obedient and hearken.' And in the sixth house they judge them in the like way; and Micah is with them; and he who scourgeth them is Pusiel: and Micah is freed from all these things, because they said in Sinai, 'We will be obedient and hearken.' And the seventh house likewise; and Elisha the son of Abuia[k] is with them, and he who-smiteth them is Dalkiel. And Elisha is freed, because he is of the sons of those who said at Sinai, ' We will be obedient and hearken.'

'And in all the seven thousand [*chambers*], I saw in each chamber, they judge all the wicked with the like judgement; and they see not each other, because all darkness, which was before the world was created, is there.'

In each hell, according to this teaching, were ten of the 70 nations, among whom they supposed the world to be divided, and mostly one man who was

[k] He was a Rabbi, who had apostatised to a belief of two first principles, and was in their belief rescued from hell by prayer after his decease. (See Bartolocci T. ii. 511, 512.) Extracts from Eisenmenger's treatise on the Jewish belief in hell were made by Rev. J. P. Stehelin F.R.S., in what is now one of the scarcest books (I am told) of the last century, ' Rabbinical literature, or the traditions of the Jews contained in the Talmud and other mystical writings.' Lond. 1748.

in the Jewish covenant, Absalom, the parricide in will, Doeg, Korah and his company, Jeroboam, Ahab, Micah, and a Rabbi, Elisha ben Abuiah, who had apostatized. The heathen, it was taught, were punished unceasingly, the signally wicked of Israel were spared the slightest chastisement.

But even the supreme influence of R. Akiba could not extinguish the previous belief in the eternity of punishment. Nay, their Rabbins must themselves have inculcated that belief to a certain extent, in order to maintain their own authority. For they assign to their lowest hell, from which none come forth, '[1] those who mock at the words of the wise,' i.e. of themselves.

But further Chief Rabbi Weill, to whom Dr. Farrar appeals as rejecting the belief, himself expressly acknowledges the traditional belief. '[m] The Talmud and the other traditional monuments do not fail to proclaim the eternity of sufferings and of rewards in the Halacha no less than in the Agada. It is thus that certain categories of sinners are marked out to us, who are deprived for ever of the bliss of the world to come[n]; it is thus that the Mishna brings before its tribunal certain individuals and certain generations, against whom it pronounces a sentence of condemnation, devoting some to annihilation, and others to endless sufferings[o]; it is thus, that certain criminals are spoken of; "[p]Hell may come to an end, but not their punishment."'

[1] See below pp. 103, 104.   [m] Le Judaisme T. iv. p. 594.
[n] 'Talmud Sanhedrin, 90 and 99, Talmud Rosh Hashana. 17.
[o] Sanhedrin c. 11, Mishna 2 and 3.   [p] Talm. Rosh Hash. l. c.

In the one passage of the two most quoted, it seems very probable, that the eternal punishments are reserved for acts against Judaism, which excluded persons from its benefits. Sins done through the body are contrasted with sins against faith or the Jewish belief. As regards sins against the body, the benefit of the 12 months of purgatory is extended to the *sinners* of the nations: eternal punishment is reserved for sins as to faith or schism or persecutors.

' q The sinners of Israel in their body, and the sinners of the nations of the world in their body, go down to Gehenna and are punished there twelve months; after twelve months their body is consumed, and their soul is burned, and the wind scattereth them under the feet of the righteous, as it is said, "r and ye shall trample on the wicked, for they shall be dust under the soles of your feet;" but the heretics [i.e. Christians, s] and traitors and Epicurus t,' who have denied the law, and who have denied the quickening of the dead, and who have departed from the ways of the congregation, and who have put the fear of them on the land of the living, and who have sinned and caused others to sin (as Jeroboam son of Nebat and his companions), go down to Gehenna and are punished there to all generations, as it is said, "and they shall go forth and look on

^q Rosh Hashana f. 17. 1. ^r Mal. iv. 3.

^s "The *Minim* are the disciples of Jesus the Nazarene, who have turned the words of the living God to evil," Rashi (here), and, "the *Minim* are the disciples of Jesus who do not approve the words of the wise," on Chagiga f. 52; quoted, with Maimonides and others, by Edzardi, Avoda zara pp. 276, 277.

^t Epicurus is a known name for Christians. It is used by Lipmann and Abarbanel, quoted by Eisenm. i. 695, 696.

the corpses of the men, who have sinned against Me." Gehenna faileth and *they* fail not, as it is said, "[u] and their beauty shall consume in the grave from their dwelling." '

' Another tradition is at variance with this, in that it sets in the first place one of the very gravest moral offences, the adulterer. '[v] Rabbi Chanina[x] said, All who go down to Gehenna arise, save three who go down and do not arise: these are, he who goeth in to the wife of another, and he who maketh the face of his neighbour to turn white before many; and he who giveth an evil name to his neighbour.' But this in part contradicts the saying in the Sanhedrin; '[y] He who goeth in to his neighbour's wife they put him to death by strangling and he has a portion in the world to come, but he who makes the face of his neighbour to turn white before many, he hath no portion in the world to come.'

The Jewish belief is plain from their express words, that, beside the exceptional case of themselves, they assigned whole generations of mankind to Hell, as to whom Scripture saith nothing, or the contrary. They assigned to Hell the generation of the deluge[z]. Holy Scripture speaks directly of [a] our Lord preaching to those in ward, who were disobedient in the days of Noah. They had repented, too late to be saved from the temporal judgement, and waited there 2000 years, until our Lord came and delivered them. Holy Scripture speaks of the temporal death only of

[u] Ps. xlix. 14.   [v] Baba Mezia f. 58. v.
[x] 'i.e. R. Hanina b. Hama the Palestinian Amoraer.' Dr. Neubauer. (lived about 180—260.) He held rigidly to tradition. Gratz. iv. 254.
[y] Sanhedrin f. 107.   [z] See above p. 91.   [a] 1 S. Pet. iii. 19.

those who died in the wilderness, nothing whatever of the generation of the confusion of tongues.

Scripture and the Church say nothing of the heathen, whom, except, at most, 'the righteous,' as contrasted with the *sinners* of Israel, Judaism assigns to hell.

Jewish imagination occupied itself in picturing to itself the terrible dimensions of Gehenna.

'Our rabbins say, [b] The land of Egypt is 400 farsa's[c] square, and is $\frac{1}{60}$ of Ethiopia, and Ethiopia is $\frac{1}{60}$ of the world, and the world is $\frac{1}{60}$ of the garden of Eden, and the garden is $\frac{1}{60}$ of Gehenna. The whole world is as the covering of a pot to Gehenna. And some say that Gehenna has no measure, and some say that Eden has no measure.'

But such terrible dimensions imply, in their belief, a proportionate number of inhabitants, on which Christian awe has not thought.

In the N. T., Gehenna is spoken of twelve times. In all the places but one, it is our Lord Who speaks. He speaks of '[d] the Gehenna of fire,' as equivalent to '[e] everlasting fire' into which men may be 'cast,' unless they cast off their sins; and *that*, in contrast to 'entering into life.' He explains it to be '[f] the quenchless fire, where their worm dieth not, and the fire is not quenched.' This is decisive as to the meaning which our Lord affixed to it. He appeals to the Pharisees on their ways, "[g] Ye serpents, ye generation of vipers, how can ye escape the judgement of Gehenna?" He bids His own disciples, "[h] Fear not them who kill the body but are not able

---

[b] Taanith c i. p 10 quoted by Bartolocci T. ii. p. 161.
[c] see above p. 89 n. x.   [d] S. Matt. xviii. 9.   [e] Ib. 8.
[f] S. Mark ix. 43, 45, 47.   [g] S. Matt. xxiii. 33.   [h] Ib. x. 28.

to kill the soul, but rather fear Him Who is able to destroy both body and soul in Gehenna:" "¹fear Him, which after He hath killed hath power to cast into Gehenna, yea I say unto you, Fear Him." He warns against going to the verge of sin, (cost what it might to cast off the temptation,) lest it should lead to the full deadly sin, which would destroy the soul. "ᵏ It is profitable for thee, that one of thy members should perish, and not that thy whole body should be cast into Gehenna." He was warning against admitting the wish to commit adultery. His warning under the sixth commandment, "¹whosoever shall say, Thou fool, shall be in danger of the Gehenna of fire," is explained by His Apostle, in plain terms, "ᵐ Whoso hateth his brother is a murderer, and ye know that no murderer hath eternal life abiding in him." The Jews have a strong saying about filthy conversation, which does not encourage any one to lighten the weight of our Lord's words. 'ⁿ Whoso fouleth his mouth, they cast him deep into Gehenna.' The remaining place, in which our Lord uses the word Gehenna, is in His woes on the Scribes and Pharisees, "ᵒ Ye compass sea and land to make one proselyte, and when he is made, ye make him twofold more the son of Gehenna than yourselves." 'ᵖ Sons of Gehenna,' says one of their recent authorities out of the Talmud, 'are those who for ever abide in Gehenna;' only that our Lord warns them while in life, that, while there was time, they might avoid it. Yet there is a remarkable variation in the use of the term otherwise alike.

¹ S. Luke xii. 5.   ᵏ S. Matt. v. 28, 29.   ˡ Ib v. 22.
ᵐ 1 S. John iii. 15.   ⁿ Shabbath f. 33. a   ᵒ S. Matt. xxiii. 15.
ᵖ Levy, Chaldee Lexicon i. 136 from the Rosh hashana 17. a.

100 Gehenna, name of hell among Latins Greeks Syrians.

Gehenna, the name used by our Lord to designate the place of the lost, continued to be so used both by those who believed in Him and those who rejected Him. Instances of its use in post-Christian Jewish writings have occurred above. It continued so to be used by those who knew nothing of the cavils as to the word αἰώνιος, by Latin as well as Greek Ecclesiastical writers; among the Syrians it is almost the one word used for Hell. In Arabic (as derived from Mohammad's Jewish teacher) it is the place of eternal doom. It is the name used [q] in the Syriac versions of the N. T. and by all the Syrian Christians, Orthodox [r], Monophysite [s], and Nestorian [t]. S. Ephrem's hymns, in which the title is used, were received throughout the Syrian Churches, and were employed in those bodies which were broken off by heresy [u].

In the Coran, it is used as altogether equivalent to two other words; 'the fire,' the '[x] fiercely blazing fire' as the place of future punishment. It is scarcely mentioned without some addition implying its eternity. The words 'abiding eternally in it,' are added as a part of its description [y]. Mohammad transferred

[q] What follows is from Dr. Payne Smith Thes. Syr. who gives other instances also, v ܓܗܢܐ p. 707.

[r] S. Ephrem, Ass. B. O. i. 134. [add e.g. Paræn. 3. Opp. Syr. P. iii. p. 386; P. 13 p. 432; P. 23 pp 458, 459; P. 32 p. 484. P. 35 p. 488.] S. James of Sarug, Ib. 315. S. Isaac of Nineveh, Ib. 468; the translator of Methodius iii. 1. 28.

[s] Barsalebi Ib. ii. 163.   [t] Ebedjesu iii. 1. 333.

[u] Ass. Bibl. Or, Art. S. Ephrem viii. ix. T. i. pp. 433, 434.

[x] ܡܣܥܪ See Lane, Arab. Lex. 384.

[y] 'Do they not know that he who opposes God and his prophet, Gehenna is his, abiding eternally in it?' Sur. ix. 65. 'God has promised the hypocrites, men and women, and the unbelievers, the fire of Gehenna, abiding in it for ever; this is their portion, and God

to his own followers the exemption from it, which the later Jews claimed for themselves. He assigns Hell as the portion of unbelievers [z]. The exemption of Mohammedans from it is an article of their faith [a]. There are traits which remind one of its Jewish origin, and which seem inconsistent with other parts. The general impression given is, that each goes at once upon death to his own place, 'Paradise,' or 'the fire.' But Mohammad has also the Jewish be-

hath cursed them and they have an abiding punishment.' Ib. 70. 'God will not lead them any way but the way of hell, to abide in it for ever.' iv. 167. 'he shall make them enter the fire to abide for ever in it.' iv. 13. ' his retribution is Gehenna, abiding in it for ever.' iv. 92. ' They who disbelieve and charge our signs as false, are companions of the fire, they abide for ever in it.' ii. 39. The phrase 'they are companions of the fire, abiding eternally in it,' occurs ii. 81. 217. 258. 276. iii. 116, as the ' companions of the fire' are contrasted with the ' companions of Paradise.' vii. 51. add further iv. 120.

[z] 'Say to unbelievers, 'ye shall be conquered and shall be gathered into Gehenna, and ill shall be your bed.' iii. 12. 'Fear the fire which is prepared for unbelievers.' iii. 131. 'The unbelievers shall be gathered into Gehenna.' viii. 31. 'Gehenna shall encircle unbelievers.' ix. 57. ' And he must believe that the Ssirât *is*, i. e. a body stretched across the middle of hell, sharper than a sword, and finer than a hair; by the judgement of God, the steps of unbelievers slip, they fall into the fire; and the steps of the faithful are steadied and they will be conducted to the region of rest.' Alghazzali in his ' Exposition of the faith of the Sonnites' in Marracci Prodr. ad refut. Alcorani P. 3. p. 91.

[a] ' And he must believe that the Unitarians will be brought out of the fire after the punishment, so that by the mercy of God there shall not remain one Unitarian in Gehenna; and he must believe in the intercession of the prophets, then of the Doctors, then of the martyrs, then of the rest of believers, each according to the degree of his dignity; and whoever remains of believers, who have no intercessor, is by the mercy of God brought forth, and no believer abides in the fire; but every one is brought out of it, in whose heart there is the weight of an atom of faith.' Alghazzali l c.

lief that all go to Gehenna for a time and will be led round it, but that wrong doers will be left in it [b].

There is one more evidence, that the Jews, at the time when the Talmud was written, believed in the eternity of punishment, which one would have thankfully suppressed, on account of the horrible blasphemy which it involves. There are, according to the Jews, 7 divisions of hell; each of them 60 times hotter than that above it [c]. It would outrage all decency to translate the description of the lowest. I will only extract what is necessary for the purpose. "[d]The lowest dwelling is called Abaddon, and *there* are the stairs, which are called 'Zoa rothachath,' 'the boiling filth,'—And in it there is no spark of holiness;—*There* are all unclean souls;—those who have made themselves an object of idolatry, especially 'asham shishi [e]', in whom is no spark of holiness; wherefore whoever goeth down there, never cometh up."

The name 'Zoa rochachath' occurs in a Gemaric Doctor [f] of our third cent. In the Tract Ghit-

[b] Sur. xix. 65—69.
[c] See in Eisenm. ii. 331. 'They (their Rabbis) say.'
[d] It is given in Eisenm. Entd. Judenth. i. 196.
[e] Eisenmenger says that a Rabbi told him confidentially that these words meant Jesus. There is a play on the word *talui*, which might be a matter on which there was doubt (suspense) or the 'hanged One,' the Jews' common title for our Lord. Ib. p. 197. Aboda zara 'an object of idolatry' is also a name given to Him. "'That man' made himself Aboda zara." Emeck hammelech in Eis. i. 78. add Rashi on Ex. xxiii. 14. Ib.

[f] Mar or Mor was one of the Gemaric Doctors viz. Rabba Bar Nachmani, uncle of Abii who was rector of the Pumbaditan Academy A.D. 325. Wolf B. H. ii pp. 878, 867. The like saying is ascribed to Rab Papa b. Rab Acha b. Ada in the name of Acha b. Ulai, 'Whoever

Evidence from blasphemy in the Talmud. 103

tin [g], it is said more explicitly who this is. The story told is, that 'Onkelos bar Kalonikos, son of the sister of Titus, wished to become a proselyte. Onkelos brought by magic Titus, Balaam, and Jesus, and asked them, 'Who is most esteemed in the other world? They answer, 'Israel'. They are asked again, 'what is their own punishment?' Decency again forbids to translate the answer put into the mouth of Balaam. I give the rest [h] verbatim.

'Onkelos went and raised up Jesus[1] by incantation. He saith to him, 'Who is highly accounted of in that world?' He answers, 'Israel.' He saith, 'What if I cleave to him?' He saith, 'Seek their good, seek not their evil.' 'Whoever toucheth them, toucheth

mocketh at the wise is judged in the Zoa rochachath,' Erubin f. 21. 2. It is quoted by Lipmann Nizzachon p. 42. n. 68. and in Emek hammelech f. 7. 3 in Eis. i. 195, referred to in Nezach Israel f. 10. 3. (Ib. p. 196) f. 20. 4. (Ib p. 200) f. 13. 3. 4 (Ib. p. 203.) The words 'Zoa rochachath' stand in the Venice editions of the Talmud. They were omitted, by order of the Christians, in later editions. In that of Amsterdam, there is no notice of the omission The space is supplied by the insertion of דבי, " Whoso mocketh at [the words of] the wise is punished."

[g] f. 56. b. It is given in Bartolocci T. ii. pp. 154, 155.
[h] It occurs f. 57.

[1] The name Jesus is printed in the unmutilated copies, as in the two Venice editions, Ven. 1520-1523, and Ven. 1546-51, both of which are in the Bodleian. In the Bodleian copy of the edition Ven. 1546-51, a Christian reader has smeared over the passage with something of the colour of burnt-umber, leaving it however perfectly legible. Subsequently a blank was left, as in the edition of Cracow 1604, in which the space was filled up in Ms. in a copy in the Barberini Library [Bartolocci. l. c. p. 156.] by the words, 'Otho haish,' 'That man,' a title which the Jews give to our Lord. See p. 95 note s. In later editions, as Ven. 1625 and Amsterdam, the whole clause was left out and a blank space left.

the apple of His eye.' He saith to him, 'Wherein is the judgement of this man' [Himself]? He saith, 'In the boiling filth.' For Mar ʲ saith, 'Whoever mocketh at the words of the wise, is judged in the boiling filth.'

Horrible as this is, and miserable that they should thus speak of Him Who died for them, their blasphemy was consistent: for unless He had been their Lord and their God, He would have been—what they called Him. The Jews of this day are not involved in the blasphemy, unless they repeat it.

The enquiry has been long; but many might be carried away or perplexed by the confidence with which Dr. Farrar urged the argument from the supposed disbelief of Jews in the time of our Lord.

The argument is in itself imperfect; for even if the Jews had used the word Gehenna of a temporal judgement, our Lord would have corrected the impression, when He spoke of God "destroying both body and soul in Gehenna," or of "the quenchless fire, where their worm dieth not and their fire is not quenched."

But now there is no trace of any doubt among the Jews, that punishment would be eternal for those who incurred it, until the theory of the limitation of its duration *for the Jew* was invented by one who lived after the Ascension of our Lord.

We have distinct and independent evidence in the book of Enoch [k] before our Lord, in which Gehenna is described: it is named in the 4th book of Ezra [l], and the Apocalypse of Baruch [m]; in the Targum of Jo-

ʲ See p. 102 note f.   ᵏ ab. p. 52 sqq   ˡ ab. p. 59.   ᵐ ab. p. 60.

nathan[n] the name is inserted as the place of 'everlasting burning after the great Judgement Day.' The Book of Judith[o] mentions the fire and the worm as the everlasting portion of those at enmity to God in His people. The final separation of the wicked from the good, and their perishing for ever, is contained in the Psalms of Solomon[p]: the 4th book of Maccabees[q] repeatedly asserts 'everlasting punishment:' '[r]the second death' is mentioned by Onkelos in contrast with eternal life, and explained in other Targums to be 'the death whereby the wicked die in the world to come.'

Such a summary must omit more than it states; for it can only mention single expressions. Far more is the fact, there is not any one exception among those who believed in any world to come.

In the Talmud, upon which Dr. Farrar relies, there are contradictions in detail. But in the main, there are two traditions: the one assigning certain definite classes of persons to eternal punishment[s], chiefly such as had apostatized or offended against Judaism, or despised the teaching of the Rabbis, and to these they went out of their way to add Him Who came to save them[s]; the other, dating from one individual who lived subsequently to our Lord, and alleged by the Talmud itself to rest on his authority, which made Gehenna a purgatory of 12 months for the Jew[t].

Gehenna continued to be the name of the abode of the lost, both among those who received our Lord's teaching, Latins, Greeks, Syrians, and those who rejected it, even in our 7th century, when the name of Gehenna as the place of everlasting punishment

[n] ab. p. 75.   [o] ab. p. 51.   [p] ab. p. 63.   [q] ab. p. 65.
[r] ab. pp. 73, 74.   [s] ab. pp. 90 sqq. 104.   [t] ab. pp. 85—87.

was transferred into the Coran from Mohammad's Jewish teacher.

There is then absolutely no ground to think that the Jews, in our Lord's day, understood by Gehenna any thing else, than what lies upon the surface of the words, that it was the place of punishment of those, who to the end would not have God as their God.

Amid all which is so sad, Dr. Farrar may, unintentionally, render good service to the Church and to souls by forcing attention to the intermediate state. He himself is so possessed with the idea, that the one remedy for those who *seem* [wholly] to have failed in this life is, that they should have a second trial or prolongation of trial in the world to come, and *that*, through punishment in 'the æonian fire,' that he tosses aside the doctrine of purgatory, or an intermediate state in which there should be any purifying suffering, simply as something which he does not hold. He reiterates (as did Mr. Wilson of the ' u Essays and Reviews' before him) that the doctrine of Purgatory makes the belief in the eternal punishment of the lost milder in the Roman Church than with us, as though the English Church held, that any whom the Roman Church assigns to Purgatory would be cast into Hell. But he mentions it only to say, 'I do not hold it.' He casts it upon us, as an aggravation of the evil of what he represents as 'ᵛthe common, the popular view of Hell in our own Church.'

"ʷ No member of the Greek or Roman Church has to face in all their horror the two doctrines which

---

ᵘ Defence p 147. See Eiren. i. p 196 note.
ᵛ Eternal Hope, Pref. p. xxix. ᵛ Et. Hope, pp. 180—182.

I impugn—of an irreversible doom passed at death, and of torment necessarily endless for every soul that has died *in sin*. The doctrine of an intermediate state robs those popular conceptions of nine-tenths of their ghastliness, because it enables Christians to contemplate without agony the condition of all who are nearest and dearest to them, and practically of all who die with the last rites of their Church. It is quite true that of the doctrine of Purgatory, in the precise and dogmatic form of it, there is no adequate proof; but the expression of our Article, '[x] a fond thing vainly invented,' applies, I imagine, far less to the mere doctrine than to the mass of flagrant abuses with which it had become inevitably [?] identified. . . . The taunt of the Roman controversialist, Möhler, that 'Protestantism must either admit many into heaven stained with sin, or imagine that a magical change is wrought merely by death,' is unanswerable, unless we reply with Karl Hase, that both views are untenable, since most men at death are indeed not wicked enough [to be cast into] to deserve an endless hell, yet not holy enough to be admitted [at once] into heaven. And Hase proceeds to argue with justice, that our Protestantism is perfectly reconcilable (not indeed with a dogmatic and definite) but with 'a subdued and enlightened view of purgatory,' i.e. of progressive amelioration, of a purifying process after death."

Why then reject it? 'Prayers for the departed' necessarily involve the belief in some possible change in the condition of the departed. And the extrusion of those prayers from our Prayer-book was owing to

[x] Art. xxii.

the unhappy declension towards the end of the reign of Edward VIth. They are still legal, although, publicly, the departed are only tacitly included in the emphatic words, 'we and all Thy whole Church.' But pain after this life for many at least in the Day of [whether particular or general] Judgement is so laid down by S. Paul, that it is strange that any overlook it.

There must remain a feeling of dishonesty as to our treatment of God's teaching through Holy Scripture, so long as we turn aside from the question, what is meant by "building wood, hay, stubble," on the One Foundation, Which is Christ, and do not even say with the Apostles, "Lord, is it I?" But it is also an indifference to our own future. "[y] All Scripture," God tells us, "is given by inspiration of God," "that the man of God may be perfect, throughly furnished unto all good works." And yet S. Paul especially draws our attention to these words. "Let every man take heed, how he buildeth thereupon," i.e. upon the One Foundation, which he himself had laid, "other than which no man can lay, which is Jesus Christ." The solemn warning does not then relate to very grievous sins, which separate from Christ. Those who commit such sins, build on the sand, not on the Rock, Which is Christ. Nor, however it was primarily addressed to teachers, can the conscience of those who are not teachers satisfy itself, that the principle is confined to them. The words are too large. "Let *every man* take heed how he buildeth." "*Every man's* work shall be made manifest." "If *any man's* work &c."

[y] 2 Tim. iii 16, 17.

understood of old to include both life and teaching. 109

The image of building is also used by our Lord of moral action, as well as of teaching. His solemn vivid picture of those who built their houses, the one class on the sand, the other on the rock, must have been and be in the mind of every reader of S. Paul. Our Lord likens the unstable, who think to be followers of Him without counting the cost, to men who lay the foundation of a tower, and are not able to finish it [z]. S. Paul, in this very context, says, "[a] Ye are God's building;" surely, as a whole, the whole man, not his faith only. S. Paul uses the same image, as to the whole building up of the Christian Church. "[b] Ye," the Ephesians, "are built upon the foundation of the Apostles and Prophets, Jesus Christ Himself being the chief Corner stone: in Whom all the building, fitly framed together, groweth unto an holy temple in the Lord, in Whom ye also are builded together for an habitation of God through the Spirit," and again, "[c] rooted and built up in Him, and stablished in the faith." S. Peter, using the like image of being built upon Christ as the "chief Corner-stone," speaks how Christians, as "[d] lively stones, are built up, a spiritual house."

With all this wider application of the same imagery in their minds, Christians have not been able to bind the words down exclusively to a superstructure of errors in faith in lesser matters, by those who still held to Jesus Christ Himself as *the* Foundation.

Yet even if it related to teachers only, there are thousands of them among us; yet hardly any one

[z] S. Luke xiv. 28.   [a] 1 Cor. iii. 9.
[b] Eph. ii. 20—22.   [c] Col. ii. 7.   [d] 1 S. Pet. ii. 5.

seems to think of its warning, save to think, 'It does not belong to me.' Why should it not? It relates to persons who are themselves saved, whatever suffering they may undergo.

S. Paul contrasts, as a whole, the two classes, those whose work shall stand the fire of the Great Day, and those whose work shall be burned. But there must, in lax days like these, be very many of a mixed class, men and women, who do not neglect altogether to build gold and precious stones, but who also build those worthless materials. Who shall be secure that, in part at least, he is not building them? The Day of Judgement, God tells us, will be very aweful and strict. Our Lord, the Judge, saith, "[e] Every idle word that men shall speak, they shall give account thereof in the Day of Judgement." Is not the world full of idle words? People shrink naturally from the terrible enumeration of the heathen sins in S. Paul [f]. But apart from those which outrage nature, can people be so sure that, at least, they *have* not *been* guilty of 'backbiting, evil speaking, insolence, boastfulness,' not to speak of 'covetousness, envy, strife, deceit?' And if so, is there not wood, hay, stubble, for the fire to consume?

And again, who shall say that Judgement will be a momentary act? It might please God to cast such light upon the conscience, that it should see at one moment every sin, which it ever committed. It may be. But it might also be that the sight might be protracted, and the loathing of sin be burned into the soul by the lengthened unfolding of the sins, which, since it had built on the One Foundation,

[e] S. Matt. xii. 36. [f] Rom. i. 29—32.

had been forgiven, but by which it had offended its God. What, if in all that review, which might be essential to its seeing the justice of God, in that it was bid to 'take a lower place,' it should be kept in suspense as to the issue? This has not seemed improbable to holy men of old. S. Ambrose says, "[g] The soul is free from the body, and yet after the end of this life, still hangs in suspense through the uncertainty of the future judgement;" and S. Gregory of Nyssa describes how, in the sight of the glories of heaven and the punishment of hell, "[h] the whole human race, from the first creation to the consummation of all things, shall stand in suspense ($μετέωρος$) between fear and hope of the future, trembling oftentimes at the event of the things looked for either way, and they who have lived with a good conscience, mistrusting what shall be, when they see others dragged down to the fearful darkness by an evil conscience as by an executioner."

Truly there are terrible ways, in which one who builds worthless materials on the One Foundation may "escape, yet so as by fire." Yet who well nigh seems to be scared from building them by S. Paul's warning? There can be no doubt that S. Paul says, that there will be suffering in the Day of Judgement, probably the particular judgement upon the individual soul upon its departing from the body. There is no limitation of time, during which whatever is meant under the figure of the burning of the wood, hay, stubble, shall last. The materials, which symbolise it, require more or less time to consume them. The image seems to represent a more or less pro-

[g] de Cain ii. 2. [h] de beatitud. T. i. p. 609.

longed suffering in that day, according to the greater or less grievousness of the things to be destroyed in those who are saved.

S. Paul's warning, as one would expect, impressed minds much, before controversy turned away attention from it. All were to pass through the fire. We are expressly told this of those, whose works are worthless: the works are burned up and perish through the fire; they, who did them, are "saved, yet so as by fire." So then as to those whose works are good. The gold too is tested, although it abides. We could not even imagine the works of a life being tested at the Judgement-seat of Christ, without pain. To some who will yet be saved, it must be agony.

The old Christian writers embodied this in their representations, how all should pass through the fire.

S. Ambrose names Ezekiel, Daniel, S. John the Evangelist, Peter; S. Hilary, even 'blessed Mary' herself. In one thing they are agreed, that the fire will not hurt the great saints; but that others will suffer in that Day in proportion as they built the wood, hay, stubble, upon the One Foundation which is Christ.

Of writers who remain, Clement of Alexandria first speaks of it briefly [1].

'*We* say that fire purifies not flesh but sinful souls, speaking not of that all-devouring and common fire, but of that discriminating fire, which penetrates the soul which passes through the fire.'

S. Ambrose speaks of it in words of awe, lest he

---

[1] Strom. vii. 6, p. 851. Et. Hope p. 157. The passage has no bearing on the subject of endless punishment, since it incorporates 1 Cor. iii., which notoriously relates to what the Church, following S. Paul, regarded as temporary.

in day of Judgement, the wicked only perished in it. 113

should himself suffer by it; '^kBut the avenging flame shall consume the ministers of impiety. Woe is me, should my work be burned, and I suffer this worsting of my labour! Although the Lord will save His servants, we shall be saved by faith, but so saved as by fire. Although we shall not be burned up, yet we shall be burned. But how some remain in the fire, others escape through it, learn from another Scripture. The Egyptians were drowned in the Red Sea, the Israelites passed over; Moses passed through, Pharaoh sank, for *his heavy sins drowned him. In like manner the irreligious will sink in the lake of burning fire.*'

And again, '^lHe who possesses here the fire of love, will have no cause to fear there the fiery sword. But *he* shall be tried as silver, I, as lead; I shall burn till the lead melts away. If no silver be found in me, ah me! *I shall be plunged down into the lowest pit, or consume entire as the stubble.* Should ought of gold or silver be found in me, not for my works, but through the mercy and grace of Christ, by the ministry of the priesthood, I shall peradventure say, "They that hope in Thee shall not be ashamed." The fiery sword, then, shall consume iniquity, which is placed on the leaden scale. One, then, only could not feel that fire, Christ the Righteousness of God, because He did no sin; for the fire found nought in Him which it might consume ^m.'

^k In Ps. xxxvi. n. 26, Opp. i. 790 Ben.
^l in Ps. cxviii. Serm. xx. n. 12—14, i. 1225 Ben.

^m Dr. Farrar (Et. Hope p. 164.) refers to these two passages, in proof that 'S. Ambrose, though using the ordinary phraseology in some places, [in these] distinctly states the doctrine of universal restitution,' whereas he distinctly states the contrary.

S. Augustine, his convert and his disciple, speaks in aweful words of the grievousness of that amending fire, while contrasting it, like S. Ambrose, with the eternal fire. "'ⁿ Rebuke me not, O Lord, in Thine indignation.' Let me not be among those to whom Thou wilt say, 'Go into fire everlasting, which is prepared for the devil and his angels.' 'Nor rebuke me in Thy wrath,' but purge me in this life, and make me such, that I shall no longer need the amending fire. (This he says) on account of those 'who shall be saved, yet so as by fire.' Why, but because here they build on the foundation wood, hay, stubble? If they would build gold, silver, precious stones, they would have no fear as to either fire, not only that eternal fire which shall to eternity torment the ungodly, but that also which shall amend those who shall be saved by fire. For it is said, 'Yet himself shall be saved, but so as by fire.' And because it is said, 'himself shall be saved,' that fire is despised. Yet, although they 'shall be saved by fire,' more grievous will be that fire, than whatever men can suffer in this life."

S. Gregory Nazianzen says of himself, "ᵒ Perchance I shall hereafter be moulded by another moulding, cleansed by the friendly fire.'

I will only add one more father, S. Ephrem, who

ⁿ In Ps. xxxvii. n. 3. Opp. iv. 295 Ben.

ᵒ De seipso v. 496 p. 48 Toll. In Orat. iii. n. vii. p. 71, he exhorts to 'build on the foundation of faith, not wood, nor hay, nor stubble,—matter unresisting and easily consumed, when what is ours is judged by the fire or purified—but gold, silver, precious stones, which abide and are stable.'

represents all the Syriac Christians, since his hymns were used by all [p].

'[q] Both the just and the unjust shall pass through the fire which is to try them, and shall be proved by it; the righteous pass and the flame is quiet; but it burneth the wicked and snatcheth him away:' and '[r] What shall I do, who must pass over the burning flame? How shall I be able to soar high above it?' S. Ephrem connects this fire with the fire of hell, which he prays may shrink back 'through the precious Body and Blood of Christ, which' 'the saved had received; and that the Cross of the Son of the living God may be a bridge over the sea of fire [s].'

What are we, or what are we doing, that we should not stand in awe of that cleansing fire, which to such holy men and great saints of God as S. Ambrose, S. Augustine or S. Ephrem was so aweful? Are we more circumspect as to idle words, than he, who retired for the day, if any word was spoken against any one [t]?

I may repeat here what, having been written in a book which failed of most of its purpose, is now forgotten:

'[u] To thoughtful minds, whom the grace of God has

[p] See ab. p. 100 n. u.

[q] Canon xlii. Opp. Syr., t. vi. p. 298; Burgess's Hymns of S. Ephrem, p. 32.   [r] Can. ix., ib. 236; Burg., p. 18.

[s] See Canon lxxxi. init., p. 355; Paræn. iii. p. 386, P. xiii. p.432; P. xxiii. pp. 458, 459; P. lxiv. p. 535; in Dr. Pusey's "Doctrine of the Real Presence," pp. 124, 418—422. These and other passages are put together in Bp. Forbes on the Articles ii. 329—334. I have omitted Origen, although there is nothing in his words indicative of Universalism.

[t] Possidii Vita S. Aug. c. 22. Opp. x. App. pp. 272, 273 Ben.

[u] Eiren. i. pp. 191—194.

taught something of what sin is, and of the holiness and love of God and of Jesus, it is absolutely inconceivable that,—when the soul shall first behold Jesus, and, in His sight, with its powers quickened by Him, shall behold its past life as a whole; when, in His Countenance, it shall behold all which it never before saw of His goodness, and, in contrast with this, all its own ingratitude, baseness, rebellion, negligence, discontent, murmurings, not to speak of deadly, forgiven sin,—it should not have intense pain, pain so intense, that one should think that, in this life, soul and body would be severed by its intensity. There seems also to be an instinctive feeling, that a soul, which here has no longings for God, even if the man himself should die in a state of grace, would not be at once, and might not for some long period be, admitted to the sight of God. It is a common saying, that a number of souls 'seem to be fit neither for heaven nor hell,' and that purgatory seems to meet the case of this class of souls. This cannot mean, necessarily so. For this would be to limit the Omnipotence of God. The ordinary belief in England must be, that God, in one act at the particular judgement, at once frees the soul which dies in His grace from all sinfulness which clung to it while yet in the body, and fits it for its abode in Paradise[x]. The Roman doctrine of purgatory presupposes, that exactly the same number of souls will be

---

[x] S. Macarius says of one dying in battle, 'The Lord, seeing thy mind, that thou fightest and lovest Him with all thy mind, severs death from thy soul in one hour (for nothing is hard to Him), and receiveth thee to His Bosom and to the Light. For He snatches thee in the turning-point of an hour from the mouth of darkness

saved, viz. those, and those only, who die in a state of grace, and that the capacity of loving will receive no accession there. The time of gaining grace, in the belief of the Roman Church equally with our own, is over with this life, and the place of the soul in bliss is then fixed for ever. Suffering and preparation for the sight of God, which, here, might have been the channel of large grace, would, *there*, be without any increase of grace. Yet many of us, for our misdeserts, may be unfit for the immediate presence of God; or, in the great words of S. Irenæus, '[y] capere Deum,' 'to contain God,' who yet, for the Merits of Jesus, may, we trust, in His mercy be saved. God can "[z] in a short time, fulfil a long time." Publicans and harlots shall enter into the kingdom of God before the self-righteous. We know not what God may do, in one agony of loving penitence, for one who accepts His last grace in that almost sacrament of death. The question, however, is not about individuals. As a class, we could not affirm that those, who bring forth no worthy fruits of repentance, with whom, after a long period of deadly sin, repentance has been but a superficial work, may not, after death, be in a state of privation of the sight of God (the 'pœna damni'), not being admitted at once to the sight of *Him*, Whom on earth they little cared to think of or to speak to, and Whom they served with a cold and grudging service. And the absence of the sight of God, Whom the soul in grace knows to be its only Good, would, when the

and translates thee to His kingdom; for it is easy for God to do all things in the turning point of an hour.' Hom. 26. n. 18. T. vii. pp. 99, 100. Gall.   [y] Adv. Hær. v. 32.   [z] Wisdom iv. 13.

distractions of this world no longer dazzled it, be an intense suffering, above all the sufferings of this life, while the *knowledge* that it is saved, and belongs to Jesus, and that it will, in all eternity, behold God and be the object of His infinite love, would be '[a] joy and felicity' above all the spiritual joys in this life, even apart from all those consolations which God may bestow on the soul which He has made His own for ever.

"The Greek Church too[b], while it states that such souls as have departed with faith, but without having had time to 'bring forth fruits worthy of repentance,' 'may be aided towards the attainment of a blessed resurrection by prayers offered in their behalf,' still holds that 'the souls of (all) the righteous are in light and rest, with a foretaste of eternal happiness.'

"A modern approved German Catholic writer on Dogma excludes from purgatory the idea of physical fire, or of any other than mental sufferings, as matter of faith. 'About[c] *any*, or *the*, place of purifying, nothing has been decided as matter of doctrine. So neither as to the mode of purifying. About the last, the fathers have expressed themselves only problematically and hypothetically, and Doctors and believers have only assumed a fire as matter of opinion; in which mention ignorance only or malice (in order to make room for irony) can find occasion to think of our common fire. Purifying, as the sloughing-off of the imperfection ingrown as it were with the soul;

[a] Burial Service.
[b] Longer Catechism, P. i. p. 98, 99, Blackmore's Transl.
[c] Klee, Dogmatik, ii. 429, 430.

the straining of the soul to become free from all earthliness on her; the longing for the vision of God, from which the unbefittingness, yet cleaving to her, still excludes her; her struggle towards the full death of the evil in her, and towards the full life of the good in her; this stirring up of her deepest and inmost self implies fire, fiery pain enough.'"

There never was a doubt in the Church, that all who die in a state of grace, even although, one minute before, they were not in a state of grace, are saved. But we know absolutely nothing of the working of God's grace at that hour. The whole Church is at one in this, that those only will be lost who, at that last hour, shut out the grace of God and will not 'be converted and live.' There is, in this respect, absolutely no difference between the Eastern Church the Western and our own. There is not the slightest variation of our belief, thus far. How each soul may be prepared for the Beatific Vision, whether very many souls may not be detained from that Vision for a long time, we know not. Our human instincts suggest that it may be so. But if so, then those same human instincts tell us, that amid 'the rest and felicity' of knowing that they are saved, that they cannot again have the very faintest wish to commit the very slightest sin, or be guilty of the slightest imperfection, or will any thing but the Will of God, the temporary banishment from the sight of God will be intense purifying suffering. Many of us know something of the intense suffering of being parted for this life from one loved as our own souls. Time goes on and on, and the wound remains deep below. What then, when the object of love, from whom the soul is through its own fault banished for a time, is *the* One Bliss of each being whom He has created, God Who is Love—Love Infinite, Incomprehensible, Immeasurable, Unchangeable, Whom His whole Creation together could not adequately love, Whom none could adequately love, save Himself in Himself, Trinity in Unity, Father, Son, and Holy Ghost?

But this pain of being kept for a time from the sight of God has its bright side too. *Here*, we are, most of us, on too easy terms with Almighty God; we neither think how Infinitely Holy God is, or *what*, sin on the part of His creatures towards God, so infinitely good and Holy, is. We know that S. John says, " he who has this hope (to see God as He Is), purifieth himself, even as He is pure." And although our own consciences will not, if we attend to them, lie to us, few of us think at all of this condition. We know that " the Blood of Jesus Christ His Son cleanseth us from all sin," so that we should be saved, and satisfied with this, (as indeed our being saved is of God's undeserved mercy alone) we leave the rest heedlessly on one side, as a matter of course. The waiting of the intermediate state teaches the soul the holiness of Him, Who is to be its Bliss for ever. It ' [d] knows that the delay is devised by the mercy of God, because it is not yet fit to endure that excessive Goodness and that exquisite Justice.'

' [e] Cleansed from all sin, and united in will to

[d] S. Catherine of Genoa in Eiren. iii. 47.
[e] S. Catherine of Genoa on Purgatory, quoted by Bp. Forbes on the Articles, Art. xxii. T. 2. pp. 348, 349.

God, they see God clearly according to the light He imparts to them; they are conscious, too, what a good it is to enjoy God, that for this very end souls are created. Again, there is in them a conformity of will, so uniting them to God, so drawing them to Him through that natural instinct whereby God is, as it were, bound up with the soul, that no description, no figure, no example, can give a clear idea of it, as it is actually felt and apprehended by inward consciousness.'

The most imperfect souls, even while unadmitted to the sight of God, have unspeakable joy—joy beyond all possible joy in this present life, from the certainty of their salvation, from their being confirmed in grace and love, from the impossibility of their ever again, by the very slightest motion of their will, willing any thing but the all-holy Will of God, and from the unspeakable love infused into them by God. They know that, by the immutable decree of God, they shall be admitted to see and love God, and to be filled with His love, and *that*, for eternity, of which they know something, because they are already in it.

ᶠSuch a full conviction of the peace and joy of the imperfect departed, peace and joy passing every conceivable joy in this world, for which, if it were the Will of God, any would most thankfully exchange any condition in this world, enables us to contemplate without horror any consequences of God's awful Holiness. We cannot wish God to be less holy than He is. And our own consciences may tell us that, our repentance for our sins having been

ᶠ Repeated from Eirenicon iii. 109.

very imperfect, and our own longings for the sight of God, amid this whirl of duties and religious interests, such as we do not like to think of, we are not fit to behold Him. This, perhaps, more than the direct dread of hell, is the source of the fear of death to many. They trust in God's mercy in Christ, that they shall be saved; but they feel themselves unfit to enter into His Presence. To be admitted into any vestibule of His Presence, where they can sin no more, and, by longing for that Beatific Vision, may be for ever freed from the slough which has clung to them in this life,—this is not too high for their hopes; the thought of this unspeakably allays their fears [g].

So, as to others also, instead of being haunted with the thought as to some one loved as one's self, 'Was he saved?' and longing that God would in some way reveal to us that he *was* saved, we may commend our departed ones to their Father's care, sure that if they have not, by an obstinate rejection of Him to the last, shut out His grace and love, they are, in whatever mansion of His, still under the shadow of His Hand, longing for their perfect consummation both of body and soul, and prepared and perfected the more by that intense longing.

'I am not prepared,' was the exclamation of a pious, simple and humble soul, who had served God and trusted in Jesus beyond the ordinary period of mortality, when told that she was shortly to see God.

---

[g] It would be expected of such a humble soul as that of the Author of the Christian Year, that the prospect of such a preparation was an unspeakable comfort to him within a year of his death. He expressed it both to myself and to others.

For the thought of His aweful Holiness and the inadequacy of our best love stood out before her. To such a soul it would have been an unspeakable comfort to have known, that, although she was not yet prepared for the sight of His All-Holiness, there was a waiting-time, out of the reach of sin, in which she might be prepared for the Presence of Him Who had ever been her God.

Most Protestants, we are told, believe in this purifying preparation to behold God. Perrone, having the German Protestants in his mind, says;

"[h] Protestants admitted a purgatory, or state of 'expiation,' which they call 'a school of preparation.'" "If you mention Purgatory to any Protestant, he kindles up; but if you ask the same person, whether or no a state of 'expiation,' 'epuration,' or 'a school of preparation, expectation' &c, can be admitted, he will readily grant it you; yea, sometimes he contends vehemently that such a state is to be admitted."

Having quoted several German writers on this side, he says,

"[i] All agree in saying, that it is too violent to admit at once into heaven all those who only repented of their past evil life at the end, or who indulged too much in the sensualities of this life, since 'nothing defiled' enters there; also it is too harsh to assign all such to eternal torments."

Leibnitz also says in detail,

'[k] Almost all agree in a fatherly chastisement or

[h] Perrone de Deo Creatore P. iii. c. 6. art. 2. p. 319. quoted in Eirenicon P. iii. pp. 118, 119. [i] Ib. p. 119, note 7.
[k] Systema Theol. p. 350 quoted by Perrone, de Deo Creatore,

purifying after this life (of whatever sort it be), which the souls themselves, on their departure from the body, being illumined, and seeing thoroughly the imperfection of their past life and the foulness of sin, touched with exceeding sorrow, invite to themselves willingly, and would not wish to attain in any other way to the summit of beatitude. For many have excellently noted, that this purifying affliction of the soul, thinking over its acts, is voluntary; amongst others there is a remarkable passage of [Luis] of Granada, which brought great consolation to Philip II. in his last illness.'

Dr. Farrar did not observe that in his eagerness against everlasting punishment, he, while rejecting the Roman Purgatory, assumed the most terrible teaching about Purgatory, held of old and now in the Roman Church, which '[1] depicts it simply as a hell not eternal.'

The picture, which continually faces us in his book, is the Æonian fire [m]. This is his one remedy. 'You can bear to think of them, as you can bear to think of yourself, suffering as they never did on earth, the aching pang of God's revealing light, *the willing agony of His remedial fire.*' This, which might be a description of the most appalling Roman doctrine of Purgatory, belongs, he says, '[n] to the vast mass of mankind.'

P. iii. c. 6. art. 2. p. 319 note. [alleged in my Eiren. iii. p. 117.] Perrone subjoins, 'These things he seems to have drawn from that most beautiful tract which S. Catherine of Genoa wrote on Purgatory.' Ib.

[1] Faber, 'All for Jesus' c. 9, pp. 333—337. quoted Eirenicon iii. pp. 99, 100.   [m] Et. Hope pp 111, 112.   [n] Ib. p. 108.

But then minds may be the more disposed to believe in a preparation of souls, by which, '°in entire freedom from the guilt of sin,' with a will perfectly transformed into the Will of God, and in continual union with Him, with a love perfected, pure, disinterested, diffused in their heart, assured of their salvation, comforted by Angels, refreshed and their waiting-time shortened through the prayers of survivors and the Sacrifice of the Altar, they may cast off their slough, and amid whatever process of purifying it may please God to employ, and after whatever time, be admitted to the Beatific Vision of the All-Holy God.

PRAYERS FOR THE DEPARTED.

JERUSALEM LITURGY.

'ᵖ Remember, O Lord God, the spirits and all flesh, those of right faith whom we have mentioned and whom we have not mentioned, from Abel the just to this day. Do Thou Thyself give them rest in the region of the living, in Thy kingdom, in the delights of Paradise, in the bosoms of our holy Fathers Abraham, Isaac, and Jacob, whence sorrow, grief, and lamentation are banished away: where the light of God's countenance visits and shines continually.'

° The language is that of S. Catherine of Genoa, speaking of the condition of souls in Purgatory.

ᵖ Assem. Cod. Lit. v. 46, quoted by Bp. Forbes on the Articles, p. 312.

CLEMENTINE LITURGY.

'ᑫ Let us pray for those who rest in faith.'

'We further offer to Thee for all Thy saints who have pleased Thee from the beginning of the world, patriarchs, prophets, just men, apostles, martyrs, confessors, bishops, elders, deacons, sub-deacons, singers, virgins, widows, laymen, and all whose names Thou Thyself knowest.'

ALEXANDRINE LITURGY.

'ʳ Do Thou rest the souls of our fathers and brethren who have fallen asleep before us in the faith of Christ, remembering the forefathers, fathers, patriarchs, prophets, apostles, martyrs, confessors, bishops, saints, just, every soul perfected in the faith of Christ; and those whom on this present day we commemorate, and our holy Father Mark, the Apostle and Evangelist, who shewed us the way of faith," "and of all these do Thou rest the souls in the tabernacles of Thy saints in Thy kingdom, granting them the good things of Thy promises which eye hath not seen, nor ear heard, neither have entered into the heart of man. Refresh their souls and vouchsafe to them the kingdom of heaven.'

LITURGY OF CONSTANTINOPLE.

'And remember all who are fallen asleep before us in the hope of the resurrection unto eternal life; and give them rest, where the light of Thy countenance visits.'

ᑫ quoted by Dr. Luckock, Canon of Ely and examining Chaplain to the Bishop, 'After Death,' p. 109.

ʳ Assem. Cod. Lit. vii. 24—26.

LITURGY OF S. BASIL.

'For the rest and forgiveness of the soul of Thy servant *N*. In a lightsome place, where grief and lamentation are fled away, give him rest.'

SACRAMENTARY OF S. GREGORY.

'[s] Remember also, O Lord, Thy servants and handmaidens (*N.* and *N.*) who have gone before us with the seal of faith, and sleep in the sleep of peace. To them, O Lord, and to all who are at rest in Christ, we intreat Thee to grant a place of refreshment, of light and peace.'

'[t] Be favourable to the souls of Thy servants with an everlasting compassion, that they may be set free from the bonds of death and kept in eternal light.'

PRAYER OF S. ANSELM (as is thought.)

'We pray Thee also, O Lord, Holy Father, for the souls of the faithful departed, that this great Sacrament of Thy love may be to them health and salvation, joy and refreshment. O Lord my God, grant them this day a great and abundant Feast of Thee, the Living Bread, Who camest down from Heaven, and givest life to the world; even of Thy Holy and Blessed Flesh, the Lamb without spot, Who takest away the sins of the world; even of that Flesh, which was taken from the holy and glorious womb of the Blessed Virgin Mary, and was conceived of the Holy Ghost; and of that Fountain of mercy which, through the soldier's lance, flowed from Thy most Sacred Side; that thence recreated and satiated, refreshed and comforted, they may rejoice in Thy praise and in Thy glory.'

[s] S. Greg. Opp. iii. p. 11.   [t] S. Greg. in 'After Death,' p. 112.

FROM THE ROMAN BREVIARY.

'Absolve, we beseech Thee, O Lord, the soul of Thy servant N., that, being dead unto the world, he may live to Thee, and whatsoever, through the frailty of our mortal nature, he did amiss in the conversation of this world, do Thou, through the pardon of Thy most merciful pity, cleanse away. Through our Lord.'

'Incline Thine ear, O Lord, to our prayers and supplication, who entreat Thy mercy for the soul of Thy servant, whom Thou hast called out of this world, that Thou wouldest place it in a region of peace and light, and bestow upon it a fellowship with Thy saints. Through our Lord.'

'O God, Who hast bidden us honour our father and mother, have mercy upon the soul of my father and mother, forgive their sins, and grant me to see them in the joy of eternal brightness. Through our Lord.'

APPENDIX.

1. On the Condemnation of Origen in the Fifth General Council.

The question whether Origen was condemned by the vth General Council has assumed importance in people's eyes on the supposition, that General Councils were the only way, in which false teaching was condemned by the Church, and that the supposed absence of any condemnation previous to that Council implies, that the Church was previously indifferent to his misbelief.

The facts are these;

1. The book, in which most of the heresies, known under the name of Origen, were contained, and among them the præexistence of souls and their subsequent restoration, was unknown to the Church until it was translated by Rufinus A.D. 398. It was written while Origen was yet quite young, when he had just 'emerged from the philosophical schools [a],' '[b] before he had left Alexandria,' about A.D. 231.

2. One heresy, involved in the doctrine of universal restitution, the restoration of Satan, he indignantly denied at the time, in a public letter, as what could not be asserted by any one, 'not even of unsound mind [c].

[a] Marcellus, accepted by Eusebius in Euseb. c. Marcell. L. i. p. 23.
[b] Eus. H. E. vi. 24.
[c] 'Although they say that the father of malice and of the perdition of those who shall be cast out of the kingdom of God, can be

3. He taught the received belief in his popular writings [d].

saved; which no one can say, even if bereft of reason.' Origen ad quosd. amicos Alex. Opp. T. i. p. 5. 'Of them' [Israel] 'there will be a conversion even at the end of the world, then when the fulness of the Gentiles shall come in and all Israel shall be saved; but of him who is said to have fallen from heaven, not even in the end of the world will there be any conversion.' in Ep. ad Rom. L. viii. n. 9. T. iv. p. 634.

[d] in Jeremiam Hom. 18. 1. Opp. iii. 241. Sel. in Jerem. xxiv. 6. Ib. p. 303, ' Perhaps the basket of bad figs is the gehenna of everlasting fire; that of the good figs the kingdom of heaven.' Hom. 6. in Exod. n. 4, 'We must come to the furnace. But when we come there, if any one bring many good works and little iniquity, that little is dissolved by the fire and cleansed, and the whole remains pure gold. And if any one bring thither more lead, he is more burned, that, although there is but little gold, it may issue cleansed. But if any one come, all leaden, as is said of that one here, he will be sunk in the deep, like lead in the mighty waters.' Hom. 8. in Levit. n. 5. T. ii. p. 231, ' Of those very sins, which pass with us after this life, it is to be understood, that some are so fixed in the souls themselves that they cannot be done away; but that others can receive cleansing according to the inspection and judgement of that High Priest, to Whom hidden things are known, and Who will dispose of the souls of each, as He sees in them the stains of leprosy, which can or cannot be expiated.' Comm. in S. Matt. Tract. xxxiv. p. 889, ' And consider, that he speaks of the kingdom as prepared from the foundation of the world for no other than the righteous, and therefore Christ their King will give it them; but the eternal fire is not said to be prepared for those to whom it is said, "Depart from Me, ye cursed," as the kingdom is for the righteous, but "for the devil and his angels." Because on His part He created men, not for perdition, but for life and joy. But they, sinning, joined themselves to the devil, and as they who are saved are made equal to the angels and are sons of the resurrection and of God and are angels, so they who perish are made like unto the angels of the devil and become his sons.' In the translation of Ruffinus, he so speaks even in the de principiis, Lib. i. Præf. n. 5, 'The soul having a substance and life of its own, when it departs from this world, will

Origen; 'truth what had come from the Apostles.' 131

4. He laid down beforehand as the rule of faith, that '^e that only was to be believed as truth, which is in no way out of harmony with the ecclesiastical and apostolic tradition.'

5. In contrast with what he had taught as to the Holy Trinity, he says that, in the matter of 'the end or consummation,' what he said, "^f is said with great fear and caution, discussing and treating, rather than laying down anything as certain and defined. I have indicated already above, what those things are, which are to be determined with doctrinal precision, which I think I did according to my ability when speaking of the Trinity. But now I am employed, as far as I see, rather in discussing than defining.'

He closed his first book, according to S. Jerome, '^g These things, according to our meaning, are not dogmas, but only matter of enquiry put forth lest they should seem altogether unconsidered.' Pamphilus dwells at length on this undogmatizing character of his speculations, in his Apology for Origen[h].

6. In the discussion itself he often[1] uses the words

be dealt with according to its merits, either obtaining the inheritance of life eternal, if its deeds gain this for it; or to be given over to eternal fire and punishment, if the guilt of its ill-deeds should turn it aside to this.' He subsequently explains the ' fire' (L. ii. 10.) not, the ' eternal.'

^e 'Since there are many who think that they hold the things of Christ and some hold things diverse from those before, but the ecclesiastical teaching is preserved, being delivered by a regular succession from the Apostles and abiding till now in the Churches, that only etc.' (as in text) de Princip. L. i. Præf. n. 2.

^f de Princ. i. 6. 1.   ^g Ep. 124 ad Avit. n. 4.

^h In Huet App. T. iv. p. 18.

[1] Cave (tit. Origenes) mentions that Wetstein notes, 'how often

'ʲ we think,' 'I suppose,' or 'I opine,' 'whence I think, as far as I may have an opinion,' 'ᵏ another perhaps will think—but how the matter will be, God only knows, and whoever are friends of God through Christ and the Holy Spirit.' 'I suppose, according as it appears to me,' 'but *we* think,' 'we, as men (not to encourage by silence the insolence of heretics,) will thus answer what according to our ability can occur to us;' 'by which language this seems to be indicated,' 'we must consider too whether that language may not perhaps signify also,' 'unless perhaps,' 'perhaps ˡ.'

τάχα 'perhaps,' or δοκεῖ 'it seems,' occurs in his writings, if hè mentions any thing new or unwonted.' Not. Ep. Orig. ad Africanum, p. 169. This appears in S. Jerome's translation of passages in his Epistle to Avitus Ep. 124 ed. Vallars, arbitramur, possit (twice) forsitan, posse, n. 3. dubitat, forsitan (twice), si, arbitror n. 5. prudenti investigatione rimandum est. n. 11.

ʲ Putamus, de princ. i. 6. 1. ego arbitror Ib. ut opinor Ib. ex quibus existimo, prout ego sentire possum, Ib. n. 2. Puto ergo secundum quod mihi videtur, i. 8. 6. nos vero existimamus. ii. 7. 2. nos quasi homines (ne hæreticorum insolentiam reticendo nutriamus) quæ pro viribus nostris occurrere nobis possunt ad ea quæ obtenderunt hoc modo respondebimus. ii. 9. 6. per quos sermones hoc videtur indicari. ii. 10.6. Videndum quoque est, ne forte etiam illud iste sermo significet, Ib. 8, nisi forte. Ib. (S. Jerome's version.)

ᵏ de Princ. i. 6. end.

ˡ 'They are cast into outer darkness, *perhaps* until they understand so as to be converted and made worthy to come forth from it; *perhaps* also for some other reason which we know not of, since we read of one before us expounding the darkness of the abyss, and saying that the abyss and darkness is without beyond the world. Let us consider then whether his exposition can be true, that some, as being unworthy, are cast from the whole world into that abyss, which he expounded, in which is darkness unillumined by any one, since they are beyond the whole world.' Comm. Lat. in S. Matt. Opp. iii. 886.

laid down the faith of the Church, as his rule.

There is also language, in which he seems distinctly to fluctuate. '[m] If what preceded as an image shall be restored after so long a time, when shalt thou be restored, *if indeed thou art restored at all?*'

7. His own mind is mostly clear enough, that he did hold *as* opinions all the wild opinions, which have since been condemned under his name, but still, in modern language, as ready to submit himself to the judgement of the Church. He distinctly lays down the faith of the Church, as *his* rule. '[n] Now then let us consider what those things are, which we have to discuss in what follows, according to our doctrine, i. e. according to the faith of the Church.'

He himself thought that the speculations would not be obtruded on others. He held them as *opinions*, but not with confidence enough to promulgate or press them upon others. S. Jerome says [o], 'Origen himself, in an epistle which he wrote to Fabian, Bp. of Rome, expressed regret for having written such things, and threw the blame upon Ambrose, who made public what he had written privately.'

So S. Athanasius separates the man, 'the labour-loving Origen,' from the heretical speculations in his book [p].

... 'Hear again from the labour-loving Origen also. For what he has written, as if inquiring and exercising himself, that let no one take as expressive of his own sentiments, but of parties who are disputing in the investigation, but what he definitely

---

[m] quando tu restitueris, si tamen restitueris? on Ezekiel, Hom. 10. n 3.   [n] de princip. i. 7. 2.
[o] Ep. 48 ad Pammach. et Ocean. n. 10. Opp. i. 527, 528. Vall.
[p] On the Nic. Def. p. 48. Oxf. Tr.

declares, that is the sentiment of the labour-loving man.'

S. Athanasius does not speak 'ᵠ with oblique and kindly disapproval of his opinion on the restitution.' He simply, in praising himself, speaks of the sentiments as *not* his; as others thought them the interpolation of heretics ʳ.

When Origen's opinions were brought before the Church, on occasion of Theophilus' censure of the Nitrian monks, we have mostly heads only of the ground of the condemnation ˢ, having no Acts.

The errors in the 'de principiis' are so interwoven together, that S. Augustine, in mentioning that the Church rejected Origen for teaching, that punishment would not be eternal to those who should be sentenced to it, generally adds some aggravation of the error. Speaking of the Universalists of his day, he adds ironically ᵗ, that 'Origen was yet more merciful, in that he believed, that, after heavier and more lasting punishment, according to their deserts, the devil and his angels were to be withdrawn from those torments and associated with the holy Angels.' 'But,' he adds, 'both for this and for other things,

ᵠ Dr. Farrar p. 163.

ʳ Ruffinus in his Liber de adulteratione Librorum Origenis in App. ad Origenis Opp. T. iv. p. 48 sqq., alleging other instances of interpolations, which however S. Jerome denies.

ˢ As in the Paschal Epistles of Theophilus Ep. 96, and Ep. 98. S. Epiphan. Hær. 44., S. Jerome Ep. 124 ad Avit. Theophilus, in his Synodical Epistle in S. Jerome Ep. 92, having enumerated several, says, "for there are many other things, which cannot be comprised in an Epistle." n. 5.

ᵗ De Civ. Dei xxi. 17. S. Augustine dwells upon the same points in his de hæres. c. 43., de gestis Pelagii c. iii. n. 9. S. Aug. Opp. T. x. p. 196.

and most of all for the unceasing alternations of bliss and misery, and the stated intervals of ages, and endless going and returning from the one to the other, [i. e. from bliss to misery and from misery to bliss] the Church hath with reason rejected him; for he lost the semblance of mercy by assigning to the saints true sufferings in punishment, and false bliss, in which they should not have true and secure, i.e. certain joy in the everlasting Good, free from all fear.'

The fact that the belief, that those who should be condemned in the great Day would eventually be restored, was, by itself, condemned by the Church, was brought out by the action of Pelagius at the Synod of Diospolis. His accusers being absent, so that they could not explain the meaning of their charge, Pelagius had his own way. The proposition, as quoted in the Acts, was very simple. '^tIn the day of judgement the wicked and sinners will not be spared, but will be burned with eternal fires.' Pelagius answers, 'that he had said this according to the Gospel, in which it is said of sinners, These shall go into eternal punishment and the righteous into life eternal,' subjoining, 'If any believe otherwise, he is an Origenist.' '^u This,' S. Augustine says, ' the judges understood of that which in truth the Church most worthily detests in Origen, i.e. that they too who, the Lord says, will be punished with eternal punishment, and the devil himself and his angels, will after a time, although prolonged [prolixum], be freed from punishment, being purged, and will be united in a society of blessedness with the saints who reign with God.' The Synod then said, ' that this is not alien from the

^u de gestis Pelagii c. iii. n. 10.

Church,' 'not,' S. Augustine adds, 'in the sense of Pelagius, but rather according to the Gospel, that such sinners and wicked persons will be burned with eternal fire, whom the Gospel judges worthy of such punishment; and that *he* agrees with Origen, in a way to be detested, whoever says that their punishment can come to an end, which the Lord said would be eternal.'

Those who brought the charge against Pelagius understood the words of Pelagius to relate to *all* sinners, those also included, who, S. Paul says, when their work has been burned, shall themselves be saved, but so as by fire.

The dogma 'that there is no everlasting punishment,' is set down by an anonymous defender of Origen, whose book Photius had read[x], as a distinct but unfounded charge.

The heresies in Origen's book were thus for the time silenced. No one any more uttered them. East and West had agreed in their condemnation. In the East they had been condemned 1) in a Synod at Alexandria, convened by Theophilus, of the Bishops of all Egypt, Libya and Pentapolis; 2) in a Synod of Cyprus, held by S. Epiphanius; 3) by Anastasius Bishop of Rome, with many Bishops of the West. These were accepted by the Church, and the Church had rest. No one maintained, even hesitatingly, what the Church had condemned.

There was then no ground, why the errors of Origen should again be brought before a Council. It was 'actum agere.' The universal reception of the decision of a particular Council by the Church gave

[x] Cod. 117 p. 92 ed. Bekker.

it the authority of the Church. Heresies had often been condemned by particular Councils, as those of Paul of Samosata and of Noetus at Antioch, that of Pelagius at Carthage and Milevis. Origenism came before the fifth General Council through the fondness of Justinian for mixing himself up in Theology. He was applied to by the Abbot Conon and his companions[y] on occasion of the violences of Origenist monks in Palestine. ' [z] The Emperor consented most readily, being glad to pass a judgement on such causes.' Justinian was applied to apparently, as a Civil Ruler, to quell evil-doers. He went beyond his province in the Edict which he issued.

The faith was secured already by the previous decisions. A new decision, identical with the preceding, could add nothing to its weight. It was not a question for a General Council; for the Church was not disturbed. The only object was to still a certain number of turbulent monks in Palestine. However, through Justinian, Origenism was brought before the fifth General Council and was condemned by it.

Of the fact of the condemnation of Origen by the Council, there is no question. In the 11th Anathematism, the name of Origen is added after those condemned in the 3rd and 4th, Nestorius and Eutyches[a]. There is no doubt that it is not a later addition, since, (as Hefele[b] notices) it was so read[c] in the Lateran Synod A.D. 649. from the Roman copy of the Acts of the Fifth.

[y] Cyrilli Scyth. Vita Sabæ p. 374. [z] Liberatus Breviar. c. 23.
[a] Conc. Const. ii. Collat. viii. Conc. vi. 232 Col.
[b] Conciliengesch., ii. 838 note 2.
[c] Conc. Later. Secr. iv. Anath. xi Conc. vii. 259 Col.

This is decisive of the fact that Origenism was condemned in the 5th General Council. After the name of Origen follows, 'and all their impious writings.'

The only question which remains is, whether the detailed proceedings, recorded by Evagrius and Nicephorus, belong to the 5th Council or no.

Those who have maintained eagerly that Origen was not condemned in the fifth General Council have directed their attention to bye-issues; such as 1) May not the 'domestic synod' (i.e. Bishops habitually resident in Constantinople to be ready to advise the Patriarch,) have discussed as well as accepted the Epistle of Justinian, in which he requested Mennas to gather them together, and condemn Origenism [d]? 2) May not Evagrius, the contemporary historian, who says that the Council condemned Origen, have confused the 'domestic synod' under Mennas with the General Council under Eutychius? 3) May not Cyril of Scythopolis, a monk, have been ill-informed? 4) May not others have copied their mistakes unwittingly?

The answer is, The question is not about a condemnation of Origen alone. Justinian asked Mennas to 'assemble the Bishops and prefects of monasteries at that time resident in this royal city, and get them to condemn Origen and all the chapters appended.' He did not herein ascribe any preeminent authority to 'New Rome.' He tells Mennas that he (Justinian) had 'sent a copy to the other 4 Patriarchs, Vigilius the most blessed Pope and Patriarch of the elder Rome, and the other most holy Bishops and Patriarchs

---

[d] Baronius published the Epistle (as Justinian calls it) Ann. A. 538. n. 34—82.

of Alexandria, Antioch, and Jerusalem, that they too would consider the matter, that what he wrote might be authenticated. When they had received and subscribed it, Liberatus tells us [e], Origen 'was condemned being dead, who before had been condemned while living.'

But those who have been eager to shew that Origen's errors were not condemned in detail in the 5th General Council, have overlooked the fact that three contemporary writers, Cyril of Scythopolis, Evagrius the historian, Victor of Tununum, say that, besides Origen, two others were condemned; Didymus and Evagrius. These, Victor says, were the two eminent men, 'Evagrius the eremite Deacon, and Didymus the monk and confessor of Alexandria.' It is obvious that there must have been some great abuse of their writings, at that time, that it should have seemed necessary to condemn Origenism, not only under the name of its author, but also under that of one who had rendered such services to the Church as Didymus the blind. And this we find in the contemporary application of a 'brother' to the Abbot Barsanuphius, then in his old age.

The brother wrote in perplexity;

"'I fell, father, I know not how, upon the books of Origen and Didymus and the Gnostics of Evagrius. They say that the souls of men were not created with their bodies, but existed before them, being naked i.e. incorporeal, intelligences, &c.; and again, that the future punishment is to have an end, and that

[e] Breviar. c. 23.
[f] Doctrina Barsanuphii circa opiniones Origenis Evagrii et Didymi, in Gallandii B. P. xi 592—596.

men angels and devils have to return to be naked intelligences, as they were; which they call 'restitution.' Since then my soul is troubled and in doubt, whether these things are true or no, I beseech you, lord, shew me the truth, that I may hold fast and not perish. For nothing of all this is said in Holy Scripture, as Origen himself affirms in his exposition of the Epistle to Titus, 'that it is no tradition of Scripture nor the Church, that the soul is older than the formation of the body,' characterising one who affirms these things as heretical. And Evagrius too attests in his Gnostic chapters, that no one disclosed any thing of all this, nor did the Spirit declare it [g].— But that there is no restitution nor end of punishment, the Lord Himself hath shewed in the Gospel saying, "these shall go away into everlasting punishment," and again, "Their worm dieth not, and the fire is not quenched." Whence then, lord, since neither the Apostles delivered it, nor the Holy Spirit declared it, as those attest, and the Gospels have the contrary, have they these dogmas? Have compassion, father, on my infirmity, and declare to me what these doctrines are.'

The same brother put the like question to 'the other aged man, the Abbot John.' He asked also 'Ought we not to read the writings of Evagrius? Why do some of the fathers of these days receive him?' &c.

This is but a single instance of perplexity; but it shews that a collection of writings of Origen Evagrius and Didymus was in circulation, inculcating 'restitution' with other heresies. Stephen bar

[g] The enquirer quoted Evagrius Cent. ii. c. 64 and 69.

Sudaili, an Origenist, when rejected at Edessa, betook himself to Palestine ʰ; so that there was risk of its becoming a focus of Origenism.

Yet it would have been absolutely unexampled, (as it would have been against all justice) that any individual should be condemned without previous enquiry into the matters alleged against him. "ⁱDoth our law judge any one, before it hear him, and know what he doeth?" Justinian, following the uniform rule, had produced such proofs against the teaching of Origen. There is no reason to think that it would be departed from in the case of Evagrius and Didymus. The statements then of those of the following authorities, who relate that Origen Evagrius and Didymus were condemned, and those who mention that passages were adduced from them and examined, harmonise together. For, according to the whole law and practice of the Church, they could not have been condemned without their writings being examined.

But those who assert that Origen Didymus and Evagrius were condemned in the fifth General Council are; two who had read the Acts of the Council, Photius, and Nicephorus; three contemporaries, who had good means of accurate information, Cyril of Scythopolis, Evagrius the historian, and Victor of Tununum; the Emperor Heraclius in his Epistle to the Lateran Council A. 649, and that Council itself, which implies a knowledge of the fact by the then Bishop of Rome, 95 years afterwards; two other Bishops of Rome, Leo ii. in a public letter to the Emperor in the 6th General Council, and another,

ʰ Assem. B. O. ii. 33.　　　ⁱ S. John vii. 51.

(probably Gregory ii. A.D. 714) in a Profession of faith which he made at his accession; a Patriarch of Constantinople in a Synodical letter written 80 years after the fifth General Council, and read in the sixth; an Imperial Edict also in the 6th Council; an Encyclical letter of a Patriarch of Constantinople, read in the second Council of Nice, and the 2nd Council of Nice itself.

To give these in detail.

i. Cyril of Scythopolis was one of the monks, who were chosen by Eustochius Patriarch of Jerusalem to replace the Origenist monks, who had been expelled by command of Justinian for refusing to communicate with the Church, after it had condemned Origen. Eustochius, being at Constantinople, was made Patriarch of Jerusalem by Justinian at the instance of Conon, Abbot and Pastor of the Laura, to which Cyril belonged. Conon himself had been persecuted at Constantinople by the Origenist Ascidas, but, on a hasty consecration of Macarius by the Origenists to the see of Jerusalem, vacant by the death of Peter, the Emperor was very angry with Ascidas and the Origenists, and being instructed by Conon as to 'the whole impiety of the Origenists, decreed that Eustochius should be Patriarch, and that a general Council should be held[1].' '¹ The Abbot Conon, when parting with Eustochius to Jerusalem, exhorted him to send Eulogius, Hegumen of the monastery of the B. Theodosius, that he too might be present in the assembled Synod. Eustochius, coming to his Patriarchate, sent three Bishops to

---

[1] Cyrill. Scythop. vita Sabæ in Coteler. Eccl. Græc. Monumm. iii. pp. 374, 5. ¹ Ib. p. 374.

i. *Cyril of Scythopolis.* 143

take his place in the Synod, and the Abbot Eulogius and two other Hegumens.' Cyril then had good means of being informed, and he tells us that he enquired diligently as to what he wrote about.

His account is,

'[k] So then, when the holy and Œcumenical 5th Synod had been assembled at Constantinople, Origen and Theodorus of Mopsuestia, and what Evagrius and Didymus had uttered 'about præ-existence and restoration,' were subjected to a common and universal anathema, the four patriarchs being present, and approving thereof. Our God-protected king, having sent to Jerusalem what was done in the Synod, and all the Bishops in Palestine having confirmed and ratified it with hand and mouth, the Nea-Laurians separated themselves from the Catholic communion. But the Patriarch Eustochius, having treated them in different ways, and having for eight months used admonitions and exhortations towards them, and not persuaded them to communicate with the Catholic Church, making use of the Emperor's commands, expelled them from the Nea Laura by the Duke Anastasius and freed the whole Eparchy from their pestilence.'

In his life of Euthymius[l], he connects his own removal to the Nea Laura with the Council. 'But subsequently, when the fifth holy Œcumenical Council had been convened, and the doctrines of Origen and Nestorius [viz. the three chapters] had been anathematized by it, and the Origenists who had possession of the Nea Laura had been expelled from it, and faithful and orthodox fathers again migrated

[k] Ib. 374, 5.   [l] c. 161. in Coteler l. c. T. ii. pp. 338, 339.

unto it, I too, at the injunction of the admirable solitary John, the Bishop, removed from the Cœnobium and came to their Laura.'

He must have known what he relates, as occasioning this change in his life.

ii. Evagrius was a contemporary, who was about 16 or 17 at the time of the Council[m], and was at Constantinople in 589, 5 years before he closed his history.

His account is [n], that the monks, sent from Palestine, stirred, in the first place, the matter against Origen, Evagrius and Didymus; but that Theodorus of Cappadocia, wishing to draw them off, brought in the matters of Theodore of Mopsuestia and Theodoret and Ibas, 'The All-Good God,' he says, 'so disposing it, in order that all profane teaching might be removed.' Having given briefly the proceedings as to Theodore, Theodoret and Ibas, he subjoins,

'But when the petitions were presented from Eulogius Conon Cyriacus and Pancratius, monks, against the doctrines of Origen, also called Adimantius, and those who followed his ungodly error, Justinian enquires of the Council which was gathered concerning these things, joining also a copy of the petition, and moreover what had been sent to Vigilius touching this matter; from all which you may gather how much in earnest Origenes was to fill the simplicity of Apostolic dogmas with Greek and Manichee tares.' A relation then was made to Justinian by the Synod, after the acclamations which they had made against Origen and those who went astray like him, beginning, 'O most Christian Emperor, whose soul parta-

[m] See Valesius Præf.   [n] H.E. iv. 38.

keth of the nobility from above;' and shortly after, 'We flee then, we flee from this; for we know not the voice of strangers; and binding such an one safely, as a thief and a robber, with the cords of Anathema, we cast him out of the holy precincts;' and shortly after, 'You will know the force of what we have done by reading the same.' To this they subjoined the chapters, which those learnt who advocated Origenism, shewing both their agreements and disagreements and their multiform errors. Among these is a fifth chapter of the blasphemies uttered by individuals of the so-called Nea Laura to this effect: Theodorus Ascidas of Cappadocia said, 'If then the Apostles and Martyrs work miracles and are held in such honour, in the Restoration unless they are equal to Christ, what sort of restoration is it to them? They brought also many other blasphemies of Didymus, Evagrius, Theodorus, which they had collected very diligently hereupon.'

Evagrius distinguishes this from the former condemnation under Mennas, since he speaks of what *had* been sent to Vigilius touching this matter, i.e. Justinian's first epistle, which he sent to Mennas.

iii. A third Contemporary was Victor of Tununum, an African Bishop, whom Justinian sent for to Constantinople, hoping to overcome his hostility to the condemnation of 'the Three Chapters.' He wrote towards the end of his Chronicle,

'º In the thirty ninth year of his Empire, Justinian sent into exile Eutychius, Bishop of Constantinople, the condemner of the three Chapters and of Evagrius the eremite Deacon and of Didymus monk and con-

º Chron. ad A. 565. Gall. xii. 231.

fessor of Alexandria, whose praises we have mentioned already on the authority of illustrious men.'

iv. At the opening of the Lateran Council A.D. 649, 96 years after the 5th, Maximus, Bishop of Aquileia, mentions only an examination of the writings of Theodorus and Origen in the fifth General Council. Whether he uses those two names compendiously for those condemned with each, we cannot say. Any how he does mention an examination of writings of Origen.

'[p] Of the two ungodly heretics Nestorius and Eutyches, as also of Dioscorus, the blessed Eusebius of Dorylæum is related to have been the only accuser; but of the ill-named Theodore and Origen in the 5th Synod, there was no accuser; their writings sufficed for their accusation and censure.'

v. In the 3rd session of the Council, a profession of faith by the Emperor Heraclius was read, at the end of which, upon mention of the 5th General Council, he says,

'[q] Following these in all things, and embracing their divine doctrines, we receive all whom they received, and reject and anathematize all whom they rejected, and especially Novatus, Sabellius, Arius, Eunomius, Macedonius, Apolinarius, Origen, Evagrius, Didymus, Theodore of Mopsuestia.' This was read at the direction of Pope Martin.

Theophylact, Primicerius of the notaries of the Apostolic See, when he had finished it, said,

'I make known to your Blessedness, [the Council] what itself also knows, that we have in its Apostolic

[p] Conc. Later. Secr. i. Conc. vii. 101 Col.
[q] Ib. Secr. iii. Conc. vii. 206 Col.

vi. *Lateran Council* A. 649. vii. *Sophronius.* 147

office, also the records made by Sergius and Pyrrhus (formerly Bishops of Constantinople) in confirmation of the said exposition.'

The Roman Church had then accepted this Epistle.

vi. The Lateran Council, in its decree[r], rejects and anathematizes all who do not reject and anathematize all the heretics whom the Holy Catholic Church i.e. the five œcumenical Synods, reject and anathematize, and then enumerates Sabellius, Arius, &c., and at the end Origen, Didymus, Evagrius.

vii. Sophronius, Patriarch of Jerusalem, in a Synodical letter, written 80 years after the 5th Council to Sergius, Patriarch of Constantinople, and read in the 6th General Council[s], adds, 'But in addition to these four great all-venerable and all-holy co-equal Œcumenical Synods of the holy and blessed Fathers, I receive also another fifth holy Synod, convened besides these and after these, (which too was held in the royal city while Justinian held the sceptre of the Roman Empire) and all its glorious dogmas; which Synod was gathered to ratify the celebrated Synod of Chalcedon. But especially it destroys and casts out to destruction the insane Origen, and all his boastful dreams, and his writings full of various ungodliness; and with him the doctrines of Evagrius and Didymus, and all their heathen and monstrous sayings, and fabulous follies. After whom it plucks up Theodore of Mopsuestia, the teacher of Nestorius who fought against God, and casts him out, as tares, from the Catholic Church together with his blasphemous writings.' He then proceeds in the like way to reject

[r] Can. 18. Conc. vii. 363. Col.
[s] Read in Conc. Const. iii. Act. xi. Conc. vii. 917 Col.

148 viii. *Imp. Edict in* 6th *Gen. Council.* ix. *Leo* ii.

the writings of Theodoret against S. Cyril and the Epistle of Ibas.

viii. In the Imperial edict [t] in the 18th Action of the 6th General Council, the Emperor declares that he receives the five holy Œcumenical Councils; and, after describing the four first, adds, "We receive also the fifth Council, gathered by Justinian of sacred memory in our aforesaid God-preserved and most happy city against Origen and Didymus and Evagrius, who fought against God;" and then follow the names of those, some of whose writings were then condemned, Theodore of Mopsuestia, Theodoret and Ibas.

The above authorities were alleged by Card. Noris, in his Dissertation on the Fifth Œcumenical Synod [u]. The following are supplied by Natalis Alexander [x], and Huet [y].

ix. Leo ii., in his Epistle to the Emperor Constantine [z], after declaring his adhesion to the 5 General

[t] Conc. T. vii 1133, 1134.

[u] Diss. Hist. de Synodo v. Œcum. c. 6. Opp. i. 639—642.

[x] Hist. Eccl. T. vi. pp. 269—273.

[y] Origenian. L. ii. sect. 3. n. xiv sqq. App. to Orig. Opp. T. iv. 283.

[z] Garnier says, 'No learned man now listens to Baronius, who objects to the letters of the Emperor and of the supreme Pontiff as supposititious.' App. ad notas c. 2. § vi. de causa Honorii Lib. Diurn. p. 248. The Versailles Editors of Bossuet quote Massarelli: 'How futile that accusation is as to the acts of the VIth Synod having been adulterated by the Greeks, Massarelli himself shall be witness. 'Such a conjecture,' he says, ' has now become so improbable, that although at other times I might, with many learned and sensible writers, have suspected it; yet now, having at leisure diligently examined all the original documents, I should be ashamed, not absolutely to reject such a judgment. Nay, I see that the condemnation of the Epistle of Honorius is so connected with the condemnation of the Epistle of

Councils, 'which the whole Church of Christ also ratifies and follows,' anathematizes all heresies and their authors, and mentions those condemned by the fifth in the same order. 'Origen who is also Adamantius, Didymus and Evagrius, and in like way the writings of Theodoret against the 12 chapters of the most holy Cyril, with the letter said to be of Ibas sent to Maris the Persian [a].'

x. In the second Council of Nice, an encyclical letter of Tarasius, Patriarch of Constantinople, to the Archbishops and Bishops at Antioch, Alexandria and the holy city, [Jerusalem] was read, in which he rehearses and accepts the six General Councils. In it he says, '[b] The fifth, as the sword of the Spirit, cut off the lawless heresies which prevailed of old times, and triumphed over their inventors; viz., Origen, Didymus, and Evagrius, and I too repel them, as the fables of heretics.'

xi. The Council itself, in its definition, says, '[c] With whom [those condemned by the four first Councils] we anathematize the fables of Origen and Evagrius and Didymus, as did also the fifth Council assembled at Constantinople.'

xii. In a profession of faith of a Bishop [d] of Rome who was elected by the concurrent votes of the Electors, between the death of Constantine Pogonatus A.D. 685 and the collection of the Liber Diurnus

Sergius and of the Type of Constans, that, not only could the VIth Synod not abstain from it, but the delegates of the Pope, and the supreme Pontiff Agatho himself, and his successor Leo, ought, in consistency, to agree to it.' De Rom. Pont. Auctor. T. ii. p. 223.

[a] Conc. T. vii. 1154.
Conc. Nic. ii. Act. iii. Conc. viii. 813.   [c] Ib. Act. vii. p. 1205.
[d] Garnier, note on Liber Diurnus Rom. Pontif. p. 58.

150 *Accounts by* xii. *Gregory* ii. xiii. *Photius.*

A.D. 715, and so, probably, Gregory ii. A.D. 714, the Pope says, '^e In this [the Fifth synod], Origenes with his impious disciples and followers Didymus and Evagrius—were subjected to eternal condemnation. In it Theodore of Mopsuestia, the source of Nestorius, and likewise Diodorus and all the disciples of the execrable division who are also called semi-Nestorians, were cast out from the Church of God under the eternal censure of Anathema. With these the epistle also, said to be of Ibas to Maris the Persian, and the writings of Theodoret against the ever-blessed Cyril, were cast out with condemnation.'

xiii. Photius says that he had "*'read* the Acts of the Fifth Council, in which the so-called Three chapters were treated of; the matters of Origen, and he and his writings were anathematized; the matters of Diodorus of Tarsus and Theodore of Mopsuestia, and they were in like way anathematized: and the 12 chapters of Theodoret written against Cyril were anathematized.'

In his Letter^g to Michael of Bulgaria, he says, 'the Fifth Synod condemned and anathematized Origen, Didymus and Evagrius, who—maintained an end of the endless punishment, another consolation this, as to all sin and perdition; and they granted their ancient dignity to the evil spirits, inventing that they returned to the ancient glory, whence they fell.'

xiv. Nicephorus tells us^h, that he had from his youth lived close to the Church of S. Sophia, had

^e Lib. Diurnus p. 66. ^f Photius Biblioth. n. 18.
^g Ep. ad Michael. Bulg. in Photii Nomoc. p. 169 ed. Justell.
^h Hist. Eccl. i. 1. T. i. p. 37.

and xiv. *Nicephorus, from written documents.* 151

collected his materials with much labour, and had gathered contributions from the records there [in its great library]. Much the same interval, which separated Nicephorus from the 5th General Council, separates us from Henry I. and his struggle with S. Anselm about investitures. Now, I suppose, that if any of us had spent our time in a library, rich in MSS., from our youth, we should expect to be believed, when we produced a statement from a MS. which we had under our own eyes. But this is the case of Nicephorus. He then, having the Acts before him, says;

"[1]In the second session [after the condemnation of Theodorus &c.] after a petition had been presented by Eulogius Conon Cyriacus and Pancratius, monks of Jerusalem, against the impious doctrines of Origen (also called Adamantius) and those who followed his ungodly error, Justinian again applied to the Synod thereupon; setting forth the petition itself, and what had been written on those things to Vigilius the Pope, in which it was shewn that Adamantius sought earnestly to fill the purity of the Apostolic doctrines with heathen nonsense and Manichean tares. The Synod then referred it to Justinian, after the exclamations against Origen and those who had been deceived like him. With these they joined certain chapters, which the Origenists maintained.—The fifth of these is a chapter of the blasphemies uttered by individuals of the so-called New Laura. The same monks very diligently selected many other blasphemies out of the books of Didymus, Evagrius and Theodorus, and

[1] H. E. xvii. 27. T. ii. pp. 776 sqq. Details not given here, agree with the history of Evagrius above, pp. 144, 145.

referred them to the Synod. All these they [the Synod] included in the anathema, setting them forth in order. To these they added the chapters, which the Origenists are wont to maintain out of what he had written.' Nicephorus mentions, among others, that 'the punishment of all ungodly men and of devils has an end; and that the ungodly and devils will be restored to their former order.' He subjoins; 'From the anathemas, which the Synod pronounced against him, it will be plain what sort of man he was: they are literally these.' Out of nine specific anathemas which follow, one is, 'If any one says or thinks that the punishment of the devils or ungodly men is for a time only, and at a certain time will have an end, viz. that there is a restoration of devils or ungodly men, let him be anathema.'

This weight of evidence appeared to Huet so decisive, that he abandoned his former impression that Origen was *not* condemned in the 5th General Council, and came to think, that no one could think otherwise, who paid due attention to the evidence.

'[k]I own that I thought, what is commonly held and believed, that it was a fraudulent fiction of the Greeks, that Origen and the doctrine of Origen were condemned by the authority of the Council, and that perhaps it was fraudulently inserted into the history of Evagrius. My grounds for so thinking were chiefly these; that there is no condemnation of Origen in the Acts of the Council, or in Victor of Tununum, or Facundus[1], contemporaries and cognizant of

[k] Origenian. L. ii. Sect. iii. n. 14. p. 282.
[1] Neither Victor nor Facundus were writing a his'ory of the

the facts. But having weighed the matter more accurately, I am now not only persuaded that the cause of Origen and the Origenists were considered in the Synod, and that he, with his followers and doctrine, were condemned and anathematized, but that whoever thinks otherwise has given too little attention to the subject or been too self-confident.'

Council: Victor relates only the ills which befell those who condemned the 3 chapters, but does incidentally relate the condemnation of Didymus and Evagrius. See above n. iii. p. 145. Facundus was a passionate defender of the 3 chapters.

2. TESTIMONY OF MARTYRS TO THE BELIEF OF EVERLASTING PUNISHMENT.

The sayings of Martyrs, bearing upon everlasting punishment, are the more remarkable, because the martyrs were of every class. The sayings then attest the faith of all classes. There were Bishops among them. The heathen had a good human knowledge whom to select, though they were baffled, because they knew not that the might of Christ within His true servants was unconquerable. The heathen hoped that, should they prevail over the shepherd, the sheep would be scattered. But besides the Bishops, there were also boys and girls; men and women of noble birth, and men living by their business; matrons and widows with abundance of this world's goods and sons to suffer with them (like the Maccabee mother) or to leave behind them; women, aforetime unhappily notorious for their evil lives, or virgins devoted to Christ; men of gentle birth who had been popular as magicians, veteran soldiers. Every nation, Latin, Greek, West African, Egyptian, Goth, Persian, had its witnesses to Christ among the noble army of martyrs.

But their utterances were as calm as they were distinct, while those who spake them were in the midst of tortures, the relation of which as we read them in their Acts makes the flesh creep. They are authenticated, as belonging to a judicial process, which, in the Roman Empire, was reported to the Emperor. It was more natural to them to speak of "the joy which was set before" them, that their torturers were only working what they longed for, the end of their being, "to be dissolved and to be with Christ." The animating constraining principle was the love of Christ Who had died for them. 'For 86 years,' said S. Polycarp, 'am I His servant, and how can I blaspheme my King Who saved me?' They thanked God Who admitted them to drink the cup of Christ. The brief words, in which they spoke of the 'everlasting fire,' were mostly called forth by some appeal of their judge; but they express, in their simplicity, the rooted convictions of those who uttered them; and these, being from every part of the Church of Christ, attest the simple faith of all. Of the enthusiasm of martyrs a very graphic and instructive picture is given by Cardinal Newman[m]. My office is only to repeat one class of their sayings, which attest how they received our Lord's words in their simple meaning, and believed them, as they did the Being of God and of their own souls.

I have only added a few words of preface (of facts gathered from the Acts themselves) in order in some degree to individualise those, whose language was so uniform.

S. FELICITAS, AND HER SEVEN SONS.

A.D. 150, in the persecution of Antonine, Felicitas, a lady of noble descent with her seven sons, was required to sacrifice. Felicitas, when told, 'if you like to die yourself, at least make your sons live,' answered,

'[n]My sons will live, if they do not sacrifice to idols;

[m] Grammar of Assent. pp. 471—478.

[n] Passio S. Felicitatis et septem filiorum ejus, Ruinart Acta sincera mart. pp. 21-23. [26, 27 ed. 2.]

if they commit this great sin, they will go into eternal destruction.'

Of her sons, one, Philip, answered, when commanded to sacrifice to the almighty gods,

'They are neither gods nor almighty; but vain miserable senseless images, and they who sacrifice to them will be in eternal peril.'

To the saying, 'If ye despise the commandment of the princes, ye all hasten to your own destruction,' Sylvanus answered,

'If we fear a passing destruction, we shall incur eternal punishment. Knowing then, what rewards are prepared for the righteous, and what punishment is appointed for sinners, we fearlessly despise human law, to keep the Divine commands. For they who despising idols, serve Almighty God, will find eternal life; but they who adore dæmons will be with them in destruction and in everlasting burning.'

Alexander, when urged to regard his tender years, said,

'The tender age, which you see, has hoary prudence, if it worship the One God. But thy gods, with their worshippers, will be in everlasting destruction.'

Martialis replied,

'O if thou but knewest, what punishments are prepared for the worshippers of idols! But God yet delayeth to shew His anger to you and your idols. For all who do not confess Christ to be very God will be sent into eternal fire.'

It is added that the whole account was sent to Antonine, who sent the boys to different judges to be tortured.

S. Polycarp. S. Biblias. S. Epipodius. 157

S. POLYCARP, in answer to the threat that he should be burned, said,

'° You threaten me with fire that burns for one hour and then cools, not knowing the judgement to come, nor the perpetual torment of eternal fire to the ungodly.'

The Churches of Vienne and Lyons relate how 'ᵖ one BIBLIAS, one of those who had denied the faith of Christ,' when further tortured to make her bear testimony against the Christians, 'recovered amid the tortures, roused as it were from a very deep sleep, her present sufferings reminding her of the torments of the eternal Gehenna.'

S. EPIPODIUS OF LYONS, 'of very illustrious birth and high literary attainments, was in the first bloom of youth, and not as yet married.' He was one who survived the persecution, of which the Churches of Vienne and Lyons wrote, and was apprehended with Alexander, a friend of his early school-days. Their friendship had ripened in their early manhood. They 'ᑫ were prepared for martyrdom by sobriety, piety, parsimony, chastity, faith, works of mercy.' The two friends were tracked out to their hiding-place, but tortured separately, lest they should, by words or signs, encourage one another. Epipodius was tortured first, in the hope that, being less mature, he would yield.

The judge began, as usual, with soft words, and

º Epist. Eccl. Smyrn. n. 10. Ruinart p. 32. [34.]
ᵖ Epist. Eccl. Vienn. et Lugd. in Euseb. H. E. v. 1. Ruinart n. 7.
ᑫ literis eruditissimi, a clarissimis parentibus instituti—ambo juventutis flore conspicui neque adhuc conjugalibus nexibus implicati—sobrietate, parsimonia, castitate, fide, opere misericordiæ, ita Deo sese hostias dignas præparabant. Acts n. 3.

promises of this world's happiness. Epipodius answered;

'ʳ Your pity is cruelty; to live with you is eternal death; but to perish from you is glorious.'

S. SYMPHORIAN also was the son of a nobleman at Autun, Faustus; well instructed in letters and morals, anticipating the life of age in the fresh years of early youth. He was just passing into manhood. The judge bade him, 'ˢ Sacrifice to the gods, that thou mayest enjoy the honours of the palace.' He answered,

'The judge defiles his own tribunal, who in public is glued to the swords of the law, and brings upon his soul a death of perpetual ill.'

S. MAXIMUS was 'a plebeian, living by his business.' While being beaten with clubs, the Proconsul said, 'Sacrifice, Maximus, that thou mayest be freed from these torments.' He answered,

'ᵗ These are not torments, which are inflicted for the name of Jesus Christ my Lord, but anointings. But if I depart from the commandments of my Lord, in which I have been instructed by His Gospel, there will await me real and perpetual torments.'

S. DIONYSIA, a young girl of 16, on seeing the miserable end of one who had apostatized under torture, cried out, 'ᵘ Most unhappy and miserable man, who, for the sake of one hour, hast gained for thyself perpetual and unspeakable punishment.' She was beheaded.

ʳ Passio SS. Epipod. et Alex. n. 5. Ruinart p. 66. [76.]
ˢ Acta S. Symphorian. n. 5. Ib. p. 71. [81.]
ᵗ Acta S. Maximi n. 2. Ib. p. 145. [157.]
ᵘ Acta SS. Petri &c. n 3. Ib. p. 148. [159.]

S. Marcian. S. Claudius.

S. MARCIAN was of gentle birth. Before his conversion he had been popular as a magician. As heathen, he, and Lucian who was apprehended with him, seem to have sold themselves to Satan to do and to propagate wickedness, but they were converted on finding their powerlessness against servants of Jesus. When threatened with torments, he said,

'[x] We are prepared for any torment which you may inflict, rather than, denying the living and true God, to enter into outer darkness and unextinguishable fire, which God prepared for the devil and his angels.'

S. CLAUDIUS. In the Diocletian persecution, the officers reported that they had been able to apprehend three boys, brothers, and two women with a little infant. Claudius was first presented. Lysias the president exhorted him, ' Forfeit not thy youth with phrensy. Come, sacrifice to the gods that thou mayest escape the torments prepared for thee.'

Claudius said,

'[y] My God has no need of such sacrifices, but of alms and righteous conversations. Your gods are unclean dæmons; therefore they delight in such sacrifices, destroying for eternity the souls of those who worship them. So thou wilt never persuade me to worship them.'

While being bared for the scourge, he said,

'[z] Although thou usest more grievous torments, thou injurest me in no wise, but providest for thine own soul eternal torments.'

[x] Acta SS. Luciani et Marciani n. 6. Ib. p. 154. [168]
[y] Acta Claudii &c n. 1. pp 279, 280. [267.]
[z] Ib. p. 280. [267.]

When about to be torn by the iron hooks,

'ᵃ Thou canst not injure me by thy torments, but providest for thine own soul unextinguishable fire.'

When the three boys, after their tortures, had been led out to be crucified, the two women were presented; Domnina first. Lysias said, 'Seest thou, woman, what torments and fire are prepared for thee? If thou wouldest escape, approach and sacrifice to the gods.'

S. DOMNINA said, 'ᵇ Lest I fall into eternal fire and perpetual torments, I worship God and His Christ, Who made heaven and earth and all that is in them.' She was stripped and expired under the scourges.

S. THEONILLA was of gentle birth. When asked whether she had a husband or was a widow, she said,

'To this day, for 23 years am I a widow, and for the sake of my God, I have so remained, fasting and watching in prayer, from the time when I left unclean idols; and I know my God.'

To her too the President said, 'Thou seest, woman, what fire and what torments are prepared for those who dare to contradict. So then come, honour the gods that thou mayest escape the torments.'

Theonilla said, 'ᶜ I fear eternal fire, which can destroy body and soul, and especially of those who have impiously left God and have adored idols and dæmons.' She too expired amid the tortures.

S. VICTOR, a soldier of noble birth ᵈ and in favour with the Emperor, had, on account of his illustrious

---

ᵃ Acta Claudii &c n. 1.   ᵇ Ib. n 4. p. 281. [268.]   ᶜ Ib. n. 5.

ᵈ The title 'nobilior' stands in contrast to his 'greater instruction or fervency or renown in our religion.' Passio S. Victoris c. 2. Ib. p. 300. [292.]

birth, his cause reserved for the immediate hearing of Maximian. He was plied at greater length with arguments, and was allowed a longer reply. The following are extracts.

'[e] They are not rightly called torments but refreshments, which extinguish eternal suffering; nor should that be accounted death, but a healthful cup, by which a passage is procured to such a life. Nothing is more mad (as the conscience of all bears witness) than he who, gratuitously neglecting so great a good [as God], diligently worships as god, him who is the manifest enemy of his life, so as to gain, after this life, nothing else than the reward of eternal death, and unutterable torments without end.' '[f] Those who are like them [the heathen gods] a most just law removes and brands; and equity itself has nothing for them after this life, but the punishment of eternal death. For no one, however insane, concedes bliss to the flagitious. It remains then that the only retribution for such after this life is, that, since they are never happy, they die with everlasting misery.' '[g] All the gods of the heathen are dæmons, and therefore they, with their worshippers, have been condemned to eternal burnings.'

He addressed some of the soldiers who guarded him and had been converted, '[h] Endure momentary sufferings, that ye may triumphantly be victors as to the eternal.'

SS. TARACHUS, PROBUS, AND ANDRONICUS, three Cilician martyrs, were brought before Maximus and

[e] Ib. c. 7. p. 303. [294, 295]   [f] Ib. c. 8. ib. [295.]
[g] Ib. 9. c. p. 304. [296.]   [h] Ib. c. 12. p. 306. [298.]

tortured in three examinations. Tarachus was a veteran soldier and Roman citizen, 65 years old[1]; Probus (as he says[k]) a Plebeian; Andronicus, of noble birth and '[l]a son of the first order of the Ephesians.' He was quite young.

An officer says to him, "[l]Obey the Governor; I am thy father in years, so I counsel thee.'

Maximus says to him, "[l]Thy youth makes thee somewhat impetuous.'

In the 2nd examination, Maximus said of Tarachus, '[m]Open his hands, and bring fire to lay on them.'

Tarachus said,

'I fear not thy temporary fire; but I fear, if I give way to you, that I become partaker of the eternal fire.'

In the third, Maximus bids him, '[n]Sacrifice to the gods, through whom all things subsist.'

Tarachus said,

'[o]No good to thee or to them, that the world be governed by *them*, for whom fire and the everlasting punishment is prepared, and not for them only, but for all you who do their will.'

Maximus urged him, 'Sacrifice, that thou mayest be freed from these tortures.' Tarachus said,

'[o]Thinkest thou me utterly foolish and without understanding, that I should not hold to my God and live for ever, but to thee who for a time benefitest the body but slayest the soul for ever and ever?'

To Andronicus, the Governor, treating his endurance (as usual) as 'folly,' says, '[p]Have not the tortures touched thee, thou miserable one, so that, in

---

[1] Acta Tarachi &c. n. 1. Ib. p. 458 sqq. [423 sqq.]   [k] Ib. n. 2.
[l] Ib. n. 3.   [m] Ib. n. 4.   [n] n. 7. init.   [o] Ib. p. 477 [437.]
[p] Ib n. 3. p. 464 [427.]

mercy on thyself, thou shouldest cease this folly which profiteth thee nothing?'

Andronicus answered,

'This our folly is necessary to those who have hope in Christ; for wisdom for time procures for those who have it eternal death.'

S. CRISPINA was a celebrated [q] African martyr, a matron [r] of noble rank, of great wealth, very illustrious [q]. She had two sons, whom she left on earth [s]. The Acts still extant, probably, contain only her last audience, when she was sentenced to be beheaded. For S. Augustine mentions tortures [t], which commonly preceded the last sentence. The Proconsul asked her, 'Dost thou wish to live long or to die in suffering, like thy companions, Maxima, Donatilla, and Secunda?' She answered;

'[u] If I willed to die and to give my soul to destruction and to eternal fire, I would give my will to thy dæmons.'

S. AFRA. It is not said whether the evil part of her life was before or after her Baptism [x]. She

[q] 'Is there any one in Africa who does not know of her?' S. Aug. in Ps. 120. n. 13.

[r] Id. Serm. 354. n. 5 Serm. 286, n. 2.   [s] Id. in Ps. 137. n. 7.

[t] 'She joyed when she was apprehended, when she was brought to the judge, when she was cast into prison, when she was brought forth bound, when she was lifted up on the iron bed (catasta), when she was heard, when she was condemned.' S. Aug. Ib. n. 3.

The 'catasta' was an iron bed, under which fire could be placed, so that it became a sort of gridiron. Prudentius has, 'post catastas igneas,' Peristeph. i. 56; he calls S. Laurence's gridiron, catasta. iii. 399. Facciolati refers also to Peristeph. xiv. 467.

[u] Acta S Crispinæ n. 1. Ib. p. 495 [450.]

[x] S. Maruthas has the Acts of a martyr from the same class Theodota. Assem. Acta Mart. ii. 221—224.

says, however, that she committed her sins, while 'ignorant of God.' The three also, who were 'her servants and had been with her in sin, were also baptized together by S. Narcissus the Bishop.' Yet she speaks, as if her sins were still unforgiven. In answer also to the Judge's question, how she knew that Christ had admitted her to the name of Christian, she refers not to her Baptism, but to her being admitted to this confession of Him. But S. Paul too confesses himself the ' chief of sinners,' for what he had done 'ignorantly in unbelief,' before Jesus revealed Himself to him.

The judge knew enough of the life required by the Gospel, to be able to taunt her, ' Thou art alien from the God of the Christians.' ' Christ doth not account thee worthy. Without reason willest thou to call Him thy God, Who does not know thee as His. For she who is a harlot, cannot be called a Christian.' She met these and other revilings simply and humbly by what the Gospel says of the love of Jesus for sinners. The mention of the eternal fire occurs in a prayer to Jesus, when she was tied to the stake.

"[y]O Lord God Almighty, Jesus Christ, Who camest not to call the righteous, but sinners to repentance; Whose promise is true and manifest, that Thou hast vouchsafed to say that at what hour the sinner is converted from his iniquities, at that same hour Thou wilt remember his sins no more; Accept my penitence in this hour of my passion, and through this temporal fire which is prepared for my body, deliver me from that eternal fire which burneth soul and body together."

[y] Passio S. Affræ. n. 2. p. 502 [455.]

Venantius Fortunatus[z] A. 560, speaks of her tomb as an object of reverence.

S. FERREOLUS, a martyr of Vienne, had served in the army, while not required to do anything against the faith. The President offered him pardon for his former 'contumacious words against the gods or the emperors,' if he would repent, renounce the sect of the Christians, and sacrifice to the gods. He replied that he did no wrong by worshipping the Creator, not the creature;

'[a] Rather, ye confuse the right order of things by preferring temporal to eternal; things dead, to living; senseless, to those gifted with knowledge; falsehood to truth: and therefore ye are lapsed into pride and condemned for ever with the malignant spirits.'

S. PETER BALSAMUS (or Abselamus) was one of the martyrs of Palestine under Maximian. The President said to him, 'It has been commanded by the most gracious Princes, that all Christians should either sacrifice, or die by divers pains.' Peter answered,

'[b] And this is the command of the true and everlasting King, 'If any one sacrifice to devils and not to God alone, he shall be rooted out.' Which then is best, to perish by thee, or to be rooted out for ever by the true God?'

Again [c], 'When the crowd standing by saw the large stream of blood running over the pavement, they were grieved, and said, "Have pity on thyself, O man, and sacrifice, to free thyself from this most cruel punishment.'

[z] In Vita Martini iv. v. fin. Bibl. Patr. x. 612.
[a] Passio S. Ferreoli, n. 2. Ruinart, p. 510. [463].
[b] Passio S. Petri Balsami, Ib. n. 1. p. 558 [p. 502]. [c] Ib. n. 2.

'Peter, the saint of God, answered,

'These punishments are none, nor do they inflict any pain on me. But if I deny the name of my God, I know that I shall enter into real punishment and greater perpetual torments.'

S. JULIUS had served in the army for 26 or 27 years, had been 7 times in direct warfare, was a veteran, his prince had never found him in fault; nor had he, as a soldier been inferior to any. Maximus said to him, '[d]Julius, I see that thou art a wise and grave man: be persuaded then by me and sacrifice to the gods.' Julius answered,

'I do not what thou desirest, nor will I incur sin and perpetual punishment.'

Again, when taunted with the folly of making more of a dead Man, than of kings who lived, he answered,

'He died for us, that He might give us eternal life. But He is God abiding for ever, Whom if any one confess, he shall have eternal life; if he deny, he shall have perpetual punishment.'

A Bishop PATRICIUS [e] was bidden by the Proconsul, before whom he was brought, to worship Asclepius and Salus, to whose power the Proconsul ascribed the salutary effects of the warm baths, by which he had just been refreshed. Patricius took occasion of this, to speak of all creation, as the work of the Almighty and Eternal God through His Only-Begotten Son. He connected the internal fire in the earth with the place of the lost. He said,

'God, knowing that men would offend Himself,

[d] Acta S. Julii Ib pp. 615, 616 [549, 550].
[e] Acta S. Patricii Episc. et mart. Ib. 622 [554, 555.]

their Creator and their Lord, and casting away the true Deity, would worship images made with hands, made two abodes, besides this earth, of which He made the one resplendent with everlasting light and full of all most exquisite goods; the other with perpetual darkness and fire of never-ending chastisement, as everlasting punishment; that those who had pleased Him and had obeyed His word might live in perpetual light, but they, who through their licentious life had deserved his anger, should be cast into darkness, to all punishment, and eternal torment.'

S. BASIL, a presbyter of Ancyra, occasioned his own martyrdom by 'ᶠexhorting the people to hold fast to their own belief, and not to defile themselves with the sacrifices and libations of the Gentiles; to think nothing of the honours coming to them from the Emperor, shewing them to be but for a time, requited by perpetual destruction.—He was, for this, brought before the Governor of the Province, and having endured many torments, courageously accomplished his Martyrdom.'

S. THEODORET. Julian, Count of the East, made excuses to persecute the Christians, 'ᵍhoping to please the Emperor.' 'He alleged against S. Theodoret, a presbyter, that he had destroyed temples and altars in the time of Constantius.' Theodoret answered, 'Constantius never prohibited it.' Count Julian commanded him to be beaten, for denying the idols to be gods. Theodoret answered,

'ᵍThou sinnest, Julian, transgressing the faith, and obtainest for thyself perpetual death.'

Count Julian again commanded him to be tortured,

ᶠ Soz. v. 11. ᵍ Pass. Theodoreti Presb. n. 1. Ruin. p. 658 [589.]

saying to him, 'Thou hast befooled thy heart, obeying One Crucified and dead, rather than the king.'

Theodoret answered,

'[h] Most unhappy man, He Whom thou callest the Crucified, hath, as thou well knowest, power in the Day of Judgement to cast both thee and thy tyrant into Gehenna.'

S. SABAS was a Goth, 38 years old, eminent for his piety. The account of his martyrdom during the persecution of Athanaric is preserved in an Encyclical epistle 'of the Gothic Church to the Church in Cappadocia, and all other Christians of the Catholic Church.'

When sentenced to be drowned in the river Musæus [Mussovo], he blessed God;

'[i] Blessed art Thou, O Lord, and praised the Name of Thy Son for ever. For Athared [the son of the petty king who sentenced him] has indeed condemned himself to death and everlasting destruction, but has sent me to perpetual life.'

In the history of the martyrs in Persia, there is the less occasion for the mention of fire, because the Persians being fire-worshippers, it was not used as an instrument of their torture.

S. PHERBUTHE, or Tarbula, sister of S. Symeon, was promised life for herself and her companions, if she would worship the sun, and marry the Pontiff of the Magi. She answered,

'[k] Why speakest thou, what I cannot listen to? I wholly will to die, that I may have eternal life.

[h] Pass. S. Theodoreti n. 3. p. 660 [590.]
[i] Epist. Eccl. Gothicæ de mart. S. Sabæ n. 5. Ib. p. 677 [603.]
[k] Martyrium S. Pherbuthæ n. 3. Ib. p. 641 [574].

Never will I relax for the sake of this brief life, lest I die the everlasting death.'

S. SYMEON, Bishop of Seleucia and Ctesiphon, in the persecution of Sapor, exhorted those led to martyrdom,

'¹Soon must they die by a natural death, though no one slay them. For that this was the inevitable end of every one who was born. But what follows, being perpetual, will not be alike to all; but each will give exact account of his life here, and each will receive deathless reward of what he has done well, or will sustain deathless punishment of the contrary.'

In S. Maruthas, Acta Martyrum, S. Symeon exhorts the hundred who were going to martyrdom,

'ᵐ Know, my beloved, that this our death will live in everlasting life, but that this life [through apostasy] will die by an eternal death.'

S. MILES, a Bishop of Susa, says to his proud judge,

'ⁿ Wo to thee—God shall judge you in the world to come in Gehenna and darkness, and will requite to your pride weeping and gnashing of teeth for ever and ever.'

Towards the close of the 40 years of the persecution of Sapor, which closed with his life, the Magi concentrated their tortures to break the faith of three old men, Acepsimas a Bishop, 80 years old, Joseph, a Priest of 70 years, Aithilahas, a Deacon of about 60. S. Maruthas describes Acepsimas as 'ᵒ a venerable old man, strong in frame, of noble birth, merciful, bearing the burdens of the poor and strangers, who by the word of God converted many heathen,

---

¹ Sozom. H. E. ii. 10. thence in Ruinart 656 [569, 570.]
ᵐ Assem. Acta Mart. i. 33.   ⁿ Ib. p. 77.   ᵒ Ib p. 179.

fasted, prayed, wept daily, till the ground was moistened with his tears.'

S. Acepsimas was asked in the midst of his tortures, '[p] Where is thy God? Let Him come and deliver thee from my hand.' Acepsimas answered, that 'God could deliver him, and bade him not boast, for that he was as a flower, which should soon fade; that he was dead, while he lived, because he did not live in God his Maker; that he would die the temporal death, and again by the death for ever in Gehenna, and that that fire, which he honoured, in it, by the righteous judgement of God, would his soul and body be tormented.'

S. Aithilahas, S. Maruthas pictures as '[p] acute, powerful in speech, patient in mind, cheerful in countenance, his whole self fervent in the love of God, and with his whole soul, intensely and tenderly loving Christ.' When bidden to worship the sun &c., so that he might escape the tortures, he answered,

'[q] It is better for me to die, that I may live for ever; than to live that I may die for ever.'

S. Joseph is also described by S. Maruthas [p] as 'a venerable old man, zealous, full of the fear of God, excellent in Priesthood and conversation, diligent.'

He spoke in warning to his torturer,

'[r] O guilty of judgement and punishment, which is for ever!'

And, in answer to the threat to destroy his body,

'[s] Our soul you cannot destroy, for it is written to

[p] Assem. Acta Mart. p. 181.   [q] Ib. p. 183.
[r] Ib. p 193.   [s] Ib. 194.

us, "Fear not them, who kill the body, and cannot destroy the soul, but fear Him, Who killeth the body and soul and casteth them both into the Gehenna of fire." Thou destroyest my body: it is in thy power; but thou canst not annul the good hope of my soul which is to come, or the resurrection to life which is promised us; in which for you, ye wicked, there is prepared weeping and gnashing of teeth for ever and ever.'

Such were the sayings of those, by whose blood, as sanctified by the Blood from our Redeemer's Side, the Church was watered and grew abundantly, and heathenism was conquered.

3. Witnesses to the belief in eternal punishment in writers of the early centuries.

The following writers have been set down, not as authorities (although very many *are* authorities, to whom any one might well be ashamed to be opposed), but as Witnesses. The Church, according to the Vincentian rule, 'what has been taught, always, every where, and by all,' is the guide to faith. No father, however gifted, is necessarily, by himself, a safe guide in every thing. One who is no guide at all, may be a good witness of the belief in his time. Arnobius and Lactantius, although ill-instructed themselves, are competent witnesses of what was the belief in their time; or Origen, although his own speculations went against the belief which he attested.

S. Irenæus is even of more value, as a witness to 'what was written on the hearts of the faithful every where, even among those who to the Greeks seemed Barbarians,' than in his own thoughtful writings, or as reporting what he had heard from S. Polycarp, as the disciple of S. John. The 'elders' probably misled him about the Millennium. The misinterpretation of Gen. vi. 3. (perhaps under the influence of the book of Enoch,) was almost universal. S. Dionysius of Alexandria judged that one who, having been baptized with words of heresy, had been admitted to Holy Communion for many years, need not be baptized. The judgement of the Church, since, has been, that he was mistaken. Some things, which S. Augustine held undoubtingly, have been tacitly dropped; and yet he has, more than any other, formed the mind of our Western Christendom. The confession of Pelagius on the Holy Trinity and the Incarnation of our Lord Jesus Christ[t] would, if needed, be in itself good testimony to the faith of the Catholic Church of his day, because, in order to withdraw attention from his own heresy, he used scrupulous care in wording it.

The collection might have seemed needless. But some have been busy in selecting what would discommend the doctrine to many minds. Some of the following passages may commend to some minds the truth which they repeat. Else, a flippant writer, Theophilus Alethinus, (made much of in the Antwerp edition of the Dogmata Theologica,) says, '[u] I wonder that the very learned man [Petavius] heaped together so many passages on a matter, *which is confessed to have been received by all, except the Origenists,* and yet did not attempt a word to refute the grounds of the Origenists or of those who hold in part or altogether with them.'

1. S. IGNATIUS. '[v] Err not, my brethren; they who corrupt houses shall not inherit the kingdom of God. If then they who do these things according to the flesh, how much more, if one, in evil teaching, corrupt the faith of God, for which Jesus Christ was crucified! One so defiled will go into the unquenchable fire, and in like way he who heareth him.'

2. The words of S. POLYCARP, the disciple of S. John, are preserved in the account of his martyrdom in the Epistle of the church of Smyrna[x].

[t] Libell. fidei Pelagii ad Innocentium ab ipso missus, Zosimo redditus, in Append. ad S. Aug. Opp. T. x P. 2 p. 96.
[u] on Petav. Opp. T. iii. p. 116 note.   [v] Ep. ad Eph. n. 16.
[x] See Testimony of Martyrs p. 157.

3. EPISTLE OF THE CHURCH OF SMYRNA.

'ʸWho would not wonder at their nobility and endurance and love of the Lord, who, being torn by scourges, so that the whole frame of the flesh even to the veins and arteries within, was visible, so that the bystanders too pitied and grieved; but they themselves were so noble that no one of them either sighed or groaned, shewing to us all, that the Martyrs of Christ at that hour while tortured were absent from the body; or rather that the Lord stood by them and was with them, and they, their minds fixed on the grace of Christ, despised the torments of this world, redeeming the eternal punishment by one hour: and the fire of the savage torturers became cool to them, for they had before their eyes to escape the eternal fire which is never extinguished, and with the eyes of their heart they looked up to the good things stored for those who endured, which neither ear hath heard nor eye seen, nor came into the heart of men.'

4. HERMAS, PASTOR OF, quoted as Scripture by S. Irenæus ᶻ, and read publicly in the Churches ᵃ.

In the parable of the building of the tower, [the Church,] Hermas is supposed to see certain stones [souls] fitted into it, and two classes rejected, the one finally, the other for a time.

'ᵇThe young men rejected some of them; some they cut down and cast far away from the tower'—'I saw others falling into the fire and burning.'

ʸ Epist. Eccl. Dei ap. Smyrnam Ecclesiæ Dei ap. Philomelium et omnibus ubique sanctæ Catholicæ Ecclesiæ parœciis. Euseb. H. E. iv. 15. The entire Greek text of the Epistle, from which Eusebius made extracts, was published by Abp. Ussher. It is given too by Valesius in his notes on Euseb. l. c.   ᶻ c. Hæres. iv. 20. 2.

ᵃ Euseb. Hist. Eccl. iii. 3.   ᵇ Vision third. c. 2 p. 334. Ed. Tr.

The explanation of the first is,

'ᶜ Those which fell into the fire and were burned, are those who have departed for ever from the living God; nor does the thought of repentance ever come into their hearts, on account of their devotion to their lusts and to the crimes which they committed.'

Of the others, he asks,

'ᵈ Have they repentance, and will they have a place in this tower?' It is answered, 'They have repentance, but cannot fit into this tower: they will be put in another much inferior place, and that too, only when they have been tortured and completed the days of their sins. And on this account will they be transferred, because they have partaken of the righteous word; and then only will they be removed from their punishment, when the thought of the evil deeds which they have done has come into their hearts. But if it does not come into their hearts, they will not be saved, on account of the hardness of their hearts.'

Coteler ᵉ explains this of penitence; he says,

'Those are mistaken, who understand this of purgatory: undoubtedly he speaks of penitence.' Grievous sinners being excommunicated, some were cast away from the Church [the tower] until the close of life; nor were they received then too, unless they repented. If they repented not, they were not saved, Hermas says.

The like sentence of eternal condemnation is repeated in other places.

'ᶠ You see that repentance involves life to sinners, but non-repentance death.'

ᶜ Ib. c. 7 p. 338.　ᵈ Ib. p. 338.　ᵉ ad loc. Patres Ap. T. i. p. 80.
ᶠ Similitude eighth c. 6. p. 401. Ed. Tr.

'ᵍ As many as do not repent at all, but abide in their deeds, shall utterly perish.'

'ʰ How, sir, I said, did they become worse after having known God?' 'He who does not know God,' he answered, 'and practises evil, receives a certain chastisement for his wickedness; but he that has known God, ought not any longer to do evil but to do good. If, accordingly, when he ought to do good, he do evil, does he not appear to do greater evil, than he who does not know God? For this reason they who have not known God and do evil are condemned to death; but they who have known God and have seen His mighty works, and still continue in evil, shall be chastised doubly, and shall die for ever¹.'

5. THE EPISTLE OF BARNABAS. It is counted among spurious works by Eusebius ᵏ, apocryphal by S. Jerome ˡ; quoted by Clement ᵐ of Alexandria as of S. Barnabas in seven places. Bishop Lightfoot's judgement is, 'ⁿ The Epistle of Barnabas can hardly have been written many years after A.D. 120 at the very latest, and may have been written much earlier.'

The writer sums up a list of Christian duties

ᵍ Ib. c. 7. ʰ Ib. c. 18. pp. 421, 422. Ib.

¹ Dr. Farrar (Cont. Rev. June 1878, p. 572) alleged the Pastor of Heimas, in proof 'that *it* (Eternal Hope or Universalism) was held in the very earliest ages of the Church.' Hermas, in the passage referred to (Pastor iii. 16), only says, 'that the death of the Son of God was preached to those who had descended into the water dead;' which is only an application of S. Peter's statement, that our Lord went and preached to the spirits in prison, which sometime were disobedient, 1 Pet. iii. 19, 20.   ᵏ H. E. iii. 25. vi. 13.

ˡ De virr. ill. n 6. Comm. in Ezek. xliii. 19. L. xiii.

ᵐ See Vett. Testim. Ep. S. Barnabæ, prefixed by Coteler to his Epistle, Patr. Ap. T. i   ⁿ 'S. Clement of Rome Appendix' p 311.

Ancient Homily before A.D. 150.

with the words, 'This is the way of light,' and begins the contrast, 'But the way of the black one is crooked and full of curses. It is the way of eternal death with punishment [o].'

6. ANCIENT HOMILY, attributed to S. Clement of Rome, and formerly known as 'a Second Epistle' attributed to him, yet not owned as his by Eusebius[p]. It is impossible to epitomise the recent discussions upon it and its date. The very cautious critic, Bp. Lightfoot, thinks the date was probably between A.D. 120—140 [q]; another laborious critic [r] supposes it to be A.D. 130—150. Bryennius, $\rho\nu\theta'$, a learned Greek, still supposes it to be the work of S. Clement of Rome [s].

'[t] For, if we do the will of Christ, we shall find rest; but if otherwise, then nothing shall deliver us from eternal punishment, if we should disobey His commandments.'

'[u] But the righteous, having done good and endured torments and hated the [evil softness [v]] of the soul, when they shall behold them that have done amiss and denied Jesus by their words or by their deeds, how that they are punished with grievous torments in unquenchable fire, shall give glory to God saying, There will be hope for him that hath served God with his whole heart.'

[o] c. 20. The cod. Sinait. has 'the eternal way of death,' αἰώνιος for αἰωνίου. But this is probably only one of the many incorrectnesses of the text of this Epistle, spoken of by Bp. Lightfoot.
[p] H.E. iii. 38.   [q] 'S. Clement of Rome, Appendix' p. 310.
    [r] Harnach, quoted Ib.   [s] quoted Ib. p. 313.
    [t] Clement. Hom. p. 383 Bp. Lightfoot.   [u] Ib. p. 389.
    [v] In no. 17 he has, 'For if we bid farewell to these ἡδυπάθειαι and overcome our soul in not doing its wicked lusts.'

N

7. S. JUSTIN MARTYR, in his defence of the Gospel to the Roman Emperor, lays down the belief in everlasting punishment as the universal faith of Christians,

'ˣ Briefly what we look for, and have learned from Christ, and what we teach, is as follows; Plato said to the same effect, that Rhadamanthus and Minos would punish the wicked when they came to them; we say that the same thing will take place; but that the Judge will be Christ, and that their souls will be united to the same bodies, and will undergo an eternal punishment; and not, as he said, a period of a thousand years only.'

'ʸ We believe—I should rather say, we are fully convinced—that each will suffer punishment by eternal fire, according to the demerit of his actions; and that an account will be required of every one, in proportion to the powers which he received from God, as Christ has declared in these words, "For unto whomsoever God has given much, of him shall the more be required."'

'ᶻ We [Christians, in contrast with the vices attributed by the heathen to their gods,] 'have been taught, that they only will attain to immortality, who lead holy and virtuous lives, like God: and we believe, that all who live wickedly, and do not repent, will be punished in eternal fire.'

He tells the Emperor that this belief of Christians would, if received, keep his subjects from sin.

'ᵃ We in fact are, above all men, your helpers and assistants in the promotion of peace, who hold these doctrines, that it is impossible for the worker

---

ˣ Apol. i. 8. p. 5. Oxf. Tr.   ʸ Ib. n. 17. p. 13.
ᶻ Ib. n. 21 p. 17.   ᵃ Ib n. 12. pp. 7, 8.

of wickedness, or the covetous, or the treacherous, or again for the virtuous man, to escape the notice of God, and that every one is advancing either to eternal torment or to salvation, according to the quality of his actions; for if all were aware of this, no man would be found to prefer sin for a season, knowing that he was passing to eternal condemnation through fire, but he would by every means practise self-control, and adorn himself with virtue, that he might obtain the blessing of God, and escape His punishments.'

He tells him, that the infliction of death on Christians, as being unjust, injures, not Christians but themselves.

'ᵇ Although death is decreed against those who teach, or in any way confess the name of Christ, we every where both embrace and teach it. And if you also should read these words as enemies, you can do no more, as I have already said, than put us to death; which to us indeed involves no loss, but to you, and to all who persecute us unjustly and do not repent, brings eternal punishment by fire.'

He speaks of the sentence to be pronounced by Christ at His second Coming, as having been foretold by the prophets.

'ᶜ The prophets foretold two advents of Christ, one which has already been, as of a Man dishonoured and suffering; and the second, when, it has been declared, He shall come with glory from Heaven, attended by His host of Angels; when He shall also raise up the bodies of all men that have been, and shall clothe those of the worthy with incorrupti-

ᵇ Ib. n. 45. p. 35.   ᶜ Ib. n. 52. p. 39.

bility; but shall send those of the wicked with the evil spirits into the endless suffering of eternal fire.'

In his second Apology, he relates an incident in domestic life, which was made an occasion of putting Christians to death; how a wife, who lived intemperately, 'ᵈ when she knew the doctrines of Christ, was brought to self-control and endeavoured to persuade her husband to the same, relating these doctrines and teaching him that there would be a future punishment in eternal fire, for all who do not govern their lives by moderation and right reason.'

Later on, he speaks of it as the result of free-will. 'ᵉ Because God in the beginning created the race both of Angels and of men, with free-will, they will justly suffer in eternal fire the penalty of whatever they have done amiss; for it is the nature of every creature to be capable of vice and of virtue; nor would any of them be praise-worthy, if it had not the power of being turned toward either.'

He affirms that the doctrine is, in his belief, essential to the belief in the Being of God.

'ᶠ They [the devils] will undergo a fitting punishment and vengeance, when they are shut up in eternal fire. For if they are even now defeated by men through the name of Jesus Christ, this is a warning of the punishment which is in store for themselves, and for all who serve them, in eternal fire; for thus both all the Prophets foretold that it should be; and Jesus our Teacher instructed us.

'But that no one may repeat what is said by those who are considered Philosophers, that what we say about the wicked being punished in eternal fire, is a

ᵈ Apol. ii. n. 2. p. 58.   ᵉ Ib. n. 7. p. 63.   ᶠ Ib. nn. 8, 9. p. 64.

mere boast and a bugbear; and that it is through fear, and not for the sake of what is good and pleasurable, that we would have men live virtuously; I will briefly reply to this, that if it be not so, there is no God; or if there is one, He cares not for men, and virtue and vice are nothing; and, as I have said, the lawgivers punish unjustly those who transgress their good ordinances.'

In his dialogue with Trypho, having answered that those who, before Christ came, 'did things by nature universally and eternally good' are well-pleasing to God, and through this Christ of ours shall be saved in the resurrection equally with their righteous forefathers, Noah, Enoch, Jacob, and others together with those who acknowledge Christ as the Son of God, he says that

' [g] Christ took flesh, that the serpent who wrought wickedness from the beginning and the angels who resemble him might be overthrown, and death set at nought, that, at the second coming of Christ, it might henceforth be utterly deprived of all power over those who believe in Him and have lived in a manner that is pleasing to Him; having no longer any being, when the one sort shall be sent into the judgement and condemnation of the eternal fire to be tormented, but the others shall live together free from suffering, and corruption, and sorrow, and in immortality.'

And again,

' [h] We know from Isaiah that the limbs of the transgressors shall be devoured by the worm and the fire that cannot be quenched, remaining immortal for a spectacle to all flesh.'

[g] Dial. n. 45. p. 125.   [h] Ib. n. 130. p. 231.

The aged man, to whom S. Justin owed the beginning of his conversion, arguing against Platonism, denied the immortality of the soul independent of its Author, and so said, '¹Such as are worthy to see God die no more, but others shall undergo punishment as long as it shall please Him that they shall exist and be punished;' but he had just before affirmed absolutely, that 'souls *never perish*, for this would indeed be a godsend to the wicked.'

8. S. IRENÆUS, in paraphrasing the Apostles' Creed, distinctly mentions eternal punishment as part of the universal belief, derived from the Apostles.

'ᵏ The proof therefore being so abundant, we ought no more to look for the Truth elsewhere, which it is easy to obtain from the Church, the Apostles having therein most abundantly deposited, as in a rich storehouse, whatsoever appertains to the truth; so that "Whosoever will, may take from her the draught of life." For this is the entrance into life, but all the rest are "thieves and robbers." Wherefore we ought, shunning them, with all diligence to love what belongs to the Church, and to lay hold of the Tradition of the truth. For why? Though the dispute were but of some ordinary question, would it

---

[1] Ib. n. 5. p. 78. 'He would only shew that souls do not exist of themselves, but of the will of God, Who, if He pleased, could reduce them again to nothing, of which He first created them.' Otto ad loc. quoted l. c p. 79 Oxf. Tr.

On the strength of this passage, which is not S. Justin's but only related by him, Dr. Farrar states that 'Universalism or a view more or less analogous to it was held by Justin Martyr, one of the earliest fathers' (Eternal Hope p. 84), although S. Justin in twelve passages distinctly states his contrary belief.

[k] adv. Hæres. iii. 4. 1. p. 209. Oxf. Tr.

not be meet to recur to the most ancient Churches where the Apostles went in and out, and from them to receive, on any present question, that which is certain and clear indeed? And what, if not even the Apostles themselves had left us any Scriptures? Ought we not to follow the course of that Tradition, which they delivered to those whom they entrusted with the Churches?

'And to this rule consent many nations of the Barbarians, those I mean who believe in Christ, having salvation written by the Spirit in their hearts, without paper and ink, and diligently keeping the old tradition: who believe in One God the Framer of Heaven and Earth and all things that are in them, by Christ Jesus the Son of God; Who for His surpassing love's sake towards His creature, submitted to the birth which was to be of the Virgin, Himself by Himself uniting Man to God; Who suffered also under Pontius Pilate and rises again, and being received in brightness, will come in glory as the Saviour of them who are saved, and the Judge of them that are judged, and to send into eternal fire them that counterfeit the truth, and despise His Father and His coming.'

In another place, he says, that the truth as to eternal punishment is certain, since our Lord has declared it: other questions we must leave to Him.

'[1] As therefore "we know in part," so ought we also concerning all questions to give way to Him, Who giveth us grace in part. That eternal fire is prepared for those who should transgress, both the Lord openly affirmed, and the other Scriptures prove. And that

[1] Ib. ii. 28. 7. p. 179 Oxf. Tr.

God foresaw that this would be, in like manner the Scriptures prove, even as He prepared from the beginning eternal fire for those who should transgress: but the cause itself of the nature of the transgressors, neither hath any Scripture related, nor Apostle said, nor hath the Lord taught. We must therefore leave this knowledge to God, as the Lord Himself doth that of the Hour and Day; and not adventure ourselves so far, as to leave nothing even to God; and *that*, receiving grace (as we do) but in part; nor should we, through seeking what is above us and whereto we may not reach, proceed to so great boldness, as to be unfolding God.'

Elsewhere, having spoken of the unquenchable fire, he speaks of that separation from God, as the result of man's free-will, and of the pain of loss through that eternal separation.

'[m] If then the Advent of the Son cometh indeed upon all alike, yet is judicial and a separater of believers and unbelievers, because, of their own purpose, believers do His Will, and of their own purpose the disobedient draw not nigh unto His teaching; plain it is, that His Father also made all alike, having every one his own purpose and free way of thinking.—And whatever beings keep their love towards God, to them He affords communion with Himself. Now Communion with God is life and light and enjoyment of the good things which are from Him. But whosoever in their purpose withdraw from God, upon them He bringeth separation from Himself. Now separation from God is Death; and separation from light is darkness, and separation from God is cast-

[m] Ib. c. 27. p. 514.

ing away all the good things which come from Him. Those then, who by rebellion have cast away the things aforesaid, as being deprived of all good things, come to be in all manner of punishment. For though God punish them not by express dispensation, yet that punishment followeth after them, because they are deprived of all good things: and the good things from God being eternal and endless, the privation of them also is, of course, eternal and endless. Just as light being perpetual, those who have blinded themselves, or have been blinded by others, are in perpetuity deprived of the enjoyment of light: not that the light inflicteth on them that penalty of blindness, but that the blindness of itself bringeth the distress upon them.'

' ⁿ As in the New Testament the faith of men towards God is amplified, receiving as an additional object the Son of God, that man may even become partaker of God... So again the punishment of such as believe not the Word of God, and despise His coming and turn backward, is extended: in that it is made not only temporal, but likewise eternal. For to whomsoever the Lord shall say, "Depart from Me ye cursed, into perpetual fire," those will be for ever condemned; and to whomsoever He shall say, "Come, ye blessed of My Father, receive the inheritance of the Kingdom which is prepared for you for ever," these receive the Kingdom and go on profiting for ever.'

' ᵒ Since the Coming of the Lord, he [Satan] plainly learning from Christ's and His Apostles' discourses, that everlasting fire is prepared for him, departing as he doth from God of his own will;—as also for all who

ⁿ Ib. iv. 28. p. 394. Oxf. Tr.   ᵒ Ib. c. 26 and 27 pp. 512, 513.

abide without repentance in their apostasy;—by men of that kind he blasphemes that God Who is bringing in the judgement, as one already condemned.'

'If the Father judgeth not, either it is nothing to Him, or He consenteth to all that is done here;—Therefore the Advent of Christ will be nugatory, and inconsistent with itself, in respect of His not judging. For He came—in the end to bid the reapers gather together first the tares, and bind up bundles, and consume them with unquenchable fire, but gather the wheat into the barn: and to call the lambs into the Kingdom prepared, while He dismisses the kids into fire everlasting, which is prepared by His Father for the devil and his angels.'

'[p]The whole curse discharged itself on the Serpent who had beguiled them. "And the Lord," we are told, "said unto the serpent, Because thou hast done this, thou art cursed above all cattle, and above all the beasts of the earth." Now the very same the Lord also saith in the Gospel to those who are found on the left hand; "Go, ye cursed, into everlasting fire, which My Father hath prepared for the devil and his angels:" implying that not for man in the first place was prepared the eternal fire, but for him who beguiled man and caused him to offend; him, I say, who is chief of the Apostasy, chief of the separation, and for his angels who became apostates with him. However these too will justly receive it, who, like them, persevere in works of wickedness without repentance and without return[q].'

[p] Ib. iii. 13. 3.

[q] Dr. Farrar says (Et. Hope p. 154), 'In the earliest of them [the Fathers], Justin Martyr and Irenæus, are some well-known passages

9. S. THEOPHILUS, the sixth Bishop of Antioch from the Apostles, succeeded to that office, in the eighth year of Marcus Aurelius A.D. 168.

'Admitting, therefore, the proof which events happening as predicted afford, I do not disbelieve, but I believe, obedient to God, to Whom, if you please, do you also submit, believing Him, lest, if now you continue unbelieving, you be convinced hereafter, when you are tormented with eternal punishments.—But do you also, if you please, give reverential attention to the prophetic Scriptures, and they will make your way plainer for escaping the eternal punishments, and obtaining the eternal prizes of God. For He Who gave the mouth for speech, and formed the ear to hear, and made the eye to see, will ex-

which seem clearly to imply either the ultimate redemption ['restoration,' for all were redeemed] or the total destruction of sinners.'

These theories, although both contradictory to that of everlasting punishment, are likewise contradictory to one another. S. Irenæus is accordingly to have taught three contradictory doctrines; 1) eternal punishment, *as* a part of the Christian Creed; 2) the universal restoration of all the lost, after those æonian punishments; 3) the infliction of those æonian punishments, with no purpose whatever. How it can be supposed that any mind could, at one and the same time, earnestly inculcate one doctrine as the faith of the Church, and yet hold two other doctrines, contradictory of each other and of the faith of its Creed also, I know not. Yet Dr. Farrar supposes him to have taught them all in his one book 'against heresies.'

However, in the passage alleged for Universalism (iii. 23. 6. pp. 300, 301. O.T.), S. Irenæus only teaches what, I suppose, all of us learned from Gen. iii. 23, that temporal death was, at once a punishment and a mercy to Adam after his fall. It follows immediately after a passage in which he had written of eternal death.

'For God hated him who beguiled the man: but on him who was beguiled, by slow degrees He took pity. Wherefore also He cast him out of Paradise, and moved him to a distance from the Tree of

amine all things, and will judge righteous judgement, rendering merited awards to each. To those who by patient continuance in well-doing, seek immortality, He will give life everlasting, joy, peace, rest, and abundance of good things, which "neither eye hath seen, nor ear heard, nor hath it entered into the heart of man to conceive." But to the unbelieving and despisers, who obey not the truth, but are obedient to unrighteousness, when they shall have been filled with adulteries and fornications, and filthiness, and covetousness, and unlawful idolatries, there shall be anger and wrath, tribulation and anguish, and at the last everlasting fire shall possess such men. Since you said, 'Shew me thy God,' this is my God, and I counsel you to fear Him and to trust Him [r].'

Life: not grudging him the Tree of Life, as some dare to say, but in pity on him, that he might not last for ever as a sinner; and that the sin which was in him might not be immortal, and an infinite and incurable evil.'

In the other (ii. 34. 3 pp. 199, 200. O.T.), S. Irenæus is speaking of real life, life in God, which is forfeited by what Holy Scripture calls the second death.' [' It refers not to annihilation, but to privation, of happiness.' Edinb. Tr.]

'And again about saving man, thus He speaks, " He asked Life of Thee, and Thou gavest Him length of days for ever and ever"— as though the Father of all bestowed continuance for ever and ever upon those that are saved. For life is not of ourselves, nor of our own nature, but is given according to the grace of God. Wherefore he who shall have preserved the gift of life, and been thankful to the Giver, shall receive also length of days for ever and ever. But whoso shall have cast it away, and become unthankful to his Maker, even because he was made, and will not recognize Him that bestoweth it, that man deprives himself of perseverance for ever.' [i. e. of continuance in that, which alone is life, as S. John says, " He that hath the Son hath life, and he that hath not the Son of God, hath not life." S. John v. 12.]   [r] ad Autolycum i. 14. Edinb. Tr.

10. TATIAN was still a disciple of S. Justin, when he wrote his Oration against the Greeks. He was writing against the Platonist who believed that the soul was in itself immortal, but himself believed a deathless death, an immortality of ill [s].

'[t]The soul is not in itself immortal, O Greeks, but mortal. Yet it is possible for it not to die. If, indeed, it knows not the truth, it dies, and is dissolved with the body, receiving death by punishment in immortality.'

'[u]These beings [dæmons] do not indeed die easily, for they do not partake of flesh; but, while living, they practise the ways of death, and die themselves, as often as they teach their followers to sin. Therefore, what is now their chief distinction, that they do not die like men, they will retain, when about to suffer punishment; they will not partake of everlasting life, so as to receive this instead of death, in a blessed immortality. And as we, to whom it now easily happens to die, afterwards receive the immortal with enjoyment, or the painful with immortality, so the dæmons, who abuse the present life to purposes of wrong-doing, dying continually even while they live, will have hereafter the same immortality, like that which they had during the time they lived, but in its nature like that of men, who voluntarily performed what the dæmons prescribed to them during their lifetime.'

11. TERTULLIAN, when not bent on producing an effect on the heathen [v], writes calmly of the fear

[s] See Ben. Pref. to S. Justin M. c. xi. nn. 3, 4. pp. xlix-li.
[t] Address to the Greeks c. 13. p. 18. Edinb. Tr.
[u] Ib. c. 14. p. 19.
[v] de spect. c. 30, and note p. 219. Oxf. Tr. His own feelings, as a

of eternal punishment, as keeping Christians from evil.

'ˣ We, of whom an account is taken by the God Who looketh upon all, and who see before us an eternal punishment at His hands, we are with good cause the only men who attain unto innocence, both from the fulness of our knowledge, and the difficulty of concealment, and the greatness of the punishment, which continueth, not for a long time but for ever.'

'ʸ There is One God, Who when this world shall have been brought to an end, shall judge His own worshippers unto the restitution of eternal life, the wicked unto fire equally perpetual and continual.'

He addresses the soul,

'ᶻ Thou continuest after the consummation of life, and thou art doomed according to thy deservings either to be tormented or to be comforted, in either case eternally.'

12. CLEMENT OF ALEXANDRIA [a]. It is not incon-

man, come out in another part of the treatise, c. 19; 'It is a good thing when the guilty are punished. Who but a guilty man will deny this? And yet an innocent man cannot rejoice in the punishment of another; for it more befitteth the innocent to grieve, because that a man like unto himself hath become so guilty as to be so cruelly punished.' p. 210. Oxf. Tr.   ˣ Apol. c. 45. p. 92. Ib.
   ʸ Ib. n. 18. p. 41. Ib.   ᶻ de test. an. n. 4. p. 136. Ib.

[a] Dr. Farrar claims the support of Clement, because (like so many fathers) 1) he speaks, after S. Paul (1 Cor. iii.), of the fire through which men should pass in the Day of judgement and calls it ' discerning,' in that it would burn the wood, hay, stubble, not the gold (see ab. p. 108). 2) He says that Clement seems to imply an ultimate amendment of every evil nature, Pædag. i. 8—10. whereas he there speaks of ' everlasting death ' and of 'the punishment of enmity' (see bel. pp. 186, 187). 3) He refers also to 'a striking passage in Fragm. in 1 Joh. ed. Potter p. 1019,' in which Clement explains S. Paul's

sistent with the saving Word, to administer rebuke dictated by solicitude. For this is the medicine of the divine love to man, by which the blush of modesty breaks forth, and shame at sin supervenes. For if one must censure, it is necessary also to rebuke; when it is the time to wound the apathetic soul not mortally, but salutarily, securing exemption from everlasting death by a little pain [b].'

'The blame,' he echoes Plato, 'lies with our own free-will.' '[c] God does not inflict punishment from wrath, but for the ends of justice; since it is not expedient that justice should be neglected on our account. Each one of us, who sins, with his own free-will chooses punishment, and the blame lies with him who chooses [d]. But if our unrighteousness commend the righteousness of God, what shall we say? Is God unrighteous, who taketh vengeance? God forbid. It is clear, then, that those who are not at

---

words, that " at the name of Jesus every knee should bow, of things in heaven and in earth and under the earth," (Phil. ii. 10.) 'i.e. angels and men and the souls *which passed out of this life before His coming*,' in which he obviously refers to our Lord's preaching to the spirits in ward, as he does in Strom. vi. 6. In that passage he, from some source, enlarges the received teaching of our Lord's preaching to them, by extending the like preaching to 'the Apostles, following the Lord.' He supposes, that the Apostles preached in Hades to righteous Heathen, as our Lord to the Hebrews. But still it was to those 'possessed of greater worth in righteousness, or whose life had been pre-eminent,' (p. 330 Ed. Tr.) and he in the same place asks, 'who in his senses can suppose the souls of the righteous and those of sinners in the same condemnation?' For one who does so would, he says, 'charge Providence with injustice.' (Ib. 329.) This absolutely excludes Universalism.

[b] Pædag i. 8. n. 74. p. 163. Ed. Tr.
[c] Ib. p. 159.   [d] Rep. x. 617 E.

enmity with the truth, and do not hate the Word, will not hate their own salvation, but will escape the punishment of enmity.'

13. APOSTOLIC CONSTITUTIONS. Substance ante-Nicene, but date uncertain.

[e] The substance of the Apostolic Constitutions is probably very old; the forgery consisting in a stupid and transparent interpolating of the Apostles' names, which mostly admit of being easily detached.

The claim is put forward, in very different degrees, in different parts of the work. Thus in the first book, there is nothing except the four lines prefixed: which need form no part of it. In the second, which is by far the longest, there are but three places, and those very subordinate. In the third book, there are two places in chapters which interrupt the context. In the fourth book there is but one place, in which the words "to me" may have been interpolated (iv. 7). There is none in the twelve last chapters of the sixth book (19—39): and with the exception of one chapter (46), only one very trifling passage in the forty-nine chapters of Book vii.

In book viii. the two sets of passages are strangely out of keeping. The greatest part of it (as is well known) consists of prayers for Ordinations, including the Liturgy for Catechumens, Energumens, those to be baptised, the faithful, before and after communion &c. These are dovetailed in, with (mostly) little dry injunctions, ascribed to eleven of the Apostles, including James, the brother of John, who elsewhere in the Constitutions is spoken of as martyred. Without them the greater part of the eighth book would be a collection of prayers.

"[f] There are indeed many and various things said [in the O.T.] concerning the resurrection, and concerning the continuance of the righteous in glory, and concerning the punishment of the ungodly, their fall, rejection, condemnation, shame, eternal fire, and endless worm.'

[e] From Dr. Pusey's 'Doctrine of the Real Presence,' No 65 c pp. 605—609. See further Ibid.

[f] Apost. Const. Book v. c. 7. p. 122. Edinb. Tr.

14. MINUTIUS FELIX (later than Tertullian whom he imitated, about A.D. 220.) Cæcilius objected to Christians, as their known belief,

'ᵍ Deceived by this error [the resurrection of the body] they promise to themselves, as being good, a blessed and perpetual life after their death; to others, as being unrighteous, eternal punishment.'

Octavius retorts, that their own poets believed it:

'And yet men are admonished, in the books and poems of the most learned poets, of that fiery river and of the heat flowing in manifold turns from the Stygian marsh; things which, prepared for eternal torments, and known to them by the information of dæmons and from the oracles of their prophets, they have delivered to us. And therefore among them also even king Jupiter himself swears religiously by the parching banks and the black abyss; for, with foreknowledge of the punishment destined to him with his worshippers, he shudders! Nor is there either measure or termination to these torments ʰ.'

15. S. HIPPOLYTUS, Bishop of Portus opposite Ostia, was martyred, probably, under Maximin, and so between A.D. 235—239.

'ⁱ He [Christ], in administering the righteous judgement of the Father to all, assigns to each what is righteous according to his works. And being present at His judicial decision, all, both men and angels and dœmons, shall utter one voice, saying,

---

ᵍ Minut. Felix, Octavius c. xi. Ed. Tr. T. xiii. 466.

ʰ Ib. c. xxxv. I have omitted what follows as an individual theory.

ⁱ Disc. ag. the Greeks fragm. Gall. Bibl. Patr. ii. 451. T. ii. 2. p. 49. Edinb. Tr.

"Righteous is Thy judgement." Of which voice the justification will be seen in awarding to each that which is just; since to those who have done well shall be assigned righteously eternal bliss, and to the lovers of iniquity shall be given eternal punishment. And the fire, which is unquenchable and without end, awaits these latter, and a certain fiery worm which dieth not.'

'ʲ These [the Pharisees] likewise acknowledge that there is a resurrection of flesh, and that the soul is immortal, and that there will be a judgement and conflagration, and that the righteous will be imperishable, but that the wicked will endure everlasting punishment is unquenchable fire.'

'ᵏ By means of this knowledge [of God] you [the heathen] shall escape the approaching threat of [the] fire of judgement, and the rayless scenery of gloomy Tartarus, where never shines a beam from the irradiating voice of the Word! [In this manner you shall never have to breast] the boiling flood of hell's eternal lake of fire, and the eye ever-fixed in menacing glare of [wicked] angels chained in Tartarus as punishment for their sins. [And you shall never be gnawed upon by] the worm that ceaselessly coils for food around the body.'

16. S. CYPRIAN. His doctrinal accuracy is recognised by S. Augustine, and was owing, probably to 'ˡ direct Divine instruction,' which was poured into him so abundantly at his Baptism, so habitually vouchsafed to him in guidance ᵐ. He speaks of the

ʲ Refutation of all heresies, ix. c. 23 p. 360. Ed. Tr.
ᵏ Ib. 30. Ed. Tr. p. 401.   ˡ See Pref. to his Epistles p. xi. Oxf. Tr., and his, ad Donatum n. 3. Treatises p. 3. Ib.   ᵐ Ib. p. xxv.

fear of hell, as the only ground of the fear of death, to any one;

'ⁿ Let him fear to die, who is to pass from death here into the second death; let him fear to die, on whom, at his going away from life, an eternal flame will lay pains that never cease.'

'ᵒ Believe in Him, Who never deceives. Believe in Him, Who foretold that all these things should be; believe in Him, Who to them who believe will give the reward of life eternal; believe in Him, Who on them that believe not, will bring down eternal punishments in the fires of Gehenna. What glory will faith then have, and what penalty will faithlessness, when the day of judgement comes! What joy for the believers, what sorrow for the faithless; to have refused to believe here, and now to be unable to return, in order that they may believe! Gehenna ever burning will consume the accursed, and a devouring punishment of lively flames; nor will there be that, whence their torments can ever receive either repose or end. Souls with their bodies will be saved unto suffering, in tortures infinite.'

'Then there will be pain of punishment without the profitableness of penitence, lamentation will be vain, and entreating ineffectual. Too late will they believe in an eternal punishment, who refused to believe in the life eternal. Wherefore while it may be done, give heed to safety and life.'

'Believe and live; you have been our persecutors in time; in eternity be companions of our joy.'

'Once gone forth from hence, there is no more place

ⁿ de mortal. n. 10. p. 223. Oxf. Tr.
ᵒ ad Demetrian. nn. 13—15. pp. 213—215. Ib.

for repentance; no satisfaction can be accomplished; it is here that life is either lost or saved; it is here that eternal salvation is provided for, by the worship of God and the fruit of faith.'

In his Epistles, he speaks of

'ᵖ gains which sever men from the feast of Abraham, Isaac, and Jacob, and bring them down, ill and to their ill, fattened in this world, to the punishment of hunger and thirst eternal.'

He has the contrast so frequent in the martyrs,

'ᑫ Having before our eyes the fear of God and eternal punishment, more than the fear of man and brief suffering.'

'ʳ Ye, who have sowed glory, reap the fruit of glory and, placed on the floor of the Lord, see the chaff burnt up with inextinguishable fire.'

'ˢ To us it is of no moment, by whom or when we be slain, since we shall receive from the Lord the recompense of our death and our blood. Their 'concision' is to be bewailed and lamented, whom the devil so blinds, that, thinking not of the eternal punishments of hell, they endeavour to imitate the advent of Antichrist who is now approaching.'

17. THE RECOGNITIONS OF CLEMENT are quoted by Origen in his Commentary on Genesis, written A.D. 231. Ruffinus, in the Preface to his translation, speaks of it as the work of S. Clement of Rome. It is of course only given as evidence of the prevailing belief[t].

---

[p] Ep. ii. p. 4. Ib.   [q] Ep. viii n. 2. p. 18. Ib.
[r] Ep. xxxvii. ad Moys. et Max. n. 2. p. 84.
[s] Ep. lix. ad Corn. n. 25. p. 170.
[t] S. Epiphanius thought, that, except a few genuine parts, "the

'ᵘGod made two kingdoms, the present and the future, and appointed to each its time, and that the Day of Judgement which He fixed should be waited for, wherein there is to be a sifting of things and of souls; so that the ungodly for their sins shall be given over to eternal fire, but they who lived according to the Will of God their Creator, receive a blessing for their good works, shining in brightest light, brought to the eternal dwelling-place, and abiding in incorruption, so to receive the eternal gifts of goods ineffable.'

'ᵛ But those who shall refuse to receive those things which are spoken by us, shall be subject in the present life to diverse dæmons and disorders of sicknesses, and their souls after their departure from the body shall be tormented for ever. For God is not only good, but also just; for if He were always good, and never just, to render to every one according to his deeds, goodness would be found to be injustice. For it were injustice, if the impious and the pious were treated by Him alike.'

'ʷ For the patience of God waiteth for the conversion of men, as long as they are in this body. But if any persist in impiety till the end of life, then as soon as the soul, which is immortal, departs, it

Travels of Peter" were Ebionite. Hær. 30. n. 15. Ruffinus thought the Recognitions interpolated by an Eunomian, de adulterat. libb. Orig., in App. ad Orig. Opp. T. iv p. 50 ed. de la Rue. On what grounds Dr. Farrar calls them 'the malicious Clementines,' I know not, nor on what supposition of the date of the Clementines, he says that 'the view of endless torments was first *distinctly* formulated in them.' (Et. Hope p. 180.)

ᵘ Recogn. S. Clementis. i. 24. Coteler Patres Apostolici. i. 493.
ᵛ Book iv. c. xiv. p. 290. Edinb. Tr.   ʷ B. v. 27, 28. p. 320. Ib.

shall pay the penalty of its persistence in impiety. For even the souls of the impious are immortal, though perhaps they themselves would wish them to end with their bodies. But it is not so; for they endure without end the torments of eternal fire, and, to their destruction, they have not the quality of mortality.'

'[x] If any are evil, not so much in their mind as in their doings, and are not borne to sin under the incitement of purpose, upon them punishment is inflicted more speedily, and more in the present life; for everywhere and always God renders to every one according to his deeds, as He judges to be expedient. But those who practise wickedness, of purpose, so that they sometimes even rage against those from whom they have received benefits, and who take no thought for repentance—their punishment He defers to the future. For these men do not, like those of whom we spoke before, deserve to end the punishment of their crimes in the present; but it is allowed them to occupy the present time as they will, because their correction is not such as to need temporal chastisements, but such as to demand the punishment of eternal fire in hell; and there their souls shall seek repentance, where they shall not be able to find it.'

Spurious Epistle of Peter to James prefixed to the Clementine Homilies.

'[y] In addition to all these things, if I shall lie, I shall be accursed living and dying, and shall be punished with everlasting punishment.'

'[z] If any one, after taking this adjuration, shall act otherwise, he shall with good reason incur eter-

[x] ix. 13. p. 409. Ib. [y] c. iv. n. 4. [z] Ib. c. v. Edinb. Tr.

nal punishment. For why should not he, who is the cause of the destruction of others, be destroyed himself?'

Epistle of Clement to James.

'[a] Be faithful with respect to your trusts. Moreover you will persevere in doing these things, and things similar to these until the end, if you have in your hearts an ineradicable remembrance of the judgement that is from God. For who would sin, being persuaded that at the end of life there is a judgement appointed of the righteous God, Who only now is [now is alone] longsuffering and good, that the good may in future enjoy for ever unspeakable blessings; but the sinners, being found as evil, shall obtain an eternity of unspeakable punishment?'

CLEMENTINE HOMILIES. '[b] Though by the dissolution of the body you should escape punishment, how shall you be able by corruption to flee from your soul, which is incorruptible? For the soul even of the wicked is immortal, for whom it were better not to have it incorruptible. For being punished with endless torture under [by] unquenchable fire, and never dying, it can receive no end of its misery.'

18. CELSUS and ORIGEN are both witnesses, that Christians believed in an eternity of punishment. Celsus, to weaken the force of the argument from the sufferings which the martyrs underwent sooner than abjure Christianity, tells Origen that Heathen priests

[a] c. x. Ib. p. 11.
[b] Hom. xi. c. 11. On the quotation of the words 'For the soul' &c. as S. Clement's see Coteler ad loc. Patr. Ap. i. 694.

taught the same doctrine of eternal punishment as the Christians, and that the only question was, which was right.

'*c* Just as you, good sir, believe in eternal punishments, so also do the priests who interpret, and initiate into, the sacred mysteries. The same punishments, with which you threaten others, they threaten you. Now it is worthy of examination, which of the two is more firmly established as true: for both parties contend with equal assurance, that the truth is on their side.'

ORIGEN answers, 'He would, then, have us believe, that we and the interpreters of the mysteries equally teach the doctrine of eternal punishment, and that it is a matter for inquiry, on which side of the two the truth lies. Now I should say, that the truth lies with those, who are able to induce their hearers to live as men, who are convinced of the truth of what they have heard. But Jews and Christians have been thus affected by the doctrines which they hold about what we speak of as the world to come, and the rewards of the righteous and the punishments of the wicked. Let Celsus then, or any one who will, show us, who have been moved in this way in regard to eternal punishments by the teaching of heathen priests and mystagogues. For surely the purpose of him who brought to light this doctrine was, not only to reason upon the subject of punishments and strike men with terror of them, but to induce those who heard the truth to strive with all their might against those sins which are the causes of punishment.'

c c. Cels. viii. 48. p. 532. Edinb. Tr.

ORIGEN'S answer acknowledges that the doctrine of eternal punishment had been taught to Christians, that One had taught it, and that it has produced the effects, which He had in teaching it, to set Christians to strive with all their might to conquer the sin, which caused it.

19. ARNOBIUS. A.D. 303. In his time the heathen ridiculed the Christians for their belief of hell and of fires which cannot be quenched. They assumed it then to be a part of the Christian faith. Arnobius, as his way is, retorted on the heathen, that their philosopher, Plato, teaches the same. His own opinion is obscure, but of no moment, since, although sincere, he was never well-instructed.

'[d] Do you dare to laugh at us, when we speak of hell and fires which cannot be quenched, into which we have learned that souls are cast by their foes and enemies? What, does not your Plato also, in the book which he wrote on the immortality of the soul, name the rivers Acheron, Styx, Cocytus and Puriphlegethon, and assert that in them souls are rolled along, engulfed and burned up?'

20. LACTANTIUS, a disciple of Arnobius, was also imperfectly acquainted with the Christian faith. 'Would,' says S. Jerome[e], 'he could have established what is our's, as readily as he destroyed the things of others!'

His teaching as to eternal punishment is distinct.

'[f] If the soul, which has its origin from God, gains the mastery, it is immortal, and lives in perpetual

---

[d] adv. Gentes ii. 14. pp. 79, 80. Edinb. Tr.
[e] Ep. 58 ad Paulinum n. 10. Vall.
[f] Institt. Div. II. xiii. T. i. p. 121. Ed. Tr. add VI. iv. p. 358 Ib.

light; if, on the other hand, the body shall overpower the soul, and subject it to its dominion, it is in everlasting darkness and death. And the force of this is not, that it altogether annihilates the souls of the unrighteous, but subjects them to everlasting punishment. We term that punishment 'the second death,' which is itself also perpetual, as also is immortality. We thus define the first death; 'Death is the dissolution of the nature of living beings:' or thus: 'Death is the separation of body and soul.' But we thus define the second death: 'Death is the suffering of eternal pain;' or thus: 'Death is the condemnation of souls for their deserts to eternal punishments.''

'[g] At the same time shall take place that second and public resurrection of all, in which the unrighteous shall be raised to everlasting punishments. These are they who have worshipped the works of their own hands, who have either been ignorant of, or have denied, the Lord and Parent of the world. But their lord with his servants shall be seized and condemned to punishment, together with whom all the band of the wicked, in accordance with their deeds, shall be burned for ever with perpetual fire in the sight of angels and the righteous.'

'[h] The power of God is so great, that He perceives even incorporeal things, and manages them as He will. For even Angels fear God, because they can be chastised by Him in some unspeakable manner; and devils dread Him, because they are tormented and punished by Him. What wonder is it, therefore, if souls, though they are immortal, are never-

[g] Ib. VII. xxvi. p. 482 Ed. Tr.   [h] Ib. VII. xxi. p. 473. Ib.

theless capable of suffering at the hand of God? For since they have nothing solid and tangible in themselves, they can suffer no violence from solid and corporeal beings; but because they live in their spirits only, they are capable of being handled by God alone, Whose energy and substance is spiritual. But, however, the sacred writings inform us, in what manner the wicked are to undergo punishment. For because they have committed sins in their bodies, they will again be clothed with flesh, that they may make atonement in their bodies; and yet it will not be that flesh with which God clothed man, like this our earthly body, but indestructible and abiding for ever, that it may be able to hold out against tortures and everlasting fire, the nature of which is different from this fire of ours, which we use for the necessary purposes of life, and which is extinguished unless it be sustained by the fuel of some material.'

21. JULIUS FIRMICUS (about A.D. 340) may be added here, since he, like Lactantius and Arnobius, wrote against heathenism. He also is a writer of no weight in himself. He wrote to advocate the suppression of heathenism, on account of the immorality of the fables about the heathen gods and goddesses.

Using our Lord's contrast of Dives and Lazarus, he says,

'¹ The deserts of each are weighed with the like goodness: on him life is bestowed, for the evils of this world; to thee, for this world's goods, the perpetual punishment of torments.'

Of heathen idolatries,

'ʲ On that food [received in the mysteries] death ever followeth and perpetual punishment.'

¹ de err. prof. relig. p. 38 Ouz. ʲ Ib. p. 36.

Of the evil spirits, as objects of heathen worship, '*k* This result and end awaits you; this the punishment, which God has appointed for deceiving mankind, that *he* should burn in perpetual flames, who against the will of God deceived or destroyed unhappy man.'

22. S. METHODIUS, whom Epiphanius calls '*l* a learned man, who contended earnestly for the truth,' died by martyrdom A.D. 303. He introduces Susannah, in a sort of litany, saying to the elders,

'*m* It is much better for me to die than by betraying to you, adulterers, the bed of my husband, to suffer eternal punishment from the fiery wrath of God. Save me, O Christ, from this present evil.

For Thee, O Christ, I keep myself pure; and holding a lighted torch, O Bridegroom, I go to meet Thee.'

23. S. JAMES OF NISIBIS A.D. 325. '*n* We should fear the second death, which is full of weeping and gnashing of teeth, of groans and anguish and tribulations; that death which dwelleth in outer darkness. To the wicked who believe not that resurrection, woe is reserved. It were better for them, not to rise at all, even as they do not believe that they shall rise— The ungodly, stricken with terror, fears that morning; for he is to be set as guilty before his Lord. For our faith teacheth, that, when men sleep, the souls of those who are just go to God; but those who are sinners to Gehenna.'

24. S. ATHANASIUS. '*o* Wherefore the Lord hath declared that for such things the punishment shall be

k Jul. Firm. p. 32.   *l* Hær. 64. n. 63.
m Conv. Virg. Orat. xi. Bibl. Patr. iii. 702.
n Serm. 8. de resuri. mort. n. 8. p. 267. ed. Anton.
o Ep. iv ad Serapion. fin.

to both [Arians and Pharisees] without pardon, in that He says, "Whoso shall speak against the Holy Ghost, it shall not be forgiven him, neither in this world nor in the world to come." And with reason; for he who denieth the Son, on whom should he call, to obtain propitiation? Or what life or rest shall he obtain, who hath rejected Him Who saith, 'I am the Life,' and, 'Come unto Me, all ye who are weary and heavy laden, and I will give you rest?' These then being thus punished, it is manifest that they who are pious towards Christ and adore Him both in flesh and spirit, and are neither ignorant that He is the Son of God, nor deny that He was made the Son of Man, but who also believe that "in the beginning was the Word," and "the Word was made flesh," will reign eternally in heaven, according to the holy promises of our Lord and Saviour Jesus Christ Himself, "these shall go away into everlasting punishment and the righteous into life eternal."'

'p Consider this, ye that forget God. As a Lover of mankind, after rebuking, He adds exhortation also, giving place for repentance. Understand ye, that I am longsuffering, not as having pleasure in the things ye do, but giving place to repentance. If not, the ungodly one or ungodliness snatcheth us away, there being none to deliver us. For I deliver those who understand, who cease their evil and say, 'We have transgressed, we have committed iniquity, we have been ungodly.' For he who still doeth evil cannot confess. 'Lest he pluck you away and there be none to deliver you:' i.e. repent, lest death rend away thy soul, for there is none to deliver those

p on Ps. xlix. [l.] 22.

who in Hades are taken in their sins: for the soul is plucked away, as having wholly fallen from God.'

25. Even EUSEBIUS has,

'ᵠWho those were (whose worm dieth not) he shewed in the beginning of the prophecy, "I have nourished and brought up children and they have set Me at nought." He spoke darkly then of those of the Jews, who set at nought the saving grace. Which end of the ungodly our Saviour Himself also appoints in the Gospel, saying to those who shall stand on the left hand, "Go ye into the everlasting fire, prepared for the devil and his angels." As then the fire is said there to be 'everlasting,' so here 'unquenchable;' one and the same substance encircling them according to both Scriptures.'

'ʳThey lie in the hell like sheep; death shall feed them.' Having said what befel the ungodly before death, he now says what they shall suffer in hell itself. For they shall be like sheep of death, being pastured by it. According to Symmachus, 'they made themselves like sheep of hell.' For they would not be placed under the good Shepherd. Therefore they became sheep of death, and some he will lead away to everlasting fire; some, where there is weeping and gnashing of teeth; some into the outer darkness.'

26. THEODORE, BISHOP OF HERACLEA A.D. 234. 'ˢa man of singular learning,' a Semi-Arian.

'ᵗThis corruptible must put on incorruption, and

ᵠ on Is. lxvi ult. in Montfaucon Coll. Nova T. ii. p. 593.
ʳ on Ps. xlviii. [xlix.] 15 Ib. i 207.
ˢ Theodoret H. E. ii. 3. S. Jerome de Virr. Ill. calls him 'elegant and clear in language and of historical understanding.' c. 90.
ᵗ Extract in S. Jerome Ep. 119 ad Minerv. et Alex. n. 2. Petavius (de Ang. iii. 8. 10) quotes this, as S. Jerome's own saying.

this mortal must put on immortality, that on either side it may be able to abide for ever, either in punishment (pœnis) or in the kingdom of heaven.'

27. ACACIUS, a disciple of Eusebius of Cæsarea whom he succeeded in his see A.D. 340, was an unscrupulous and changeable heretic, but '^uno common man, with great natural powers both of thought and speech.' The Benedictines suggest, that he may be the person designated by S. Gregory, as '^vthe first in speech of those among the [Arian] Bishops who were eloquent.'

'^xWe read in the same Epistle [1 Cor.] the discourse of the Apostle of a sacred diversity of resurrection, not in the nature of the body, but in the variety of glory, in that some rise to a perpetual punishment, others to everlasting glory.—In which opinion the Church most acquiesces, that we all die by a common death, but are not all changed into glory, according to what Daniel writes, "Many sleeping in the dust of the earth shall rise again, some to everlasting glory, some to shame and everlasting contempt." For those who shall rise again to shame and everlasting contempt shall not rise again to eternal glory, into which Paul and those who are with him shall be changed. This being so, and so understood by us, to acknowledge the 'change' in those only, who shall rise again to glory; but of sinners and unbelievers, who are called dead, and shall arise incorrupt, it is not to be called 'change,' but perpetual punishment.'

28. S. CYRIL, Bishop of Jerusalem, in Catechetical Sermons on the Creed.

'^y Though the resurrection is common to all men, it

^u Soz. H. E. iv. 23.   ^v Orat. 23 n. 21.   ^x in S. Jerome l. c. n. 6.
^y S. Cyril Lect. iv. n. 31. p. 48. Oxf. Tr.

is not alike to all; for we all indeed receive everlasting bodies, but not all the same bodies. For the just receive them, that through eternity they may join the Choirs of Angels, but the sinners, that they may undergo for everlasting the torment of their sins.'

'[z] We shall be raised therefore, all with onr bodies eternal, but not all with bodies alike: for if a man is righteous, he will receive a heavenly body, that he may be able duly to hold converse with Angels; but if a man is a sinner, he shall receive an eternal body, fitted to endure the pains of sins, that it may burn eternally in fire, nor ever be consumed.'

29. LUCIFER OF CAGLIARI. '[a] Thou, on the contrary, if thou willest to persevere in thy faithlessness, shalt have to be in the outer darkness, as a deserter of the warfare and an assailant of the truth, who doest the will of the devil, whence, unless thou extricate thyself from his snares, thou must be tormented with him in the quenchless fire, as it is written. This we say, not of any one of ourselves; for of you prevaricators, of you blasphemers, who deny the Only-Begotten Son of God to be that true Son, and of all who decline to believe in Him, we read it said in the most holy prophet, "Their worm shall not die and their fire shall not be quenched."'

30. S. HILARY. '[b] But if, considering the long patience of God, which is lengthened out to the advancement of man's salvation, he shall behave insolently to his fellow-servants, and give himself up to the evils and vices of the world, living only for things present in provision for the belly, the Lord will come, on a

---

[z] Lect. xviii. n. 19. p. 249. Oxf. Tr.   [a] Moriendum esse pro Dei Filio, to the Emperor Constantius. Bibl. Patr. Tom. iv. 248.
[b] S. Hil. in S. Matt. cap. 27. n. 2.

day unlooked-for, and sever him from the good things which He had promised, and will appoint his portion with hypocrites in an eternity of punishment, because he gave up hope of His coming, because he obeyed not His commands, because he studied things present, because he lived the life of the heathen, because, giving up thought of the judgement, he harassed the household committed to him with hunger, thirst, slaughter.'

'^c An eternity of the body is destined for the heathen too, so that there shall be in them eternal matter for the eternal fire, and in all being everlasting, everlasting punishment shall be put in force. If then the heathen have a corporeal eternity, only that they be destined to the fire of judgement, how profane is it, that the holy should doubt of the glory of eternity, when the ungodly have eternity for punishment!'

31. S. ZENO, eighth Bishop of Verona, in the latter part of the fourth Century [d]. He comments on the first psalm, "The ungodly shall not arise in the judgement, nor sinners in the council of the just."

'[e] In different stages and sentences, according to their deserts, he marks in very few words the judgement of the whole human race. For the ungodly differs from the sinner, as the sinner from the just. He himself assigns no judgement to the ungodly, because, by their ungodliness, they have been judged already; nor did he think sinners, who are to be judged, worthy of the Council of the just, who shall not

[c] Ib. cap. 5. n. 12.   [d] Diss. Ballerini i. c. 3. p. lxix.
[e] Lib. ii. Tract. xxi. pp. 221—224. ed. Ballerini. On the passage itself, see the Ballerini's. Diss. ii. c. ix. pp. cxvii—cxix.

be judged. Now we ought to know (since the just are destined to perpetual life and the ungodly to eternal punishment, and no further enquiry awaits) who they are, for whom judgement is in store. And from whom should we know this, except from the Lord Himself Who continues His own word ["whoso believeth in Me shall not be judged"] "this is judgement, that light is come into the world, and men loved darkness rather than light." He marked out doubtful and slippery Christians, who are intermediate between godly and ungodly, holding fully with neither, since they cease not to hold with both.—So then it is meet that there should be three judgements. One, of the just, who not only shall not be judged, but who shall judge this world, as the Apostle says, "Know ye not, that the saints shall judge this world?" A second, of the ungodly, who are not to be judged, because they have been judged already, but shall perish, as Scripture says, "The way of the ungodly shall perish." A third, of sinners, the secrets of whose crooked and dubious life must needs be examined.—So it will be, that the just shall receive a crown; sinners, being either excused or amended, forgiveness; but to the ungodly shall be assigned everlasting punishment.'

32. S. CÆSARIUS, youngest brother of S. Gregory Nazianzen, a pious layman and physician, disputed with the Emperor Julian on the faith. He says, "I have not set down things extemporised of my own, but in the meadows of the celebrated and blessed fathers, I have collected from their rosebeds.'

'g With him [David] agreeth the sublime prophet

---

f Dial. i. Interr. i. Gall. Bibl. Patr. vi. p. 5.
g Dial iii. Interr. 140. pp. 97, 98. Gall.

Isaiah, "Let the ungodly be taken away, that he may not see the glory of the Lord," which S. Paul confirmeth, saying, "As many as have sinned without law, shall perish without law," speaking of their entire desertion by God and His aversion, and the punishment for endless ages. This same do the prophets also shew, that the ungodly shall not, when raised, be presented for judgement, but shall be forthwith led off to condemnation with their prince the devil.'

'[h]In every generation we remember the Name of Christ, having been made by Him rulers of the Enemies and lords, through Baptism and the Holy Spirit given us in it; which let us take heed to honour, living virtuously, not inflicting on them spot or stain of unclean life, lest the Lord, when He judgeth, cut us in two, and destroy us with the rulers who believed not, into the everlasting fire, depriving us of the spiritual grace and baptism. Not as one of the fablers thought, soothing the ears but not nourishing the soul, that the vengeance on sinners shall have an end, because the Lord only called the avenging fire 'eternal' and not 'eternal of eternities[1].' For when the prophet saith, "Thy word, O Lord, endureth for ever in heaven," should we therefore think that God the Word is in heaven, but, after the æon, goeth forth out of the heaven? And again the same saith, "And the truth of the Lord abideth for ever." Shall then after the lapse of a certain time the Lord not be true?—And the Judge Himself saith in the Gospels to His holy Apostles, "I am with you always to the end of the Æon." Are we to conceive that He will be with the saints for a time, and not

[h] Ib. pp. 99, 100.   [1] See above p. 39 note j.

rather eternally and without end? How were it not extremest madness to assign an end to the æon, and that the devil, with the wicked men driven away to him, shall be freed from suffering, being punished no more? For so contrariwise it would happen to the just, that having, till some æon, lived happily and without fear, they should again die, or undergo something, their æon being concluded. For the Judge declared, "These shall go away into everlasting life, and the others into everlasting punishment." It must then needs be, that when the punishment of the one is ended, the life of the other should be ended, as those say, who are deprived of real life.'

'[k] By 'the floor,' I understand the Church of all people, and the resurrection of all mankind from the dead, in which the Divine sentence, like a fan, scatters to the fire to an everlasting burning, the chafflike and unstable, blown about with every wind of sin, and become light and unfruitful.'

33. TITUS, Bishop of Bozra, about A.D. 362.

In contrast with the first judgement on the Jews, he says,

'[l] In the Second Coming of Christ our true God, they will all, as in a sort of internecine war, be given over to punishment which shall have no ending.'

34. S. EPIPHANIUS A.D. 368. Of him it is not necessary to say any thing, since he held a local Council, in which the errors of Origen were condemned[m].

35. S. EPHRAEM. A.D. 370. '[n] For it is a place of

[k] Cæsar. Dial. iv. Interr. 187 p. 141. Ib.
[l] on S. Luke c. 19. Bibl. Patr. T. iv. p. 458.
[m] See above p. 136.   [n] Can. necr. 12. Opp. Syr. iii. 243.

sentence and has no ending: for the judgement is true and kings cannot undo it; the light there grows not dark, and the darkness there shines not; the glory there cometh not to nought, and the weeping there ceaseth not; the bliss there faileth not, and the disgrace there waneth not.'

'° And I go up to doom and to chastisements which have no ending; and in torment that passeth not, I abide and am tormented.'

'ᵖ Sooner is there hope to come out of the midst of hell.'

'ᑫ That fire which is unquenchable, not consuming what it devoureth, for it was not appointed to consume, but to cause suffering and agony.—It burneth with mingled darkness and gnashing of teeth: it devoureth and wasteth and consumeth; darkness and not light; causing suffering and not extinguished; for it is for ever, as it is written.'

36. S. BASIL. 'ʳ Blessed he who, in the day of the righteous judgement of God, "ˢ when the Lord shall come to lighten the works of darkness and to make manifest the counsels of the heart," shall with all boldness come under that light of examination and return unshamed, having his conscience undefiled by evil works. For they who have done evil shall arise to reproach and shame, seeing in themselves the foulness and the marks of their evil deeds. And perhaps more fearful than the darkness and the eternal fire is that shame, which sinners will have as their companion in eternity, having ever before their

⁰ Ib. 244. ᵖ Rhythm 2 on the faith p. 413 Oxf. Tr.
ᑫ Serm. exeg. in Script. Opp. Syr. ii. 354.
ʳ In Psalm 33. n. 4. Opp. i. 147. Ben. ˢ 1 Cor. iv. 5.

eyes the traces of that sin in the flesh, as a dye which cannot be washed out, abiding for ever in the memory of their souls.'

'ᵗ Let no one deceive thee with vain words: for sudden destruction will come upon thee, and the overthrow shall overtake thee, like a whirlwind. The dark angel will come, carrying away by force, and dragging thy soul bound with sins, often turning back to the things here and mourning voicelessly, the organ of lamentation being now closed. O, how wilt thou tear thyself! how groan! repenting uselessly of thy counsels, when thou shalt see the gladness of the righteous in the bright distribution of gifts, and the dejection of sinners in the deepest darkness! What wilt thou then say in the sorrow of thy heart? Woe is me, that I did not cast from me this heavy weight of sin, when it was so easy to lay it aside, but I dragged upon myself the heap of these evils! Woe is me, that I washed not away the stains, but am branded with the sins! Now should I have been with the Angels; now should I have had the fruition of the heavenly joys. Woe for the evil counsels! For a brief enjoyment of sin, I am tormented deathlessly: for pleasure of the flesh, I am given over to the fire. Just is the judgement of God. I was called, and I obeyed not; I was taught, and I attended not: they bore witness to me, and I mocked.'

'ᵘ What must their minds needs be at this [the revelation of the whole self in the general Judgement] who have lived amiss? Where will that soul sink

---

ᵗ Hom. 13 in S. Baptisma n. 8. Opp. ii. 121, 122.

ᵘ Ep. 46 ad virg. lapsam n. 5. Opp. iii. 139.

down, which is suddenly seen in the gaze of so many spectators, full of shame? With what body shall it endure those interminable and unendurable scourges, where is the quenchless fire and the worm punishing deathlessly, and the dark and horrible abyss of hell, and the bitter groans, and the vehement wailing, and the weeping and gnashing of teeth, where the evils have no end? For there is no liberation from these things after death, nor any device or means of escaping those bitter prisons.'

37. S. GREGORY NAZIANZEN. '[x] I will not speak of the tribunals there [after death], to which the sparing here delivers over, so that it is better to be disciplined now and cleansed, than to be transmitted to the torment there, when it is the hour of punishment, not of cleansing. For as he who remembers God is superior to death (and well has the divine David uttered this truth), so there is not to those who depart to Hades, confession or amendment. For God hath concluded here life and action, but there the sifting of what has been done.'

'[y]That sentence, after which is no appeal, no higher judge, no defence through subsequent works; no oil, from the wise virgins or from those who sell, for the failing lamps; no repentance of a rich man wasting in flame, and seeking amendment for his relations; no appointed time of transformation; but one last fearful judgement, even more just than formidable, yea rather the more formidable, because it is also just; when thrones are set, and the Ancient of days sitteth, and books are opened, and a stream of fire sweepeth,

---

[x] S. Greg. Naz. Orat. 16 in patrem, n. 7. pp. 304, 305 Ben.
[y] Ib. n. 9. pp. 305, 306.

and the light is before, and the darkness prepared, and they that have done good shall go to the resurrection of life, which is now hid in Christ and which hereafter shall be made manifest with Him : and they who have done evil, to the resurrection of judgement, wherein those who believe not have been already condemned by the Word Who judgeth them: and the unspeakable light shall receive the one, and the contemplation of the holy and royal Trinity, now shining in them more clearly and purely, and wholly mingling Itself with the whole mind, which I conceive alone to be especially the kingdom of heaven; but to those others, the torment will be, with the rest or rather above all the rest, to be cast off from God, and that shame in the conscience which hath no end.'

> '[z] Whene'er I snatch an hour of sleep,
>   Ruthless is night to me;
> Mid scaring dreams I lie and weep;
>   A place of doom I see,
> And forms that stand in chill dismay
> Before a Judge Whom nought can sway.
>
> On this side, boiling fierce and high,
>   A fount of quenchless fire;
> On that, the worm that cannot die
>   Feeds on with gnawings dire;
> Betwixt, with no indictment scroll,
> Stands Conscience to accuse the soul.'

[z] Carm. Iamb. xix. (comparatio vitarum) T. ii. p. 223. ed. Morell. Carm. L. 2. sect. 2. c 8. T. ii. p. 400 ed. Caillau. For the translation I am indebted to my friend Dr. Bright. ˙ I subjoin the Greek of the most salient part in its marvellous condensation,

πηγὴ παφλάζουσ᾽ ἔνθεν ἀσβέστου πυρός,
ὁ κώληξ ἐκεῖθεν ἐσθίων ἀϊδίως,
μέσον συνειδὸς, ἄγραφος κατήγορος.

S. GREGORY was not one, who would assert positively, what he did not certainly believe. These explicit statements then require, that inferences should not be drawn from others, so as to contradict them. Such are those, adduced by Petavius [a], according to his wont of disparaging individual fathers.

1. S. Gregory invites the Novatians to a milder discipline as to sinners.

'[b] How is that unlovingness of Novatus a law for me, he who did not punish covetousness, that second idolatry, but punished fornication so severely, as though he were fleshless and incorporeal? What say ye? Shall we persuade you with these words? Come, stand with us [who are but] men. Let us magnify the Lord together. Let none of you dare to say, however confident in himself, "Touch me not, for I am pure," and who is as I? Give us too of your brightness. Shall we not persuade you? We will weep for you.'

And then follow the words relied on, in proof that S. Gregory did not hold punishment to be eternal.

'Let them then, if they will, go our way and Christ's: if not, let them go their own. Perhaps there they shall be baptized with fire, the last Baptism and more laborious and more enduring, which devoureth what is coarse like hay, and consumeth the lightness of all evil.'

Apart from the manifest allusion to 1 Cor. iii, and so to temporary punishment, there is nothing in the passage to shew that S. Gregory held that the Novatians by their discipline, which, severe as it was, was out of mistaken zeal for holiness, incurred God's ex-

[a] Pet. de Ang iii. 7. 13. [b] Orat. 39. n. 19. p. 690. Ben.

tremest displeasure. It is altogether one assumption, that S. Gregory held that they were cast into hell; it would be another, that hell was not eternal for any.

2. '^c I know of a cleansing fire, which Christ came to cast upon the earth, Who Himself is mystically called also a fire. And the quality of this fire is to consume what is material, and evil dispositions, which also He willeth to be kindled very quickly. For He longeth to do good quickly, since He giveth coals of fire also to our succour. I know also a fire, not cleansing, but also punishing; whether that fire of Sodom, which God raineth on all sinners, mingled with brimstone and storm; or that which was prepared for the devil and his angels; or that which goeth before the face of the Lord, and shall burn up His enemies round about; and that which is more formidable than these, which is joined with the sleepless worm, which is not quenched, but is coenduring throughout eternity with the wicked. For all these belong to destructive power, unless any one willeth to understand this too in a milder way, and worthily of Him Who punisheth.'

Since S. Gregory mentions four kinds of avenging fire, and one of them is that 'prepared for the devil and his angels,' it is clear that whatever this last clause means, it cannot refer to the fire 'prepared for the devil and his angels,' to which our Lord says that in the Great Day, He shall bid those on the left hand to depart. The Benedictine note is, 'a milder fire, which does not destroy, like that of Sodom and that reserved for the ungodly, but which should punish the evil in time and cleanse from sins. Of which

^c Orat. 40. n. 36. p. 720.

Augustine says, 'Burn here, cut here; only spare for eternity.'

The remaining passage simply states, that he will discuss the subject elsewhere. In prose it is

'Who formed them, when they were nothing, and afterwards
Shall both form them, being dissolved, and bring them to another life,
To have for their portion, either the fire, or God illuminating.
But whether all shall hereafter (partake) of God, be it discussed elsewhere.'

S. Gregory is not one to give hints of what he held, but dared not speak of.

38. S. GREGORY OF NYSSA, (however he at times Origenises) also expresses the common belief of Christians.

'[e] The tail and extremity of the enemy will be destroyed, i.e. death. And thus will be the complete effacement of wickedness, when all are called up to life by the resurrection; the just being removed to the portion above, those held fast by sins being delivered over to the fire of Gehenna.'

He speaks also of the rich man in the Gospel,

'[f] Who was clad in purple and fine linen, and whom every sort of luxury and enjoyment of delicate fare nourished as the fuel for the quenchless fire.'

And to those who delayed Baptism, in order that they might continue in sin, yet have the forgiveness through Baptism in the end, he appeals,

[d] Naz. in 1mo carm. heroico de vita sua sub fin. Ed. Gr. Lat. p. 41.
[e] in diem Nat. Christi. Opp. iii. 343.
[f] contra eos qui differunt Baptisma. Opp. ii. 220.

'ᵍ Provoke not by lingering Him Who baptizeth, nor anger Him by deferring day by day, consuming in promises the ebbing time, lest He, like the Baptist, call thee a generation of vipers, or a deaf adder which is angered by the voice of the charmer, or shew thee the axe sharpened and flashing, lying by the tree and threatening to cut it down. But to choose the lesser evil, better were it, that one to whom had been vouchsafed the saving laver, should be again in sin, than to end life, without partaking of the grace. For upon offence perhaps pardon or clemency may be bestowed, of which there is much hope among the good; but the other hath salvation altogether precluded by that definite sentence. For when I hear that Voice of truth, saying, "Verily, verily, I say unto you, unless one be born again he cannot see the kingdom of God," I can expect nothing good for the unbaptized. For what pardon is it indeed right to impart to those, who insulted the royal grace, and accepted not the remission of their debt, nor received their freedom adoring, nor embraced it coming of itself to them from heaven, but through their contempt of the gift insulted the Giver.'

Again, 'ʰ Then he resumes what he had said before about those who return in the evening and are hungry like dogs and go about the city; shewing, I think, through this repetition that men, eitherwise, will be hereafter also in the same good or evil, in which they now are. For he who walketh around in ungodliness, and doth not live in the city, nor in his own life maintain the character of man, but becomes wilfully beastlike and like a dog, will be punished

ᵍ Ib. pp. 219, 220.   ʰ In Ps. xviii. Opp. i. p. 367.

in the hunger of all good things; but he who conquereth the enemy and goeth on from strength to strength and gaineth victory after victory, saith, "I will sing to Thy might and rejoice in the morning in Thy mercy."'

Here is the same abiding in good or bad, although eternity is not mentioned.

The above clear and explicit preaching to his people, shews what was the faith of S. Gregory. Whatever be the explanation of the mists of Origenism, which, at times, floated over his own imaginative mind, or that of his saintly sister, S. Macrina¹, to whom he owed so much, nothing but a want of conviction of the truth of the speculations could have made him preach the exact contrary. Origen rightly dreaded the effect of his speculations, to let loose the passions of man, which, even with the dread of hell, were, with difficulty, restrained[k]. This might have been ground enough to withhold any one from teaching positively, what he held as his own personal opinion only. Modesty might say to any one, 'I may be wrong, and then what untold evil should I be doing!' But it would be morally wrong, to teach any thing contrary to what any one believed to be true. And so, judging one's neighbour as one's self, we are bound to think, that those who taught the truth as to eternal punishment, had no convictions opposed to it. It is little to claim for S. Gregory, that he was an honest man. But even heathen honesty "[l] hated, like the gates of hell, one who concealed one thing in his breast, and uttered another." Even

---

¹ de anima et resurr. Opp. ii. 66.
[k] c. Cels. vi. 26.   [l] Hom. Il. 9. 313.

Synesius, in his memorable condition of being made a Bishop, while not holding the Christian faith as to the resurrection, only stipulates that he '[m] might philosophise at home, and mythologise abroad; i. e. teach fables:' but this too he explains to be, 'although not teaching, yet neither unteaching, but letting them remain in their preconceived opinion.' To teach, as Dr. Farrar suggests to have been done, φωνᾶντα συνέτοισι, would be cowardly and vain as well as hypocritical, letting those who would, see that any one has attained a higher wisdom than he ventured to speak plainly.

39. S. ANDREW, Bishop of CESAREA, is said to have been the successor of S. Basil[n].

'[o] By this casting of death and hell into the lake [of fire,] it is conveyed, that among those who are written in the book of life, no death or corruption shall further reign, but only life and incorruption. Nor wonder thou that all who are not written in that book, shall be cast into one lake of fire. For as with God the Father there are many mansions of those who shall be saved, so there too will be divers places of punishments. For some will be severer, others milder, by which those shall be assailed for ever, who are not written in the book of the living.'

40. S. MACARIUS of Egypt, A.D. 373, was called the Great; he was a contemporary of S. Athanasius, and a friend of S. Anthony. He dwells on the different degrees of punishment in Gehenna, in contrast with the different degrees of bliss in heaven.

[m] Ep. 105. Euoptio fratri, p 249. ed. Petav.
[n] Series auctt. in Bibl. Patr. T. v.
[o] Comm. in S. Joann. Apoc. c. 63 on c. xx. 14. Bibl. Patr. v. 629.

'ᵖ Some say that there is one Kingdom, and one Gehenna; but we say, that there are many degrees and differences and measures, both in the Kingdom and in Gehenna.—In the world some are murderers, some fornicators, some robbers; others again give their own to the poor. The Lord regardeth both, and giveth rest and reward to those who do well. For there are surpassing measures and little measures; and in the light itself and glory there is a difference, and in Gehenna too and in punishment there are poisoners and robbers, and others who commit small offences. But they who say, "There is one Kingdom and one Gehenna, and there are no degrees," speak ill.'

He knew then of two lasting abodes; as we say, Heaven and Hell.

41. S. MACARIUS of Alexandria, head of the Catechetical school of Alexandria A.D. 373.

He pictures the angels shewing to the lost soul 'ᵍ the glory of the Angels and all the heavenly hosts, saying, Of all these Jesus Christ, the Son of the living God, is Lord, Whom thou wouldest not know and worship; go to the ungodly like thee and their ruler the devil, and the everlasting fire, prepared for the devil and his angels, whom in thy life thou didst worship as gods.'

42—49. The sayings of the great Ascetics, which Cassian diligently set down, are the more remarkable, as shewing the absence of Origenism even in the country, where S. Epiphanius said that it had

ᵖ Homil. 40 n. iv. Gall. Bibl. Patr. vii. 133, 134.
ᵍ Sermo de excessu justorum et peccatorum fin. Gall. vii. 239, 240.

its birth, and that it still existed among the monks [r]. For the 'Long brothers,' against whom the charge of Origenism was brought by Theophilus were (Sozomen relates) of the desert of Scete [s], and so, of the same monasteries, which those great Ascetics governed. The sayings of the Ascetics range over a century; for they lived from 90 to 113 years [t]. The mention of the eternity of punishment is, in these also, wholly incidental.

42. S. SERAPION, BISHOP OF THMUIS, was at the Council of Sardica A.D. 347. He was '[u]called Scholasticus' for his good natural talent, was a friend of S. Antony and S. Athanasius, and was sent with two other Bishops to clear S. Athanasius with Constantius A.D. 355. S. Jerome calls him a '[x] column of Christ.'

'[y]Vain glory and pride are wont to be consummated without any aid from the body. For wherein do *they* need any action of the flesh, who, through the will alone of gaining praise and human glory, abundantly effect the ruin of the captive soul? Or

[r] Hær. 64. n. 4.

[s] Soz. viii. 12. Palladius says, 'Nitria' (Vita S. Chrys. c. 6. p. 22. Ben.). Perhaps he uses the term vaguely. The two deserts, each thronged with populous monasteries, were only 85 miles apart. Cassian Collat. vi. 1.

[t] Paul the hermit lived above 113 years (S. Jerome Vita S. Pauli n. 7.); S. Antony 105 years (S. Ath. Vita S. Antonii); S. Paphnutius above 90 (Cassian Coll. iii. 20.); Arsenius, in early years teacher of Arcadius and Honorius, 120; James the Eremite, a Persian, 104 (Theodoret Hist. Relig. n. 2.); S. Macarius above 90.

See Comm. Alardi Gazæi on Cassian Collat. iii. 1. Sozomen (vi. 34.) thinks that the life of many was prolonged for the furtherance of religion; for many heathen were converted by them, as S. Athanasius also says, Ep. ad Dracont. n. 7.

[u] S. Jer. de Virr. Ill. n. 99.

[x] Id. Ep. 108. ad Eustoch.   [y] Coll. v. 7.

what bodily effect had the ancient pride of the aforesaid Lucifer, which was conceived only in mind and thought, as the prophet saith, "[z] Who didst say in thy heart, I will ascend into heaven, I will exalt my throne above the stars of God: I will sit also upon the mount of the congregation, in the sides of the north: I will ascend above the hights of the clouds; I will be like the most High." As he had no one to incent him to this pride, so did the thought alone perfect the consummation of his sin and endless ruin, even although no works of the tyranny, which he has effected, had followed.'

43. THEODORUS, probably the successor of the Abbot Pachomius (A.D. 350.), '[a] of singular sanctity and perfect knowledge in practical life but also in the knowledge of Scripture, which he obtained, not by study or the literature of the world, but by purity of heart alone, since he could understand or speak very few Greek words.' He attributes 'the various errors of interpreters to their rushing to interpret, without having diligently cleansed the heart.'

In answer to the question, '[b] If a righteous man who was slain, not only suffered no evil but also gained the reward of his suffering, how is *he* to be held guilty, who did not injure him by killing him, but benefited him?' he says,

'The ungodly will not therefore remain unpunished, because his malice could not injure the just.—For neither did the patience of Job gain any reward to the devil who, by his temptations, only made his praise the greater, but to him who endured them bravely. Nor will an immunity from eternal pu-

[z] Is. xiv. 13. [a] de cœnob. Instt. v. 33, 34. [b] Coll. vi. c. 7—9.

nishment be granted to Judas, because his treason served to the salvation of the human race. For we have to consider, not the benefit of any act, but the feeling of him who enacts it.'

44. PAPHNUTIUS, '^ca great and virtuous man,' 'He thirsted, inseparably to cleave to God.'

'^d We ought to hasten with all earnestness, that our inner man also should cast away all the possessions of his vices, which he contracted in his former conversation; for these, ever cleaving to body and soul, are properly ours, and unless, while we are yet in this body, they are cut off and cast away, they will not cease to accompany us after death. For as the virtues, or charity itself which is the fountain of them, having been gained in this life, make their lover beautiful and radiant, so the vices transmit the soul, darkened and stained, to that eternal dwelling-place. For the beauty or foulness of the soul is caused by the quality of virtues or vices.—These are our true possessions, which dwell evermore with the soul, which no king, no enemy can either bestow upon us or take from us. These are our own possessions, which not even death itself can separate from the soul: by renouncing which we may arrive at perfection, or bound to which be punished with eternal death.'

45. DANIEL, Abbot, '^edesignated by Paphnutius as his successor, but died before him; equal to all who dwelt in Scete in all virtues, but adorned especially by the graces of humility purity and meekness.'

'^fA spiritual substance, not bound by any union

---

^c Palladius Hist. Laus. c. 62.   ^d Collat. iii. 8.
^e Collat. iv. 1.   ^f Ib. 14.

with the flesh, as it has no excuse of an evil will arising in it, so it shuts out excuse for its malignity; because it is not, as we, harassed into sin from without by the assaults of the flesh, but is kindled by the fault of that evil will alone; therefore it hath sin without pardon and sickness without remedy.'

46. SERENUS, Abbot, 'ᵍa man of singular sanctity and a mirror of his name, whom we admired with singular reverence.'

'ʰ They are to be accounted truly wretched and miserable, who, while they stain themselves with every crime and wickedness, not only shew no visible mark of the work of Satan, but have no temptation proportioned to their acts nor any scourge of chastisement. For they do not deserve the speedy and expeditious medicine of this time, whose hardness and impenitent heart, exceeding any punishment of this present life, treasureth to itself wrath and indignation in the day of wrath and the revelation of the just judgement of God, in which their worm shall not die and their fire shall not be quenched.'

'ⁱ The serpent, who first incited to this offence, is punished with a perpetual curse. Wherefore we must beware of evil counsels with the greatest anxiety and circumspection; because while they bring punishment to the author, they do not exempt the deceived from either sin or punishment.'

47. MOYSES, Abbot, 'ᵏ a very chief Saint,' 'ˡ a remarkable and incomparable man.'

'ᵐ Wherefore let every one, while in this body,

ᵍ Coll. vii. 1.   ʰ Coll. vii. 31.   ⁱ Coll. viii. 11.
ᵏ Cassian de cœnob. institt. x. 25.   ˡ Id. Coll. vii. 27.
ᵐ Collat. i. 14. Condemnation to eternal death is mentioned also

know that he will be assigned to that religion or ministry, whereof he made himself in this life a partaker and worshipper, and let him not doubt that, in that everlasting world also, he shall be a partaker of *Him*, to Whom he now chooses to make himself a minister and associate, according to that sentence of the Lord, "[n] If any man serve Me, let him follow Me, and where I am, there shall also my servant be." For as one subjects himself to the kingdom of the Evil one by a correspondence of vices, so the kingdom of God is gained by the practice of virtues, by purity of heart and spiritual knowledge. But where the kingdom of God is, there doubtless is also eternal life, and where the kingdom of the Evil one is, there, no doubt, is death and hell, in which whoso is, cannot praise the Lord, as the prophet says, "[o] The dead shall not praise nor all they that go down into hell" (of sin doubtless)—For souls, after the separation from this body, are not insensible, as that parable of the Gospel sheweth, of the poor man Lazarus, and the rich man in purple; of whom the one obtains that most blessed abode, the rest of Abraham's bosom, the other is burned by the intolerable heat of the quenchless fire.'

48. ISAAC, Abbot. '[p] Some tears flow, when the thorn of our sins pricks our heart, of which it is said, "[q] Every night wash I my bed, and water my couch with my tears." Others, from the contemplation of the eternal goods, and the longing for that brightness to come, for which large streams of tears

in Coll. i. 20. In Coll. ii. 3, Ahab is spoken of as 'given over in darkness, condemned to an irrevocable death.'

[n] S. John xii. 26.   [o] Ps. cxv. 17.   [p] Coll. ix. 29.   [q] Ps. vi. 6.

burst forth, out of joy too great to bear, and the immense alacrity. Other tears gush forth, which, even without the consciousness of such sins, still proceed from the fear of Gehenna and the remembrance of that fearful judgement, stricken by the terror of which, the prophet prays to God, "'Enter not into judgement with Thy servant, O Lord; for in Thy sight shall no man living be justified."'

49. CHÆREMON, Abbot, in the Thebais. 's He was found dead in his chair, with his work in his hands.' He was above a hundred, when he spoke this;

''There are three things which make men keep from sin; either the fear of Gehenna or of the present laws; or the hope and longing for the kingdom of God; or the love of the good itself and virtues. For fear hateth the contagion of evil—Hope shuts out the incursion of all vices—Charity doth not fear the ruin of sins. Faith causes men to avoid the contagion of vices through fear of the future judgement and of punishments. Hope calls our mind from things present, and despises all bodily pleasures, in expectation of the heavenly reward. Charity which, kindling us to the love of Christ and the fruit of spiritual virtues with all the ardour of the mind, makes us detest with active hatred whatever is contrary thereto.'

[To this date belong two, who once were of high repute for their intellectual gifts, but who afterwards, in their writings, were Patriarchs of those who denied the Incarnation, Diodorus of Tarsus, and Theodore of Mopsuestia. Of these, Theodore of Mopsuestia

r Ib. cxliii. 2.   s Pallad. Lausiaca 92   t Coll. xi. 6.

(as is known) after large extracts from his writings had been read, was condemned in the Vth General Council [u]. Diodorus was a very rare and sad instance of one, held in the very highest repute during his life, but whose writings after his death became (all the more through his previous reputation) a mainstay of a deadly heresy. S. Cyril collected the proof from the writings of both, that they wrote not 'about' but 'against' the Incarnation [v]; Leontius says, that Diodorus had been to Theodorus the author and leader and father of these evils and impieties [w]. In the 9th century the Nestorians counted Diodorus, Theodorus and Nestorius their 'three Fathers.' A Nestorian Patriarch elect promised, '[x] that he would adhere to the true [Nestorian] faith, and the Synods of East and West, and the three fathers, Diodorus, Theodorus, Nestorius.' Photius, while praising a work of Theodorus against those who denied free-will, subjoins, '[y] Not always; for he seems to me in many things giving birth to the heresy of Nestorius and to echo that of Origen as to the end of punishment.'

Of Diodorus, Photius had seen the Nestorianism only. '[z] From various essays of Diodorus of Tarsus on the Holy Spirit, he seems to have been sick beforehand with the disease of Nestorius.'

The extracts, alleged in proof of *this* misbelief, are contained in the works of a like-minded Nestorian, Salomo Metropolitan of Bassora, who governed that

[u] Conc. Gen. v. Coll. iv. Conc. T. vi. pp. 42 sqq. Col.
[v] Ep. 52 Opp. v. 2 p. 198.
[w] Contr. Nest. et Eutych. L. iii. de Nestorianorum impietate secreto tradito piincipio. Bibl. Patr. T. ix. p. 696.
[x] Assem. Bibl. iii. 1 p (233 arab.), 236.
[y] Cod. 177 p. 122 ed. Bekker.   [z] Cod. 102.

Church, A.D. 1222 [a], about 800 years after the date of Diodorus and Theodorus. The work of Diodorus, from which he quotes, 'de Œconomia,' is no where mentioned in antiquity, although we have long lists of his works which have perished [b]. However, the Nestorians early translated writings of the patriarchs of Nestorianism into Syriac. Heresies glide easily into one another. So it is very possible that Theodore of Mopsuestia learned his denial of eternal punishment, as well as that of the Incarnation, from Diodorus. Both statements are very commonplace. The two writers use different arguments and have different theories [c]. Theodorus rests his on Holy Scripture, "until thou hast paid the uttermost farthing [d]," and the 'many and few stripes [e],' and attributes the amendment of those who had done ill all their lives, to the discovery of their mistake. Diodorus says, that punishment must not be perpetual, lest the immortality prepared for them be useless to them: he twice repeats, that punishment, though varied according to their deserts, would be for a short time. His ground was, his conviction, that since God's rewards so far exceed the deserts of the good, the like mercy would be shewn to the evil.

They did not communicate *this* heresy to their co-religionists. Ebedjesu, Metropolitan of Soba [Nisibis] and Armenia, at the end of the 13th century [f], (who, in his Bibliography, under the title of Salomo, preserves these passages of Theodorus and Diodorus) himself held the belief of eternal punishment. He

[a] Assem. Bibl. Or. iii. 1. p. 309.
[b] See Cave sub tit.
[c] Assem. l. c. pp. 323, 324.
[d] S. Matt. v. 26.
[e] S. Luke xii. 47, 48.
[f] Ass. B. O. l. c. p. 3 note 3.

held indeed that the earth will be the place of the lost, being '^g a sea of darkness and a chaos of thick darkness ^h,' from which light should be withdrawn; and he thought that the punishment would be the pœna damni, when they would be 'burned with the fire of remorse' for the evil exchange which they had made, losing eternal life for momentary pleasure; 'and this,' he says, 'is the true Gehenna, whose fire is not extinguished, "and its worm dieth not."' He says also, that rewards and punishments will be given according to their merits, 'and these shall go into eternal torment, and the righteous to eternal life.'

Those who have simple faith will not attach any moment to any opinions of those who denied the Incarnation of our Lord. I only insert the above, because these two teachers had a great reputation, until their unbelief became known, and are paraded by Dr. Farrarⁱ on the authority of Gieseler^j as 'great teachers.']

50. DIDYMUS. '^kSinners and the lawless shall then fail, not altogether from the universe, but from the

^g Ib. p. 332 note.   ^h Ib. p. 360 note.
ⁱ Eternal Hope, p. 162.   ^j Kirchengesch. § 82. p 408.
^k on Ps. 103, 35 in Corderii catena T. iii. 92. We have no record of the passages which were brought together by the monks and laid before the Fifth General Council, upon which it condemned him, with Origen and Evagrius. But it was not unusual with Origenists to be inconsistent. S. Jerome calls him 'Origenis apertissimus propugnator.' c. Ruf. i. 6. Dr. Farrar says, (Et. Hope p. 161) 'The traces of the same doctrine which are found in the teaching of Didymus of Alexandria and Gregory of Nazianzus are slight, but φωνᾶν- τα συνετοῖσιν.' Dr F.'s authority for Didymus is Neander KG. ii. 3. p. 1407. [Eng.Tr iv. 455.]. 'We observe here another after-influence of the great Origen upon individual Chuich teachers, who formed

earth; so that they should be no longer in the earth but in another element beside the earth. For they shall be given over to the everlasting fire, according to the word which saith, "Go ye into the everlasting fire which was prepared for the devil and his angels." Wherefore, O soul, remembering these things and having them ever before thine eyes, fail not at any time to fulfil what is enjoined thee by the Divine Spirit; for this it is to bless the Lord.'

In his book on the Holy Spirit,

'[1] He who hath forsaken the Lord, and is an un-

themselves upon the study of his writings especially, as a Didymus, a Gregory of Nazianzus.' In a note, he says, 'Although in the writings of Didymus, which have come to our knowledge, there is no definite trace of the doctrine of ἀποκατάστασις [Restoration] yet in his work '.De Trinitate' published by Mingarelli (Bologna 1769) one might find an indication of this sort in his exposition and application of the passage Phil. 2. 10, where, in reference to the καταχθόνια as well as the ἐπίγεια, he speaks of the invocation of the saving name of Christ by all.' (L. iii. 10. p. 365.)

It seems to me incredible that this inference should be made from the quotation of Phil. ii. 10 by Didymus against Arians or Macedonians, and his simple explanation, 'before the Son appeared in the world, the heavenly beings alone bowed before Him and glorified Him, knowing the Equal Glory and Deity of the Holy Trinity; so that the Seraphim thrice cried ' Holy' and once ' Lord,' so as to send the hymn alike to each Person, and proclaim that All had one Lordship; but things on earth and under the earth did not know Him as they did after the Incarnation. For then they too began to bow the knee before Him and glorify Him and call Him God, and on sudden emergencies, overtaken by the sharpness of the calamity, not to use long prayers, nor, as usual, to use much repetition, but ' to call upon Him,' ' Christ, help!' in that prayer was to all unto salvation.'

Besides that ' things under the earth ' are omitted, twice at least in this treatise eternal punishment is spoken of.

[1] De Spiritu Sancto n. 47. translated by S Jerome Opp. ii. 154 Vallars.

believer, both provoketh the Holy One of Israel to anger, and angereth His Holy Spirit. For the same indignation on sinners is referred both to the Holy Spirit and the Holy One of Israel. Whence also in what follows the like Unity of the Trinity is shewn, where Scripture says, the Lord was turned to be the enemy to those who provoked His Holy Spirit, and that He delivered them to eternal torment, after that, not in speech but in deeds, they blasphemed His Holy Spirit. For He, Who became their Enemy, fought against them and subjected them to manifold and long torments, so that they should not obtain forgiveness of sins, either in this world or in that to come. For they provoked His Holy Spirit and blasphemed against Him.'

'[m] Let us consider how each thing is said, lest through ignorance we fall into the pit of error. For in other things an error, arising from the kindred use of words, brings confusion and shame to him who has committed the error; but the lapse into what is perverse as to things above and divine, leads to eternal punishment and Tartarus, chiefly when one, once deceived, wills, not to repent but shamelessly to defend his error.'

'[n] Every one, who shall call upon the name of the Lord shall be saved. But what name of the Son do they call upon, who do not call upon Him, the glorious Conqueror, the Saviour of heaven and earth and sea, the Uncreated God, or the Son Consubstantial with the Father? And John saith in like way of Him, "while ye have light, believe in the light, that

---

[m] de Sp. S. n. 59 p. 163.
[n] de Trin. i. 28 p. 87 ed. Mingarelli.

ye may be children of light." For after death, there is no place for repentance, as David says, "In the grave, who shall confess to Thee?"—He calleth the "vineyard," the world or the people, whom the teachers of heretics and Jews, by their blasphemous teaching, have made guilty of the Gehenna of fire.'

'[o] This reviling does not injure the Holy Spirit, nor do the reproaches and insolence of the heretics who think amiss go beyond the hearing, but they who utter such things will suffer interminably.'

'[p] Those who obey her [the harlot's] ways and counsels, are led away at last to everlasting destruction.'

51. S. AMBROSE. Passages have been given above, in which he speaks of the sufferings being immaterial[q], and contrasts the temporal suffering in the Day of Judgement with the eternal[r]. He does this again;

'[s] Knowing then, that all the judgements of the justice of God will endure for ever, let us take heed that our works displease Him not, and we begin to come into His eternal judgement; nor, if we have done any good, let us become supine and be relaxed, "For we must all stand before the Judgement-seat of Christ, that every man may receive what he has done, good or bad." Thou seest that Paul too will stand there, as himself says. Beware of "wood;" beware of "stubble;" lest thou bring with thee to the Judgement of God, what the fire may burn. Beware lest, in one or two works, thou have what may be approved, and

[o] Ib. ii. 3 p. 131. [p] on Prov. x. 18 in Catena Peltan.
[q] See ab. p. 20. [r] See ab. p. 113.
[s] in Ps. 118 Serm. 20 n. 58.

bring, in many works, what shall offend. "If any man's work be burned, he shall suffer loss, yet himself may be saved by fire." Whence it is gathered, that the same man is saved in part, condemned in part. Knowing then that there are many judgements, let us examine all our works. In the just man, grave is the loss; grave the burning of any work; in the ungodly, miserable is the punishment. Rather may all judgements be full of grace, full of bright crowns; lest perchance, when our acts are weighed, guilt preponderate.'

'"Lighten thou the weight of errors, that thou mayest be fit to attain without fear the rest of the future sabbath. For if thou bearest hence heavy sins, thou wilt not have rest there. Unburden then thy mind; cast away every thing, whereby the conscience is burdened or oppressed. Let the consummation of this world find thee lightened, lest, being weighted with sins, thou be unable to escape. Flee beforehand that thou escape. Flee also the wrath to come, i.e. the Day of Judgement. He flees, who does works of repentance, as John Baptist laid down, "O generation of vipers, who hath warned you to flee from the wrath to come? Bring forth then fruits meet for repentance."'

In the De fide he pictures our Lord pronouncing judgement on the Manichæan;

'"Thou, O Manichæan, thinkest that thou wert created by the devil; haste then to his abode, where is the fire and sulphur; where his conflagration is not extinguished, lest his punishment should ever die.'

[t] in Ps. 37. n. 2.   [u] de fide ii. 13. n. 119

Again,

'ˣ(David) as a stranger, hasted to that common home of all the saints, praying, as to the defilement of this sojourning, that his sins may be forgiven, before he departs this life. For he who hath not received here remission of sins, will not be there. For he will not be able to attain to eternal life; for eternal life is the remission of sins.'

Petavius thinksʸ, that in one place S. Ambrose Origenises, because he thought that Satan was not yet given over to punishment, because his punishment was to be eternal, but that Dives was punished at once because he was to be delivered.

'ᶻ The judgement of the devil is delayed, that, guilty, he may abide ever in punishment, ever be held bound in the chains of his wickedness, may undergo for ever the judgement of his own conscience. So then that rich man in the Gospel, although a sinner, undergoes penal suffering, that he may escape the sooner. But the devil is shewn, not as yet to have come to judgement, not as yet to be subjected to punishments, except what he undergoes of himself, in the consciousness of his great guilt through perpetual fear, so as never to be without apprehension.'

The Benedictines [a] answer in part, that it was the common opinion of all the old fathers, that the devil had not yet undergone his sentence [as S. Jude speaks of a further judgement, ver. 8.] It is no where laid

ˣ de bono mortis c. 2.
ʸ de Ang. iii. 7. 12.   ᶻ in Ps. 118. Oct. 20. n. 23.

[a] ad loc. The passages of the fathers are contained in Maldon. de Angelis q. 7, de pœnis dæmonum, and in Petavius himself de Ang. iii. 4.

down that Dives was in the place of the lost [b], (although it is the opinion held by almost all.)

52. S. Pacian. '[c] Darkness and hell are opening their enlarged bosoms for the wicked. After the punishment of souls in time, everlasting punishment is reserved also for the revivified bodies.'

53. S. Jerome expresses his faith in several places with abundant clearness.

He emphasises our Lord's words, "These shall go away into everlasting punishment, but the righteous into life eternal."

'[d] Careful reader, observe, that, both the punishments are eternal, and that perpetual life has no fear thereafter of being destroyed.

And in three places in his Commentary on Isaiah; '[e] They who say that the devil will be penitent and obtain pardon, let them explain to us how they take this passage, "And He shall slay the dragon who is in the sea."'

And again [f], in explanation of the words, "The sinner, being a hundred years old, will be cursed."

'In that time, when all shall be of one age, and the holy and the sinner shall be perfect in the like resurrection and shall not vary in time, but one shall be taken to reward, another dragged to punishment, and therein shall the sinner be cursed, that, his body being uncorrupt, he shall suffer eternal punishment.'

[b] Dr. Farrar says even eagerly, 'Who, be it observed in passing, was not in Gehenna at all, but in Hades, the intermediate state, whom Abraham still addresses as son; and who can speak, and speak words of sympathy and affection &c.' Cont. Rev. June 1878 p. 573. note.   [c] Paræn. ad pœnit. p. 375 Oxf. Tr.
[d] on S. Matt. xxv. 46. Opp. vii. 210. Vallars.
on Isa. xxvii. 1. p. 361. Ib.   [f] on Isa. lxv. 20. p. 791. Ib.

And again,

'ᵍ Hell and death have enlarged themselves, and opened their mouth, and without number or satiety have swallowed those who are to be punished for ever.—What I have said of the people of the Jews may be transferred to those who, taken up with the pleasures of the world and not regarding the works of God, are led captives to sin and have not the knowledge of God, and so, through hunger and thirst of good works and virtues, perish, and shall be drawn down to Gehenna, and there, delivered over to eternal torments, shall see their power and pride changed into misery and humiliation.'

And tacitly against the Origenists,

'ʰI know that very many explain the king of Nineveh—of the devil, who in the end of the world (because no reasonable creature made by God should perish) coming down from his pride will repent, and be restored to his former place.—But since Holy Scripture does not say this, and it wholly subverts the fear of God, since men easily sink into sins, thinking that the devil too, who is the author of ills and the fountain of all sins, can repent and be saved, let us cast this away from our minds. And let us know that sinners in the Gospel are cast into everlasting fire, prepared for the devil and his angels, and of them it is said, "Their worm shall not die, and their fire shall not be quenched." We know that God is merciful, and we who are sinners have no pleasure in His severity, but we read, "Merciful and just is the Lord, yea, our God is merciful."

ᵍ on Is. v. 14, 15. pp. 78, 79.
ʰ on Jonah iii. 6, 7. Opp. vi. 418, 419. Vall.

The justice of God is fenced round by mercy; and, encircled with this, He proceeds to judgement. He so spares as to judge; so judges, as to be merciful.'

He repeats this concisely on Daniel;

'¹ Some very ill refer this to the devil, that in the consummation and end of the world, he too receives the knowledge of God and exhorts all to penitence, and they will have it, that he is [designated under] the king of Nineveh, who at last came down from his throne of pride, and obtained the rewards of humility.'

After three passages in S. Jerome's commentary on Isaiah, in which he had written on the eternity of punishment, it is in itself inconceivable, that he should throw a doubt upon it in a fourth in that same commentary. But the passage has no bearing on the subject. S. Jerome speaks only of a certain class, who shall be exempted from that doom. He first declares absolutely the eternity of punishment.

'ʲ If all flesh shall worship the Lord, and yet contrariwise the corpses of the men who have transgressed against the Lord shall be delivered to everlasting burning, there will be on either side a resurrection of true flesh.'

Then he mentions that very many thought that the punishments were spiritual[k]. 'Yet,' he adds, 'so as not to deny the eternal punishment of prævaricators and of those who deny the Lord.' Then, after a digression against our having aerial bodies, he speaks of the fire which shall try every man's work and of the places of Scripture which those alleged,

---

¹ on Dan. iii. 96. Vulg. Opp. v. 644.
ʲ on Is. lxvi. 24.   ᵏ The passage is given above p. 20.

'who will have it that punishment should at some time be ended.' He sums up,

'These things they ponder upon, wishing to assert that, after sufferings and torments, there will be refreshments, which are now to be hidden from those to whom fear is useful, that, dreading punishment, they may cease from sin. Which we ought to leave to the knowledge of God, by Whom not mercies only but punishments are weighed, and Who knows whom, how, and how long He ought to punish. Let us say only, what is meet for human frailty, "Lord, rebuke me not in Thine anger, nor chasten me in Thy wrath." And as we believe that the torments of the devil and of all who deny [God], and the impious who said in their heart, "There is no God," are eternal, so as to sinners [and the impious[1]] and yet Christians, whose works are to be tried and purged in the fire, we believe that the sentence of the Judge will be moderated and mingled with clemency.'

S. Jerome seems to me too to distinguish between temporal and eternal punishment; and to say that we ought not to rule, to whom God would assign the temporal.

2. This is borne out by the other passage, alleged in proof that he did not hold the Catholic faith as to future punishment. It occurs in his Dialogue against the Pelagians.

S. Jerome rejects the doctrine of Pelagius, '[m]In the day of judgement the wicked and sinners will not be

[1] An old Ambrosian Ms. omits this word, which introduces the same class into the two opposed clauses.

[m] Dial. c. Pelag n 28. Opp. ii. 709.

spared, but will be burned with everlasting fire,' as too broad, and precluding the mercy of God. He himself sums up,

'But if Origen says, that no rational creature will be lost, and ascribes repentance to the devil, what is that to us, who say that the devil and his hosts and all ungodly and transgressors perish for ever, and that Christians, if overtaken [by death] in sin, will be saved after punishment?'

He had laid down that ungodly [impii] 'were those who had not the knowledge of God, or who, knowing it, changed it by transgression.'

Pelagius held all sin to be equal, and that '[n]a rich man, continuing in his riches, could not enter the kingdom of God, unless he sold all which he had, nor did it avail him anything, if out of those same riches he shall do what is commanded.' I think then (with Vallars) that S. Jerome means by 'sins,' lesser sins, which did not shut out the grace of God.

But this has nothing to do with the doctrine of eternal punishment in the abstract, since S. Jerome expresses his belief in this, in this very passage.

54. S. GAUDENTIUS BISHOP OF BRIXIA, A.D. 387. (deputed by a Synod of Rome to reconcile the Emperor Arcadius with S. Chrysostom.)

'[o]Let us do good to the poor and miserable, let us minister food, drink, clothing to those in need, because the Lord is the just Rewarder of such deeds, Who, when He shall come in His Majesty, shall give

---

[n] Ep. Hilarii Syrac. (Ep. 156 inter Epp. S. August. Opp. ii. 542) quoted by Vallars on S. Jerome Dial. c. Pelag. Opp. ii. 711, 712.

[o] Tract 13. de Natal. Dom. contra avaritiam Judæ et pro pauperibus. Bibl. Patr. T. v. p. 964.

the kingdom of heaven to the nourishers of the poor, placed for their good deeds on His Right Hand. Contrariwise, He shall adjudge the inhuman and ungodly to be burned by the eternal fires, saying, that He Himself in the poor was tenderly cherished, or cruelly neglected. Such were the feelings of our Saviour towards His poor.'

He gives briefly the history of the 40 martyrs, as in their Acts. They say,

'p We execrate gifts, which bring a loss of salvation; we repudiate honours, which deprive of that everlasting glory; we reject the friendships of the king, which long to separate us from the love of God; we reject too this temporal life of our body, which, preserved at the peril of the faith, gains the death of the soul; nor, lastly, are we deterred by these present tortures. We yield our flesh to the sufferings, whatever thou willest to lay upon us; lest, denying Christ our God, we be sunk down to perpetual torments, which have, from the beginning, been prepared for the devil and you his ministers.'

55. RUFFINUS. 'q The body, which shall rise from the dead, will be incorruptible and immortal, not of the just only but of sinners; of the just, that they may abide for ever with Christ; of sinners, that without perishing they may undergo the penalty due.'

'r There will be given to sinners also (as we have said above) from the resurrection a condition of incorruption and immortality, that, as to the just God ministers to a perpetuity of glory, so to sinners He

p Tract 17. Die dedicat. Basilicæ SS. xl. martyrum. Ib. p. 969.
q de Symb. n. 45.   r Ib. n. 47, 48.

should minister to a prolongation of confusion and punishment.' 'These things, if we attend to consistently, according to the rule of the tradition above expounded, we pray that, to us and to all who hear them, the Lord will grant that, keeping the faith which we have received, our course finished, we may await the crown of righteousness stored up, and be found among those who rise to life eternal, and be freed from confusion and eternal [s] shame through Jesus Christ our Lord.'

'[t] Flee also those, if there are such, who are said [u] to deny that there will be a just judgement of God towards all, or to say that the devil will be absolved from the due damnation of punishment. From all these, I say, let the ear of a believer turn away.'

'We say also, that there will be a judgement, in which judgement every one shall receive what he hath done in the body, whether good or evil. But if men shall receive according to their works, how much the more the devil, who is to all the cause of sin! Of whom we believe what is written in the Gospel, that the devil himself and all his angels, together with those who do his works, i. e. who calumniate their brethren, shall, with him, equally obtain the inheritance of eternal fire. If then any one deny that the devil will be delivered to eternal fire, let him have a portion of eternal fire with him, that he may feel what he denied [x].'

---

[s] The substitution of 'eternal' here for 'prolongation' (prolixitate) above, shews that 'prolixitas' was not adopted before, as a weak word.   [t] ib. 39.

[u] Ruffinus here rejects other heresies contained in the de principiis.

[x] Apol. ad Anastas. n. 5. Coarse as these last words are, there is

56. TICHONIUS. '^y He who hath not the wedding garment, here, is shut out from the guests, and is cast into darkness, i.e. into hardness of heart, until he go down to the fire for eternity.'

57. S. PAULINUS. '^z Let us die here to sins, lest we live there to punishment. For that which is called the second death, is nothing else than a life of punishment. Let us beware then of the lower hell [inferiore inferno] where Gehenna will torture soul and body, the soul of the sinner dying eternally, the sense abiding and the matter of corruption lasting. For the dead, as is written, shall rise incorrupt, in an immortality, not of glory, but of punishment.'

In his poems he says of the wicked, '^a Life will be to these, without end to die; and death, to live to punishment.'

58. S. AUGUSTINE A.D. 396. His belief has been already incidentally stated. One passage may be set down for the variety of the subjects which it embraces.

'^b After the resurrection, when the general Judgement hath been made and finished, then shall the two kingdoms have their accomplishment; the one, that is, the kingdom of Christ, the other, the kingdom of the devil; the one of the good, the other of the evil; either, however, both of angels and men. To the one there shall not be possible the will, to

---

no ground to suspect any evasion, which Petavius suggests to be possible. de Ang. iii. 8. 11. ^y de regulis. Bibl. Patr. T. vi. p. 66.
^z Ep. xl. ad Sanct. et Amandum, fin.
^a Poem. 32 de ob. Celsi pueri. l. 569.
^b Enchiridion c. iii. Short Treatises. p. 152. Oxf. Tr.

the other the power, of sinning, or any occasion of death; the one in eternal life living truly and happily, the other abiding unhappily in eternal death without the power of dying; since both are without end. Yet of these, continuing in their blessedness, will one man be in a higher state than another; of those in their misery, will one man be in a more tolerable state than another. For in vain certain, or rather very many, with human feelings compassionate the eternal punishment of the damned, and their continual torments without intermission, and so believe not that it will take place: not indeed in the way of opposing themselves to the divine Scriptures, but by softening, according to their own feelings, all the hard sayings, and by turning unto a more gentle meaning such things in them, as they think to be said rather to excite terror than as though true. For "God forgetteth not," they say, "to be gracious, neither will He in His anger shut up His tender mercies." This is indeed read in the sacred Psalm; and is understood without any doubt of those, who are called vessels of mercy, because that they themselves, not for their merits, but by the mercy of God, are set free from misery. Or if they think that this belongs to all, it is not therefore necessary that they think that their condemnation may have an end, concerning whom it is written, "And they shall go unto eternal punishment;" lest in this way it come to be thought, that an end will, one day, come to *their* happiness also, concerning whom on the other hand it is said, "But the just unto life eternal." But they may judge, if this pleases them, that the pains of the damned are at certain intervals of time in some measure mitigated. Seeing that even thus the wrath of God may be understood to abide on them, that is their condemnation itself, (for this is meant by the wrath of God, not any perturbation of the divine mind,) so that in His anger, that is, His anger continuing, He may yet "not shut up His tender mercies," not by putting an end to their eternal punishment, but by applying, or interposing between their tortures some alleviation. For neither does the Psalm say, to put an end to His anger, or, after His anger, but, *in* His anger. Which if it were alone the very least that there can be conceived; to perish from the kingdom of God, to be an exile from the City of God, to be an alien from the Life of God, to want "so great a multitude of God's sweetness which He hath laid up for them that fear Him, but hath wrought for them that hope in Him," is so great a punishment, that no torments, of which we know, can be compared to it, if it be eternal, and they continue through how many ages soever. There will therefore continue without end that eternal death of the damned, that is, alienation from the Life of God, and itself will be common to all, whatever men according to their human feelings may imagine concerning variety of punishments, or concerning relief or intermission of pains; as the eternal life of the Saints will remain in common the life of all, in whatever distinction of honours they harmoniously shine.'

S. Augustine states (which is the belief of the Church) that there are different degrees of suffering among the lost, as of glory among the saved; he pronounces no opinion upon any mitigation of suffering, but insists on the eternity of punishment, and that 'alienation from the life of God, which would be common to all, would be greater than any other suffering whatever.'

Origenism was not attractive to the practical Western mind. It seems that no one in the West, even if he held restitutionism, thought that Satan would be saved. S. Augustine asks,

'^c Why does [supposed] mercy flow to the whole human race and when it comes to the angelic, dry up? Yet they dare not to stretch further in compassionating, and to reach to the freeing the devil. But if any one dares, he surpasses those, and yet is found to err, so much the more unseemlily and the more perversely, against the right words of God, the more merciful he seems to himself to be.'

S. Augustine puts down, not abstract theories, but men's pleas for themselves, how, being bad men, they might, as they were, escape hell. He begins,

'^d There are also such, as I myself have experienced in my colloquies, who, while they seem to reverence Holy Scripture, are to be censured for their morals, and who, *maintaining their own cause*, ascribe to God much greater mercy towards the human race, than those others. For they say that God said truly beforehand of bad and unbelieving men that they are worthy of punishment, but that when it comes to judgement, mercy will prevail. For the merciful God will grant them to the prayers and intercessions of His saints.'

He sums up,

'These are chiefly maintaining their own cause,

^c de Civ. Dei. xxi. 17.   ^d Ib. c. 18. n. 1. init., n. 2 fin.

promising a false impunity to their own abandoned morals by a supposed general mercy of God to the human race.'

The other questions raised do not bear on the eternity of punishment in itself, but only on the exemption of certain classes from it. They are, 1) whether impunity of all sins is to be promised to all, in whatever heresy or impiety they have lived, if they have been baptized or partaken of the Body of Christ; or 2) to those only, who have been reborn among Catholics, although they have afterwards fallen into very many crimes and errors, or heresy or heathen idolatry; or 3) to those who abide in the Catholic faith, although they have lived exceeding ill; or 4) to those who give alms, but amidst their very alms live very wickedly.

This was, of course, only so much self-deceit! S. Augustine patiently tries to remove the veil off their eyes; yet so as to say, that they 'e try to go against the words of God, under the plea of greater mercy.' He himself speaks in no faltering tone, nor is there one word to shew, that he regards *that* as a matter, not of faith but of opinion, which he declares to be ''against the word of God' and which he held to have been condemned by the Church.

59. S. CHRYSOSTOM. His teaching is so full, so repeated, that it is difficult or rather impossible, by a few extracts, to give any adequate idea of it. The greater part of his Remains consisting of his sermons to his people at Antioch and Constantinople, we have more allusions to hell in him than in most fathers. We see any how, what he, with his practical wisdom

e De Civ. Dei. xxi. 24.   f Dr. Farrar Et. Hope p. 165.

and love of souls, thought to be best for his people. But we are set upon proving that S. Chrysostom did really believe what he took such pains to preach, and did preach so earnestly.

Dr. Farrar says[g], 'The doctrine of 'accommodation' οἰκονομία, συγκατάβασις) was too prevalent with some of the Fathers, and there is good reason to think that it influenced S. Chrysostom on this very question.'

The principle of 'accommodation' was that of our Lord, "I have yet many things to say unto you, but ye cannot bear them now." The Apostles were not prepared to receive His full teaching, until the Holy Ghost descended upon them. Yet on whatever subject this condescension to human infirmity was to be used, its limit was, in not declaring, as yet, all the truth on a given subject; never in saying what was untrue.

It is a somewhat circuitous office to shew that a very eloquent writer, who brought himself into trouble by his eloquent declamation against the vices of the Court, did not really mean what he continually preached. Perhaps it may be best to illustrate what he does lay down, by some of his sermons in which he mentions the subject.

Whether at Antioch or Constantinople, he had to teach those who were very like ourselves. They were worldly, self-indulgent, luxurious; and because the thought of hell is inconsistent with worldly lives, they tried to persuade themselves that there is none [h]; that God's word about it was impossible,

[g] Et. Hope p. 95, 96. note.
[h] 'Seest thou the drift of this satanical argument? how, instead of men, he [the devil] wishes to make us brutes, or rather, wild beasts, or rather dæmons. Let us not then

hyperbolical¹; or that hell is milder and only temporary ʲ; or that unbelievers only fall into it ᵏ.

He appeals to them whether, thinking of God's be persuaded by him. For there is a Judgement, O wretched and miserable man! I know whence thou comest to use such words.—Thou hast committed many sins, thou hast offended, thou hast no confidence, thou thinkest that the very nature of things will even follow thy words. Meanwhile, saith he, I will not torment my soul with the expectation of hell, I will persuade it that there is none; meanwhile I will live here in luxury.' Hom. ii. on Col. i. 14. p. 207. [The Oxf. Tr. has been used for S. Chrysostom throughout.]

¹ ' "But whosoever shall say, Thou fool, shall be in danger of hell fire." To many this commandment hath appeared grievous and galling, if for a mere word we are really to pay so great a penalty. And some even say that it was spoken rather hyperbolically. But I fear lest, when we have deceived ourselves with words here, we may in deeds there suffer that extreme punishment.... As yet these are no great things; for the punishments are *here*. Therefore for him who calleth 'fool' He hath added the fire of Hell, now for the first time mentioning the name of hell.... Again I set another punishment, the council. If thou overlook even this, and proceed to that which is more grievous, I visit thee no longer with these finite punishments, but with the undying penalty of Hell, lest after this thou shouldest break forth even to murder.' Hom. xvi. on S. Matt. v. 22. pp. 241, 242.

'When we say that he who calleth his brother a fool shall depart into hell-fire, others say, 'What? Is he that calls his brother a fool to depart into hell fire?' 'Impossible,' say they. And again, when we say that the covetous man is an idolater, in this too again they make abatements, and say, the expression is hyperbolical.' Hom. xviii. on Eph. v. 5, 6. init.

'ʲ There are many men, who form good hopes, not by abstaining from their sins, but by thinking that hell is not so terrible as it is said to be, but milder than what is threatened, and temporary, not eternal; and about this they philosophise much!' Hom. iii. on 2 Thess. i. 9, 10. init.

'ᵏ Yea,' you say, 'but that there *is* a hell, every body sees. But the unbelievers only are to fall into it.' Hom. xxxi. on Rom. xvi. 16. p. 497.

present judgements, '¹ wilt thou not even suspect against thy will that there is a hell?' 'ᵐ Where then are they who, with all this great exactness in view, yet will not allow that there is a hell?'

The whole minds of some of them were set against it. He treats them like children who had to be managed. He will approach them, so that they will be least restive.

He teaches, how gently people must be approached, as by the mention of the temporal sufferings of others, and so, while their minds were intent on this, to introduce the mention of Hell ⁿ.

His allusions to it occur in all his courses of sermons, but at times he only suggests the thought to their mind, and tells them that he is content that it should be brought there, and so leaves them. It will do good to their souls º.

'¹ When therefore you see one who has been guilty of the same things as they, or even much worse, and yet not suffering punishment, wilt thou not suspect, even against thy will, that there is a hell?' Hom. viii. on 1 Thess. iv. 18. p. 424.
ᵐ Hom. xxxi. on Rom. xvi. 16. p. 495.
'ⁿ All these things let us speak as in pity for the deceased, and as depreciating things present; in order that by fear and by pity we may soften the cruel mind. And when we see men shrinking into themselves at these narrations, then, and not till then, let us introduce to their notice also the doctrine of hell, not as terrifying these, but in compassion for others. And let us say, But why speak of these things present? For far indeed will our concern be from ending with these; a yet more grievous punishment will await all such persons: even a river of fire, and a poisonous worm, and darkness interminable, and undying tortures. If with such address we succeed in throwing a spell over them, we shall correct both ourselves and them, and quickly get the better of our infirmity.' Hom. xi. on 1 Cor. iv. 5. p. 146.

'º On this subject I will rather discourse at some other

He checks himself at times, telling them,

'ᵖ The thoughts concerning Hell and the Kingdom ye are not yet able to hear.'

He tells them that he himself trembles at having to speak of hell, that his heart is troubled and throbs at it ᑫ, but that he cannot help himself; that he must teach them of hell, that they may not fall into it. 'ʳ Let us then continually employ ourselves with talking about these things. For to remember hell prevents our falling into hell.'

To soothe his speaking to them of it, he tells them of the awe, in which he himself stands of the Judgement-seat of Christ and of the eternal doom, since he should have to give account for them, as well as for himself ˢ, but that he *must* so speak.

He tells them that he knew that he was paining

season, that we may not confuse the discourse concerning hell. In the mean time let not that slip, which we have gained. For it is no small advantage to be persuaded concerning hell. For the recollection of such discourses, like some bitter medicine, will be able to clear every vice, if it be constantly settled in our mind.' Hom. viii. on 1 Thess. iv. 18. p. 425.

ᵖ Hom. xxviii. on S. Matt. viii. 34. fin.

'ᑫ For indeed my heart is troubled and throbs, and the more I see the account of hell confirmed, the more do I tremble and shrink through fear. But it is necessary to say these things, lest we fall into hell.' Hom. ix. on 1 Cor. iii. 1, 2. p. 115.

ʳ Hom. xxxi. on Rom. xvi. 16. p. 497.

'ˢ I say not these things as merely wishing to terrify you, nor to lay a burden on your souls, but to make them wise and render them easier. I could wish also myself, that there were no punishment—yes, myself most of all men. And why so? Because whilst each of you fears for his own soul, I shall have to answer for this office, in which I preside over you. So that most of all it is impossible for me to escape. But it cannot be, that there

them by speaking of hell [t], but what could he do? that to speak of hell was the way to save them from hell [u]; flattery of God that He was so merciful that He would not punish, was the devil's language; and the suggestion that there was no hell, was the device of Satan, in order to draw them down into it [v]; that the denial of hell is '[x] Satanic reasoning,' '[y] a Satanic notion.'

is not punishment and a hell. What can I do?' Hom. viii. on 1 Thess. iv. 18. pp. 424, 425.

'[t] I know that I am galling you and giving you pain by these words, but what can I do? I would fain not speak thus; but since we are in sins the more part of us, who will give me ability to pain you indeed, and to penetrate the understanding of them that hear me? Then might I so be at rest.' Hom. xliii. on S. Matt. xii. 43—45. p. 605.

[u] see below pp. 259-261.

'[v] For when thou sayest that God is merciful, and doth not punish, if He *should* punish, He will be found in thy case to be no longer merciful. See then into what language the devil leadeth you.' Hom. xxv. on Rom. xiv. 13. p. 429.

'[v] How is it, that thou dost not see who is the teacher of these evil doctrines? For he who deceived the first man and, under the pretext of greater hopes, threw them out even of the blessings they had in possession, he it is who now suggests the saying and fancying these things. And for this reason he persuades some to suspect there is no hell, that he may thrust them into hell. As God on the other hand threatened hell, and made hell ready, that by coming to know of it, thou mightest so live, as not to fall into it.' Ib. p. 430.

[x] Hom. viii. on 1 Thess. iv. 18. p. 418.

[y] He is speaking of the heathen, 'Yea, and what of the torments of hell?' They too are but a fable. And mark the Satanic notion,—When they are told of gods who are fornicators, they deny that these are fables, but believe them. Yet whenever any shall discourse to them of punishment, 'these,' they say, 'are poets, men who turn everything into fable, that man's happy condition may be on all sides overturned.' Hom. xii. on Eph. iv. 17. p. 241.

He tells them that their favourite vices lead them to hell; that covetousness, 'the beloved object,' is '[z]the friend of hell, the enemy of the kingdom of heaven.'

He tells them that he is obliged continually to repeat his teaching, if so be he might profit them a little[a].

He tells them;

'[b] It is impossible, yea impossible for an avaricious man ever to see the Face of Christ. For this, is hell appointed; for this, fire; for this, that river of fire; for this, the worm that dieth not. I know that many hear me say these things with pain, and indeed it is not without pain I say them. But why need I say these things? I could wish the things concerning the Kingdom to be ever my discourse. But what shall I do? . . It is for this cause that I am continually speaking of these things, that we may the sooner pass over to those other. For for this cause did God threaten hell, that none may fall into hell, that all may obtain the Kingdom: for this cause we too make mention continually of hell. . . . Be not then displeased at the heaviness of our words. Better it is that ye be burned for a little space by our words than for ever in that flame.'

'[c] Such are their circumstances in this world; but

[z] Hom. xxiii. on 1 Cor. x. 12. p. 323.

[a] 'There is no pardon, no not any, for him who does not perform works of mercy. These things we say to you continually, that we may effect, if it be but a little, by the continued repetition; these things we say, not caring so much for those who receive the benefits as for yourselves.' Hom. xxxi. on Heb. xii. 17. p. 365.

[b] Hom. vi. on Phil. ii. 5-8. p. 73.

[c] Hom. xiii. on 1 Cor. x. 10-12. p 322.

those in the next, what discourse shall exhibit? the intolerable furnaces, the rivers burning with fire, the gnashing of teeth, the chains never to be loosed, the envenomed worm, the rayless gloom, the never-ending miseries. Let us fear them, beloved, let us fear the fountain of so great punishments, the destroyer of our salvation. For it is impossible at the same time to love both money, and your soul.'

'd Him that has done *thee* no wrong, whom thou art able to deliver, him thou neglectest. How shall He forgive thee, who art sinning against Him? Is not this deserving of hell?

'e Let us make then to ourselves friends of the mammon of unrighteousness. Let us do works of mercy; let us exhaust our possessions upon them, that so we may exhaust that fire; that we may quench it, that we may have boldness there.'

'f What can be more grievous than hell? Yet nothing is more profitable than the fear of it; for the fear of hell will bring us the crown of the kingdom. Where fear is, there is no envy; the love of money does not disturb; where fear is, anger is quenched, evil concupisence is repressed, and every unreasonable passion is exterminated.'

Our Lord said, "he that saith to his brother, Thou fool, shall be in danger of hell-fire."

S. Chrysostom repeats;

'g We are ever ready to make accusations, prepared for condemning. Even if no other evil thing had

---

d Hom. xi. on Heb. vi. 20 p. 145.
e Hom. i. on Heb. i. 3, 4. p. 16.
On the Statues, Hom. xv. p. 249.   g Hom. xxi. on Heb. xi. p. 250.

been done by us, this were sufficient to ruin us, and to carry us away to hell.'

Our Lord condemned the slothful servant.
S. Chrysostom says,

'ʰ They, who, though they have no evil indeed to be charged with, yet have omitted to do any good they might have done, will be hurried away with them that have done evil into hell-fire, unless one might indeed say this, that the very not doing good is a part of wickedness, inasmuch as it comes of indolence.'

'ⁱ And often not only from a bad life, but from one defect, we enter into Hell, where there are not good qualities to balance it.... Those who were pronounced accursed in the words, "Depart from Me, ye cursed, into everlasting fire,' were not accused of any such crimes, but because they had not fed Christ. Seest thou, how a failure in almsgiving is enough to cast a man into hell fire?'

If we 'ʲ shew no fruit, fire awaits us, even that of Hell and flame unquenchable.'

'ᵏ These things I say continually, and I will not cease to say them, not so much because I care for the poor, as because I care for your souls. For they will have some comfort, if not from you.... But none can rescue you from hell, if you obtain not the help of the poor,—we shall say to you what was said to the rich man, who was continually broiling, yet gained no comfort.'

ʰ Hom. xvi. on Eph. iv. 32. p. 276.
ⁱ Hom. vi. on 2 Tim. ii. 25, 6 pp. 221, 222.
ʲ Hom. xx. on Heb. x. 26, 27. p. 233.
ᵏ Hom. xxvii. on S. John iii. 16 fin. p. 228.

'[1] As many then, as do not believe there is a Hell, let them call these things to mind: as many as think to sin without being punished, let them take account of these things.'

If, after all this, any one can think that S. Chrysostom did not believe what he preached so earnestly, and, he says, unceasingly; which he had pains to induce his people to listen to [m]; which he wished them not to put out of sight [n]; that, whilst he spoke of endless [o] undying [p] punishment, he himself believed that the punishment would end; that, while he spoke of an ever-lengthened torture [q], he only believed in one which would end; that while he preached to them, that there would not be any release [r], he himself believed that there would be a release; that he enforced upon them, notwithstanding their repugnance [s], what he did not himself believe; one can only say that they treat him, in fact, as they do his Master, and accuse him of using language

[1] Hom. xxxi. on Heb. xii. 17. p. 360.
[m] 'Whence then shall I persuade you?' Hom. viii. on 1 Thess. iv. 18. p. 418 sqq.   [n] See below p. 260.
[o] below p. 265.   [p] below pp. 264, 265.
[q] Hom. xii. on Acts v. 1-16. p. 174. see below p. 264.
[r] Hom. xxv. on Rom. xiv. 13. p. 427.
'[s] There is therefore a hell, O man! and God is good.— Aye, did you shudder at hearing these horrors? [those related by Josephus, prophesied by our Lord.] But these which take place here, are nothing in comparison with what shall be in that world. Once more I am compelled to seem harsh, disagreeable, stern. But what can I do? I am set to this . . . to those to whom we do good, we seem stern and severe, troublesome and disagreeable. For we do good, not by the pleasure we give, but by the pain we inflict.' Hom. v. on Acts ii. 14-21. p. 75.

which would obviously mislead. Such an one must, I suppose, be so taken up with his preconceived prejudice, that no Father can have held the faith of eternal punishment, that he cannot understand the heart of S. Chrysostom and his earnestness, and would rather impute to him the immorality of teaching earnestly what he did not believe himself.

I will subjoin a long passage, because it contains such a variety of topics of his teaching.

'ᵗ He indeed who is exceedingly virtuous is induced neither by fear nor by the prospect of the Kingdom, but for Christ's sake alone, as was the case with Paul. But let us even thus consider the blessings of the Kingdom, the miseries of hell, and so regulate and school ourselves, so bring ourselves to the things that are to be practised. When you see any thing good and great in the present life, think of the Kingdom and you will consider it as nothing. When you see any thing terrible, think of hell, and you will deride it. When you are possessed by carnal desire, think of the fire, think also of the pleasure of sin itself, that it is nothing worth, that it has not even pleasure in it. For if the fear of the laws that are enacted here has so great power, as even to withdraw us from wicked actions, much more should the remembrance of things future, the vengeance that is immortal, the punishment that is everlasting: if the fear of an earthly king withdraws us from so many evil deeds, how much more the fear of the King Eternal? Whence then may we constantly have this fear? If we continually hearken to the Scriptures.

ᵗ Hom. ii. on 1 Thess. i. 8. pp. 475—480.

For if the sight only of a dead body so depresses the mind, how much more must hell and the fire unquenchable, how much more the worm that never dieth! If we always think of hell, we shall not soon fall into it. For this reason God has threatened punishment. If the thought of it were not attended with great advantage, God would not have threatened it: but because the remembrance of it is able to work great good, for this reason He has put into our souls the terror of it, as a wholesome medicine. Let us not then overlook the great advantage arising from it, but let us continually advert to it, at our dinners, at our suppers..... He who converses about hell incurs no dangers, and renders it more sober. But dost thou fear the offensiveness of such words? Hast thou then, if thou art silent, extinguished hell? or if thou speakest of it, hast thou kindled it? Whether thou speakest of it or not, the fire will boil forth. Let it be continually spoken of, that thou mayest never fall into it. It is not possible that a soul anxious about hell should readily sin. For hear the most excellent advice, "Remember," he says, "thy latter end and thou shalt never do amiss." A soul that is fearful of giving account cannot but be slow to transgression; for fear, being vigorous in the soul, does not permit anything worldly to exist in it. For if discourse, raised concerning hell, so humbles and brings it low, does not the reflection constantly dwelling upon the soul purify it more than any fire? Let us not remember the kingdom so much as hell. For fear has more power than the promise. And I know that many would despise ten thousand blessings, if they were rid of the punishment, inasmuch as it is even now sufficient for me to escape vengeance, and not be punished. No one of those who have hell before their eyes will fall into hell. No one of those who despise hell will escape hell. . . . It is a great evil to despise a threat. He who despises threatening will soon have experience of it in reality. Nothing is so profitable as to converse concerning hell. It renders our souls purer than any silver. For hear the prophet saying, "Thy judgements are always before me." And Christ also constantly discourses concerning it. For although it pains the hearer, it benefits him very much. . . . Let us not not then avoid discourses concerning hell, that we may avoid hell. Let us not banish the remembrance of punishment, that we may escape punishment. If the rich man had reflected upon that fire, he would not have sinned; but because he never was mindful of it, therefore he fell into it. . . . Wherefore, I beseech you, let us even now become watchful; let us keep hell before our eyes; let us consider that inexorable Account, that, thinking of those things, we may both avoid vice, and may be able to obtain the blessings promised to those who love Him, by the grace and loving-kindness of our Lord.'

Or look at the sympathy of these words. Do they look like sympathising about a thing which he thought unreal?

'ᵘ Hell, I confess, is intolerable, yea, very intolerable, but more intolerable than it, is the loss of the Kingdom . . . If in the case of men, it were a bitter thing to fall away from this glory, much more is it

ᵘ Hom. xiii. on Phil. iv. 23. pp. 153-5.

so with God, when all the heavenly Powers are present with the King, when the dæmons, bound and bowing down their heads, and the devil himself, and all might that opposeth itself, are led along in chains, when the Powers of the heavens, when He Himself, cometh upon the clouds.'

'Believe me, I have been unable to finish my words, from the grief which had hold of my soul at this relation. Consider of how great glory we shall be deprived, when it is in our power not to be deprived of it. For this is the misery, that we suffer these things, when it is in our power not to suffer them. When He receiveth the one part and leadeth to His Father in heaven, and rejecteth the other, the Angels take them, and drag them against their will, weeping and hanging down their heads, to the fire of hell, when they have first been made a spectacle to the whole world, what grief, think you, is there? Let us then make haste, while there is yet time, and take great thought of our own salvation. ... Here, thou art afflicted for a little time; rather, thou dost not perceive thy affliction, knowing that thou art afflicted for thy good. But there, the affliction is more bitter, because it has no hope, no escape in view, but is without limit, and for ever.'

He reminds them that they will never be able to forget their own evil deeds, nay, that they will see them more vividly than here, and that the memory of them will be then harder than all Gehenna and unspeakable torment.

'ᵛ If there were no streams of fire, no horrible

ᵛ quoted by Dorotheus the Archimandrite. Doctrina xii. Bibl. Patr. v. 927.

dæmons, there but only that, of those judged, on some should be bestowed the glory and triumph of heaven, the others be left inglorious and dishonoured, that they should not see the glory of the Lord; this pain, this shame, this confusion surpasses every sort of torment, all Gehenna. Besides there is the vain grief over themselves, the gnawing of conscience, and the most bitter memory of evil deeds, all which are harder than unspeakable torments. For souls remember there, what they have done in this life, words, actions, desires, concupiscences; none of them can they ever forget.—Thoughts of this world perish, when the soul goes forth from the body. Souls there neither remember nor care for any of these things. But what it did right or wrong, all these it remembers; none of these can it lose. Yea, when it has laid aside this earthly body, it perceives, acknowledges, understands every thing more clearly and in brighter light.'

I must add passages, at which some will take offence, but S. Chrysostom had to preach them to persons, as fastidious as we are, and yet he shrank not; nor would our people (I speak from experience [w],) rebel against them, if we dreaded not the fastidiousness of the fastidious.

In the early part of this century such sermons were favourite sermons with the poor, because they were stirred up by them to reverent and awe-stricken thoughts.

[w] After a sermon which was (I am told) terrific, founded on the literal meaning of Holy Scripture, on the 'pains of sense,' the only observation made by two 'commercial travellers' who happened to be in the Church, was, 'Why were we not told all this before?'

'ˣ Many like things are done now as were done before the Flood, yet no flood has been sent: because there is a hell threatened, and vengeance. Many sin, as the people did in Sodom, yet no rain of fire has been poured down; because a river of fire is prepared. Many go the lengths of Pharaoh; yet they have not fared like Pharaoh, they have not been drowned in a Red Sea: for the sea that awaits them, is the sea of the bottomless pit, where the punishment is not accompanied with insensibility, where there is no suffocation to end all, but in ever-lengthened torture, in burning, in strangling, they are consumed there. Many have offended like the Israelites, but no serpents have devoured them; there awaits them the worm that never dieth.'

'ʸ Seest thou how it is more intolerable than this fire? For it is not quenched. Yea therefore it is called unquenchable. Let us then consider, how great a misery it must be to be for ever burning, and to be in darkness, and to utter unnumbered groanings, and to gnash the teeth, and not even to be heard.'

'ᶻ Here he is speaking of Hell and of the punishment [in store for the wicked] the being delivered to an everlasting hell, and to undying punishment and vengeance.'

'ᵃ Let us be continually in mind of the aweful judgement-seat, of the stream of fire, of the chains never to be loosed, of the darkness with no light, the gnashing of teeth, the venomous worm.'

ˣ Hom. xii. on Acts v. 1—16 p. 174.
ʸ Hom. i. on Heb. i. 3, 4. p. 15.   ᶻ Hom. vi. on Heb. iii. 14. p. 82.
ᵃ Hom. xxv. on Rom. xiv. 13. p. 424.

'ᵇWhat wouldst thou that we should compare with those fearful things? What with the unquenchable fire? with the never-ending worm? Which of the things here canst thou name as equal, in comparison, with the gnashing of teeth, with the chains, with the outer darkness, with the wrath, the tribulation, the anguish? But as to duration? Why, what are ten thousand years to ages boundless and without end? Not so much as one little drop to the boundless ocean.'

'ᶜIf we shall depart into the next world with corruption about us like this, we have that corruption incorruptible and endless. For to be ever burning and never consumed, and to be ever being wasted by the worm, is corruption incorruptible; like as was the case with the blessed Job; he was corrupted and died not. Some such torment as this shall the soul undergo then, when the worms surround and devour it, not for two years, nor for three, nor for ten, nor for ten thousand, but for years without end; for "their worm," He saith, "dieth not."'

'ᵈA river of fire rolls before Him, the undying worm, unquenchable fire, outer darkness, gnashing of teeth. Although you should be angry with me ten thousand times for mentioning these things, I shall not cease from mentioning them. *There* is punishment, deathless, unallayed, and no one to stand up for us.'

'ᵉWhat are we, if we fail of that spectacle, if no

ᵇ Hom. xxviii. on Heb. xii. 3. p. 329.
ᶜ Hom. xxiv. on Eph. vi. 24. p. 382.
ᵈ Hom. ix. on 1 Thess. v. 11. p. 438.
ᵉ Hom. xii. on S. John i. 14. p. 100.

one grant us then to behold our Lord? If those who see not the light of the sun endure a life more bitter than any death, what is it likely that they who are deprived of that Light must suffer?.... But now we must look also for other vengeance. For he who beholds not that light must not only be led into darkness, but must be burned continually, and waste away, and gnash his teeth, and suffer ten thousand other dreadful things. Let us then not permit ourselves, by making this brief time a time of carelessness and remissness, to fall into everlasting punishment; but let us watch and be sober, let us do all things, and make it all our business to attain to that felicity, and to keep far from that river of fire, which rushes with a loud roaring before the terrible judgement-seat. For he who has been once cast in there must remain for ever; there is no one to deliver him from his punishment.'

'[f] It is said, he found a release. But the case is not so with the other life. For that *there*, there will never be any release, hear from His own mouth, 'Their worm will not die, nor their fire be quenched.' 'And these shall go into everlasting life, but these into everlasting punishment.' Now if the life be eternal, the punishment is eternal.'

60. S. CHROMATIUS, BISHOP OF AQUILEIA, A.D. 401. S. Jerome writes to him, '[g] my Chromatius, thou most holy and most learned of Bishops.'

'[h] To mutilate the body profits nothing to amend

[f] Hom. xxv. on Rom. xiv. 13. p. 427.
[g] Præf. ad Paralip.
[h] on Matt. c. 5 de octo beatitudinibus. Conc. i. Bibl. Patr. v. 983.

an evil mind, in which is a whole whirlpool of vices. Nay, we see many, sightless or weak in body, who yet do not cease from vices. Wherefore the Lord commands us to cut away these members of the vices of an evil mind and depraved thought, for the kingdom of Heaven's sake; lest if the vices gain the mastery, both body and soul, that is, the whole man, should, for his guilt, become liable to the eternal fire.'

'¹Woe unto him who, when he falleth, hath no one to raise him up, i.e. because the flesh to which, for its unfaithfulness, the fellowship of the Spirit is not vouchsafed, is not raised aloft to eternal life, but is raised to perpetual punishment by Him Who is the Judge of quick and dead.'

61. S. ASTERIUS, BISHOP OF AMASEA, A.D. 401.

'ᵏ When that voice shall be heard, "Give account of thy stewardship," shew, how thou didst obey His commands, how thou didst act towards thy fellow-servants, whether gently and kindly and mercifully, —or defrauding them of the due portion of alms. If he could win the favour of God, and prove himself a good servant, well. If not, what is there laid up are not scourges or stripes, nor an obscure prison, nor iron chains, but an unextinguishable fire, but perpetual darkness with no interval of light, but gnashing of teeth, as the Gospel itself of old hath borne witness to us. If thou wert never to be stripped of these earthly goods, as being Another's, come, enjoy the world, and with full liberty and the aid of all thy senses, indulge in pleasure; but if all these things are to come to an end, and their enjoyment is to be

¹ ib. col. 1.   ᵏ In Divitem et Lazarum. Bibl. Patr v. 812.

allowed us but for a short time, let us fear, brethren, that day, when we must go forth, and let us pass the time of our sojourning according to the commands of God.'

62. VICTOR OF ANTIOCH, contemporary of S. Chrysostom.

He held distinctly that the punishment of the worm is to be spiritual, not corporeal; he held equally, that punishments would be endless.

'[1] He [our Lord] alleges in proof an oracle of the Prophet Isaiah, in which it is said that the worm of the ungodly will never die. For it is heavier than any punishment to bear about with one perpetually that deathless worm, without any intermission eagerly devouring and terribly gnawing. But by this 'worm' is designated an impure and wicked conscience, seeing that this pricks and gnaws the sinful soul, conscious of no good, with the stings of an useless regret, like a devouring worm. Every wicked man will be an accuser of himself. For while he shall continually weigh and revolve in his mind, what he did wickedly in this mortal life, he will be compelled against his will to own himself guilty, driven by the stings of conscience and openly convicted by its testimony against himself. In this sense then, the worm of sinners is said to be deathless; for what is here said of the 'worm' must not be transferred to any worm which should be an object of sense, which in hell should gnaw the hearts of the ungodly.'

"And their fire is not quenched." 'As the fire which burns sinners is elsewhere called eternal, so it

[1] on S. Mark ix. 44. Bibl. Patr. iv. 393.

is here called quenchless. But there are those who, by this unquenchable fire, suppose the judgement or estimate of a polluted and wicked conscience to be designated. Because that judgement, through and because of the deathless worm, like raging fire, ever feeds upon their inmost self.'

63. PELAGIUS, heretic, A.D. 405. His belief, and his rejection of Origenism, have been already stated in his own words [m].

64. S. ISIDORE OF PELUSIUM, A.D. 412. '[n] If ye neither long for the everlasting life with Christ, nor dread the judgement of the eternal flame, you either vie in contempt with the dæmons, or are mere phantoms of men, soulless and irrational and destitute of any sense of fear.'

'[o] Why carriest thou books in vain, and by thy acts castest aside their meaning? For when the Lord condemns the curious gaze—thou, as I know, lovest an enslaved life, taking a harlot as thy companion, and loving the eternal fire.'

'If no law marked thee out, nor order of war armed thee nor divine oracle sent thee to shed the blood of thy compatriot, (rather it bids to love our enemies) it were better for thee to expiate thy blood-stained hands, and give thine own blood to be shed, than retain the guilt in thy mind, and keep it for the tribunals there, and everlasting suffering.'

'[q] If any one ask, what we shall be when we return to life from death, the Lord sheweth when He

[m] Ab. p. 135. [n] Epp. L. i. ep. 223. Zosimo Eustathio Maroni.
[o] Ib. Ep. 234 Amazonio.
[p] Ib. Ep. 297 Eulampio, who had shed blood.
[q] Ep. 416 Timotheo Lectori.

saith, "the righteous shall go to life eternal, but sinners to eternal punishment."'

The above are taken from the first book of the Epistles, but shew, how the doctrine was urged in individual intercourse of the Bishop with those, chiefly bad men, under his charge. They are not all.

65. S. CYRIL OF ALEXANDRIA, A.D. 412. "*r* Our Lord therefore being good and gracious, as it is written, both bears with those who dishonour Him and aids those who insult Him, and is found, as God, superior to all the littleness of man. Yet does He, for their good, threaten to depart from them, and says plainly, "I go My way," that He may implant in them a more resolved mind, and that He may whet them on, considering that they ought not to leave their Redeemer, when present, frustrate of His work, to pass on to the faith, and may make them now at length more ready unto obedience. And having cried out, "I go My way," and threatened departure from the whole nation, He subjoined suggestively the damage therefrom ensuing unto them. For (He says) "Ye shall die in your sins;" and we shall see the nature of the thing bringing in the truth of what is said. For they who did not at all receive Him Who came to us from Heaven, that He might justify all through faith, how shall they not beyond all contradiction die in their sins, and not receiving Him Who can cleanse them, how will they not have the defilement from their impiety lasting? For to die unredeemed, yet laden with the weight of sin, to whom is it doubtful where this will conduct the soul of man? For deep Hades will, I

---

r Comm. on S. John Lib. V. c. viii. 21. p. 580. Oxf. Tr.

deem, receive such an one, and he will continue in great darkness, yea he will inhabit fire and flames, with reason numbered among those, of whom it has been said by Prophet's voice, "Their worm shall not die neither shall their fire be quenched," and they shall be for a sight to all flesh.'

66. S. MAXIMUS, BISHOP OF TURIN A.D. 422. 'ˢ A man very intent on Holy Scripture and an able teacher of the people.'

'ᵗSo blessed Laurence passed through the fire, from which, when burned, he did not shrink, but shone illumined by it; he passed through earthly fire which is for a moment, but escaped the fire of Gehenna which consumeth eternally.'

'ᵘ Remission of sins is specially to be believed, brethren, because this is the one remedy, which frees the race of man from the sentence of perpetual death.'

'ˣ Consider then the impending Day of Judgement and the quenchless flames of Gehenna, the dreadful gnashing of teeth, the last torment of darkness.'

'ʸ No one falls more grievously than he who, having heard the word of God, turns to sins, on account of which eternal punishments are prepared.'

'ᶻ The Holy Spirit operateth in that water, that they who before Baptism were held guilty of divers sins and were to burn with the devil in the Gehenna of eternal fire, after Baptism should be found worthy to enter into the kingdom of heaven.'

ˢ Gennadius, a contemporary, de Virr Ill. c. 40.
ᵗ Hom. 76 in Nat. S. Laur. p. 243 Rome 1784.
ᵘ Hom. 83. de traditione Symboli, Opp. p. 272.
ˣ Hom. 117. p. 388. ʸ Tract 1. de Bapt. Opp. p. 711.
ᶻ Tract 2 p. 713. add ib. p 716.

'ᵃ He therefore does not always punish those who despise Him, because He has decreed that a Judgement should be hereafter, where eternal condemnation and perpetual punishment is reserved for sinners, where will be weeping of eyes and gnashing of teeth, where, as the Lord Himself says, "Their worm shall not die, and their fire shall not be quenched."'

67. THEODORET. 'ᵇ That Thou mayest give him rest from evil days. He calleth everlasting punishment the evil day.'

'ᶜ Immortal is the fruition of the just, and the punishment of sinners.'

'ᵈ He (S. Paul) saith that it is just and suitable to the lawgiver of justice, both to reward us for our sufferings for the faith, and to inflict the opposite punishments on ungodliness. And this will be at the time of the end. For then the Lord cometh from heaven, and the tribes of the angels before Him, and those encompassed with the darkness of unbelief shall be given over to the unquenchable fire. He expresses more exactly the greatness of punishment, calling it 'eternal.''

'ᵉ Just is the judgement of God, and my hardheartedness does not procure for God the glory of loving-kindness. For it would be the height of injustice, that they who promoted His glory, should incur judgement from Him and endure everlasting punishment.'

He too speaks of souls "ᶠ who have not yet obtained

ᵃ Tract 3. p. 720.   ᵇ on Ps. xciii. 13. [xciv. 13 Eng.]
   ᶜ on Is. lxv. 20.   ᵈ on 2 Thess. i. 7—9.
ᵉ on Rom. iii. 7.   ᶠ on Cant. vi 7. Opp. ii. 127 Schultze.

freedom, but still are willing to serve, and for fear of Gehenna, fulfil the laws of God.'

68. CASSIAN began to write at 73, A.D. 424. He was a Semi-pelagian. One work, chiefly against the 7 deadly sins, is full of practical wisdom. Prosper wrote by name against another work of his.

'g These indications will very chiefly shew, that the deadly contagion of vain-glory cleaves to us. Which we shall most readily escape, if we consider that we shall not only wholly lose the fruit of our labours, whatsoever we have done with any purpose of vain-glory, but shall also become guilty of a great offence, and shall, as sacrilegious, incur eternal punishment, inasmuch as we chose to wrong God by doing for man a work which we ought to have done with a view to God, and so are convicted by Him Who knows the secrets of the heart, of having preferred men to God, and the glory of the world to the glory of God.'

69. S. PETER CHRYSOLOGUS (so named for his eloquence) Bishop of Ravenna A.D. 433.

'h We believe in eternal life, because after the resurrection there is no end either of good or ill.'

70. SEDULIUS, about A.D. 434. 'i There seems to be a fourfold variety in all iniquity or righteousness; the seed, the tree, the end, the fruit. The Seed is the good or evil thought; the Tree, the good or evil will; the Fruit are the works of righteousness or unrighteousness, of justification or uncleanness; the end is, death or life eternal.—There are

g Cassian de cœnob. institt. L. xi. c. 18.
h Serm. 60. de Symbolo Apost. B. P. vii. 892.
i in Ep. ad Rom. c. vi. fin. Bibl. Patr. vi. 513.

five kinds of death. The first is the separation of the soul from the body. The second, the separation of the soul from God, which comes through sin. The third, that the Devil, the author of death itself, is called death. The fourth death is named the lake of hell, in which sinful souls are kept. There is also that praiseworthy death, whereby each dies to sin, and is buried together with Christ.'

71. S. Proclus, disciple of S. Chrysostom, Patriarch of Constantinople A.D. 436.

'O perverse counsel of Judas! O madness of Judas, who had heard from Christ the Author and Teacher of life, "What doth it profit a man, if he gains the whole world, and lose his own soul or be cast away?" Yet taking pleasure for a brief time in the thirty pieces of silver, he betrayed to the ungodly, Christ the Giver of life, and made over his own soul to eternal punishment. Therefore also our Lord Jesus Christ said, "Woe unto that man, by whom the Son of man is betrayed; good had it been that he had never been born!"'

72. Valerian, Bishop of Cimies, A.D. 439. '[1] If thou willest not to face judgement to come, turn aside from evil and do good.—Those guilty persons, whom that temporal judgement does not afflict, that judgement pursues for eternity with unexhausted pangs of sufferings.'

'[m] If we knew how to maintain due reverence to His laws, Gehenna would receive none, the punishment of perpetual death would condemn none.'

[k] Orat. x. in Sanctam Quintam Feriam, Bibl. Patr. vi. 604.
[l] Hom. i. Bibl. Patr. viii. 500.
[m] Hom. xix. Ib. p. 520.

73. EUSEBIUS GALLICANUS, A.D. 449. '[n] To such it is said, "go into the everlasting fire, prepared for the devil and his angels." Of such it is declared, "It is a fearful thing to fall into the hands of the living God." Of such the Evangelist witnesseth, "Every tree which beareth not good fruit shall be cut down and cast into the fire." You see how it is a subject of condemnation, not only to have done evil, but not to have done good. Too late shall we be displeased with ourselves in sight of the eternal fire, which will search our bones and marrow and thoughts. What would every one, who is to be condemned, give, that he had never stained the garment of his body?—The burning pit of hell will be opened; there will be a going down, there will be no return. There, bared, will they be plunged for ever, to be cast into outer darkness; unhappily shut out, unhappily shut in. Of this pit the prophet speaks, "Let not the deep swallow me up, and let not the pit shut her mouth upon me." He said "shut her mouth upon me," because when it shall have received the guilty, it shall be shut above, opened below, enlarged in depth; no breathing place, no free breath shall be left, the bars pressing from above; they shall be thrust down there, bidding farewell to all living things. They will be known no more by God, who would not know God; to die to life, to live without end to death. Blessed they, who now act well, using their means, giving abundantly of their own; in themselves chaste, towards others bloodless, these save themselves from the fiery night of this depth.'

[n] de Epiph. Hom. iii. Bibl. Patr. T. vi. p. 625.

74. NILUS, A.D. 440. once Præfect of Constantinople, disciple of S. Chrysostom, afterwards a Monk.

'°Thou, who hast so many souls in thy charge, hast exiled virtue and chased it far away, and gladly buriest thy face in the darkness of wickedness and evil conversation, and castest the brethren into evil habits and storms and unceasing trouble, and art busy in destroying those who ought to be saved. And who then will ransom thee from everlasting destruction? For "it is a fearful thing to fall into the hands of the living God."'

'ᵖ Awake now, and cease thy great insatiableness, and turn to amendment and good deeds, before thou quit the tabernacle of the present world, where none of those who die in their transgressions will find room for defence, where neither friend nor slave nor relation shall be able to be thy advocate, or to help thee being punished for ever.'

'ᑫ That God may be all in all, a light to those worthy of light, but an avenging fire to those worthy of everlasting punishment.'

75. S. LEO, A.D. 440. 'ʳLest, through ignorance of the truth, the creature, formed in the image of God, should be driven to the precipices of perpetual death, He placed in the evangelical pages the character of His judgement, to recall all from the snares of that most crafty Enemy, it being now known to all, what rewards the good might hope for, what punishments the evil had to fear. For that incentor to sin and its author, who first fell through

° Epp. L. ii. 57 Platoni Archimandritæ p. 145 ed. Allat.
ᵖ Ep. ii. 147 Lycuɪgo (over-rapacious for his heir).
ᑫ Ep. i. 47 Dositheo.   ʳ Serm. ix. (de collectis iv.) c. l. pp. 30, 31.

his pride, and then in his envy injured, because he abode not in the truth, concentrated his strength in lies, and out of this most poisoned fountain of his skill brought forth all kinds of deceptions; that he might shut out the hope of human devotion from that good, which he had himself lost through his own pride, and might drag down to share in his own damnation, those to whose reconciliation he could not himself belong.'

's The just shall be separated from the unjust, the innocent from the guilty; and when the sons of mercy, after the rehearsal of works of mercy, shall have received the kingdom prepared for them, the unjust will be upbraided with the hardness of their barrenness; and those on the left, having nothing in common with those on the right, shall, by the condemnation of the Almighty Judge, be sent into the fire prepared for the torment of the devil and his angels, to have community of punishment with him, whose will they chose to do. Who then would not be in terror of that lot of eternal tortures? Who would not fear ills, never to be ended? But since severity is denounced with a view to mercy, we must, in these days, live with largeness of mercies, that it may be possible for man, after a perilous negligence, by returning to works of mercy, to be freed from this sentence.'

'ᵗIn that great and supreme Judgement, the kindness of bountifulness and the ungodliness of tenacity shall be so accounted of, that the one should stand for the fulness of all virtues, and the other for the sum of all misdeeds, and by one good the one is

ˢ Ib. c. 2. pp. 31, 32.   ᵗ Id. Serm. x (de coll. v.) c. 3. p. 36.

brought into the kingdom, and by one evil the others are cast into the eternal fire.'

'ᵘ The Word of God, God, the Son of God, Who was in the beginning with God, by Whom all things were made, and without Whom was not any thing made, was made Man, to deliver man from eternal death.'

'ˣ Let not then sinners be so in love with their sins, that the end of this life should overtake them in deeds of sin, because in hell there is no amendment, nor is there any remedy of satisfaction, where there is no longer exercise of will, as the Prophet David says, " For in death who remembereth Thee ; in hell who will give Thee thanks ?"'

76. SALVIAN, A. D. 440. Presbyter of Marseilles, native of Cologne or Trèves.

'ʸThis is a new kind of monster, to wish to provide for any one, only not for one's self. Most unhappy one! Thou art about to go to that holy enquiry, to that terrible and unbearable judgement, where the stranger and anxious soul can have no consolation except only a good conscience, except only an innocent life, or, what is next to a good life, mercy ; where to guilty man there is no help, except a bounteous mind, and fruitful penitence, and large almsgiving, like strong hands ; where, according to the diversity of deserts thou wilt find either the highest good or the deepest evil, either immortal reward, or torment without end. And thou thinkest about enriching what-

ᵘ Serm. 21 (de Nativ. i.) c. 2. p. 65.

ˣ Serm 35 (in Epiph. v.) c. iv. p. 131.

ʸ Against avarice L. iii. 3. There is much more in cc. 11 and 12 but it runs throughout.

ever heirs thou hast, sighest over the wealth of thy relations or connections; whom especially thou shouldest enrich with thy patrimony &c. Of all, most unhappy! Thou thinkest, how well others may live after thee; thou thinkest not, how ill thou thyself diest. Tell me, miserable, faithless man, when thou dividest thy patrimony among many, when thou enrichest many with thy means, deservest thou so ill of thyself alone, that thou givest not thyself a stranger's place among thy heirs? Lo, when thou shalt go forth out of this life, the holy judgement-seat awaits thee, the avenging angels and the terrible ministers of immortal torments await thee, and thou revolvest in thy mind the pleasures of worldly heirs which shall be after thee.'

'ᶻ The whole human race is rushing into eternal pains, in the order which Scripture mentions [Is. 1. 11]: first, he kindleth the fire; then he giveth strength to the fire; lastly he goes into the fire which he had prepared. When then doth man kindle for himself the eternal fire? When he first begins to sin. When does he give strength to the fire? When he heaps sins upon sins. When will he enter the eternal fire? When by the excess of his increasing sins he shall have filled up the irremediable sum of all ills, as the Saviour said to the princes of the Jews, "Fill ye up the measure of your fathers."'

'ᵃ If, according to the Word of God [S. Matt. v.] we are drawn by offences into Gehenna, right is it that we deprive ourselves even of our hands and eyes, that we may avoid Gehenna. But because our attach-

---

ᶻ Salvian de gubernat. Dei L. iv. pp. 75, 76. Baluz.
ᵃ Ib. L. iii. p. 56.

ments to certain domestic services are so necessary to us, that we make use of them as eyes, sometimes also as hands, we rightly withdraw from ourselves the offices of the present ministrations, lest we suffer the torments of eternal fire.'

77. S. PROSPER A.D. 444. '[b] The Lord, who speaketh in the prophet, announces the Day of His judgement; for it was said truly at the beginning of the Psalm, "I will sing to Thee, Lord, of mercy and judgement." Because the time of this world is a time of night and ignorance and tribulation, nor is it known to any one, to what end each shall come; the mercy of God gives place of repentance, and He acts in divers ways, that the just may profit, the fallen may be raised, those averted from Him may be converted. But this longsuffering is granted, while the night still lasts. But when the Day shall have dawned and all hidden things been revealed, the ungodly being separated from the society of the righteous, the evil will be no longer spared, but all the sinners of the earth shall be destroyed; in that morning when it shall be declared what each deserveth.'

'[c] As the preaching of the Cross of Christ was "[d] to some the odour of life to life, to others the odour of death to death," so also those coals [of fire] are of His operation, which can both illumine the faithful and punish sinners. But this punishment of the evil is in the earth, i.e. in this world and in this life, when the fire of temporal punishment falleth upon them, before the eternal fire comes.'

[b] On Ps. c. [ci.] 8.   [c] On Ps. cxxxix. 12 [cxl. 10].
[d] 1 Cor. ii. 16.

'ᵉ When God puts forth His wrath and scourgeth sinners,
He acts, that men may know what they deserve,
For, while the time of mortal flesh continueth,
The scourges themselves bring aid to miserable men,
And a brief vengeance so endeth the noxious crimes,
That the punishment due may not without end seize the guilty.'

78. S. JAMES OF SARUG, A.D. 472. ᶠwrote 'a letter to Stephen bar Zudaili to prove the eternity of Paradise and Gehenna from Scripture and reason.' When Stephen shortly after fell into open heresy,

79. PHILOXENUS of Mabug wrote to Abraham and Orestes, Presbyters of Edessa, to confute him.'

80. FAUSTUS, BISHOP OF RIEZ. A.D. 472; Semi-Pelagian.

'ᵍ Man then will, for deadly ills, die to God and live to Hell. This will be his death, that in his dolour he cannot die.'

'ʰ Whence the very things of earth thou easily despisest, or dispensest them, as one who lends on usury, when thou thinkest of that time, when sinners shall be burned up like stubble, when those who neglected the oblations, in the perpetual fury of the burning Gehenna, whose smoke goeth up for ever and ever, shall be punished by such a death, that in their dolour they may not die, dying to life and living without end to death.'

ᵉ Epigramma v. De ultione Dei.   ᶠ Assem. B. O. T. i. p. 303.
ᵍ Ep. i. ad Ben. Paulinum Bibl. Patr. viii. 551.
ʰ Ep. vi. ad Ruricium Ep. Lemovicensem, Ib. p. 556.

81. S. CÆSARIUS, Archbishop of Arles, A.D. 502. '¹ Consider, brethren, and plead with those who precipitate themselves along the wide and broad way, not with grief only but with fear, telling and protesting to them that, after a brief joy, they will have punishment without end.—Again and again I entreat you, dearest brethren, let us both consider the eternal joy of the just after slight toil, and fear the endless punishment of sinners after a passing gladness.— For as they who, with an unhappy joy, are slaves of avarice or luxury will, the journey on the broad road ended, burn with the devil in hell, so on the contrary, they who despise the false joys of the broad way or luxurious life, when they have finished the course of the narrow, will attain to the society of the angels in heaven.'

82. JULIANUS POMERIUS. 'ᵏ This too, we believe, will be, through the righteous judgement of God, in which the righteous are to be separated from the wicked for ever, not by merits only, but also in place: so that neither should those rewarded come to any end of the reward, nor those condemned, of punishment. Since incorruption and immortality will therefore be given to the bodies of the miserable, that neither should they come to an end of eternal punishment, nor should deathless punishment consume, but punish them. But to this end shall the bodies of the righteous be gifted with a blessed incorruption and immortality, that both they may abide in glory, and eternal glory ever abide in them.'

In a later book, he sums up one of those terrible

---

¹ Hom. 13. Gall. Bibl. Patr. T. xi. p. 20.
ᵏ De vit. contempl. i. 3.

antithetic descriptions of hell, by which they sought of old to scare people from sin, in which he had also dwelt on 'the pain of loss,' '[1] to think what an evil it is, to be shut out from that joy of the contemplation of God, to be deprived of the most blessed society of all the saints, to be banished from the heavenly country, to die to blissful life, to live to eternal death.'

'To think on these and many like things—is nothing else, than to repudiate all vices, and bridle all carnal blandishments. Let us now, from these terrible ills, which shake the minds of the faithful with healthful terror, and lead them away from all vicious delights, and which the lovers of their own pleasures will then prove by the experience of their own damnation, when, what is more miserable than all misery, they will not be able to amend, let us ascend from these sad and terrific ills, to those lofty things, by which the minds who advance rise to the hope of obtaining beatitude, and abjuring earthly things, long for heavenly. And since those who desire to advance begin from a healthful fear, and by advancing attain to charity, let us too, judging what we have written about the fear of beginners to suffice, treat on charity, which He Whose gift it is, shall bestow.'

He too then, like S. Chrysostom, knew that the dread of hell was often the first step towards heaven.

83. S. FULGENTIUS, Bishop of Ruspe in Numidia, A.D. 507. '[m] Eminent for his confession of the faith; abundantly learned in the Holy Scriptures,' twice banished for the faith, and on different occasions the

[1] Ib. iii. 12. 2. [m] S. Isidore de Vir. Ill. c. 35. Opp. vii. 36.

mouth-piece of 60 other Bishops, his co-exiles in Sardinia.

'ⁿ Believe most firmly and in no wise doubt—that in the end of the world the good shall be separated in the body too from the evil; when Christ shall come, having His fan in His hand, and shall " throughly purge His floor, and shall gather the wheat into His garners, but shall burn the chaff with unquenchable fire," when by a just judgement He shall separate the just from the unjust: the good from the evil; the upright from the perverse; when He shall place the good on His right hand, the evil on His left; and the everlasting and unchangeable sentence of a just and eternal judgement having been pronounced by His mouth, all the wicked shall go to eternal burning, but the just to life eternal; the wicked to burn for ever with the devil, and the righteous to reign with Christ for ever.'

I will add one more writer, although of a late date, because he is to the Greeks the representative of all their great fathers, who had been lights of the Church of old.

84. S. JOHN DAMASCENE, A.D. 730. A passage of S. John Damascene has been already cited [o], in proof that it was admissible to hold the eternal fire not to be material, provided that the eternity of punishment was not denied. He repeats the same belief in his Dialogue against the Manichees.

'ᵖ In this life, there is a dispensation and unspeakable Providence, calling sinners to conversion and repentance: but after death there is no longer turning,

[n] De fide ad Petrum c. 43. Bibl. Patr. ix. 83.
[o] de Fide L. iv. fin. above p. 21 [p] Dial. c. Manich. c. 75. i. 460.

no longer repentance, not that God would not accept repentance, for He cannot deny Himself, nor doth He cast away His compassion: but the soul is no longer converted. Wherefore, although any one do all righteousnesses, but, turning, sins and departs from life, longing for sin, he will die in his sin. In like way also the sinner, if he repent and die in his repentance, his sins are remembered no more. For as the dæmons do not repent after their fall, nor do the angels now sin, but both have come to have unchangeableness, so men too after death acquire unchangeableness. And the just, longing for God and always having Him, are in joy; but sinners, longing for sin, and not having the material for sin, devoured, as it were, by fire and worm, are punished, having no consolation whatever. For what is chastisement but privation of what is longed for? According then to the nature of the longing, those who long for God are filled with joy, and those who long for sin, are punished; for those who gain what they long for, are gladdened according to the measure of their longing, and they who miss it, according to the measure of their longing, suffer.'

Strong as the language of S. John Damascene is, that God would accept repentance, it is not stronger than words of Saint Martin, overheard by some of his brethren, and related by S. Martin's contemporary biographer [q].

Some of the brethren attested that they had heard the devil finding fault with Martin in insulting language, 'Why, on their subsequent conversion, he had received within the monastery some of

[q] Sulpicii Severi Vita S. Martini n. 24. Bibl. Patr. vi. 353.

the brethren who by divers errors had formerly forfeited their Baptism?'—detailing the crimes of each: that Martin, contradicting the devil, steadily answered, that old offences were purged by a better life and conversation, and that, by the mercy of the Lord, they who ceased to sin were to be absolved from their sins. When the devil contradicted, 'That criminals had nothing to do with pardon and that no clemency was shewn by the Lord to those who had once lapsed;' Martin is said to have exclaimed thus: 'If thou thyself, thou miserable one, wouldest desist from infesting men and wouldest repent of thy deeds, even now, when the Day of Judgement is nigh at hand, I, truly trusting in the Lord, would promise thee the mercy of Christ.' Satan's answer is not recorded. It must have been obviously one of contempt. In a like history, which I read very recently, but of which I cannot recall the authority, Satan's answer was in great anger, 'Do you think that, if I had meant to repent, I should not have repented long ago?' The history was related by the individual, upon whom Satan had tried to impose.

The controversy of 'restitutionism' turns on this, 'Which knows best the heart of the creature, whom God made and all his life long solicited by His grace, Himself, or some other of His creatures?' It has been the belief of thoughtful loving minds that no one is in Hell, who did not to the very last refuse the grace of God. Dr. Farrar owns, "[r] that it is impossible for us to estimate the hardening effect of obstinate persistence in evil, and the power of the human will to resist the law and reject the love of

[r] Eternal Hope Preface p. xxiv.

God.' How do we know that Almighty God has cast into Hell a single soul, of which He does not know in His absolute knowledge, that, under any circumstances, it would continue to 'resist the law and reject the love of God?' But then it is wasting words about that, of which we know nothing. We know nothing as to, 'who are in Hell;' 'whether on God's terms they would leave it;' 'whether heaven would be heaven to them;' 'whether any thing would replace to them those things, by their preference of which to God, all their lives long to their last breath, they displeased God;' whether the 'æonian fire' would not rather harden those, who did not already love God, and did not long to be punished, because they had offended so good a God. But these would be no inhabitants of hell. It *may be*, then, that Dr. Farrar, amid the vehement language, with which he insists on the necessity of a new 'trial' for those who have *seemingly* failed here, may in part be asking it for millions upon millions who do not need it, in part for those to whom God knows that it would be useless.

It is wisest, surely, to leave all blindly in His Hands, from Whose words Christians, as a body, have received the belief in Hell, ever since He came on earth to redeem us from it. "[s] Just and true are Thy ways, Thou King of Saints." He can reconcile His own attributes, if we abide His time.

It may be useful in conclusion to point out a few characteristics of the body of witnesses alleged, which very probably might not strike persons, who read their words here for the first time.

[s] Rev. xv. 3.

It is very rare if they use argument. Few felt any need of it. They had received their belief as part of their Creed, and mentioned it, as occasion led them. They use the word 'eternal,' when speaking of the punishment of the reprobate, as they do the word 'Almighty' in speaking of 'Almighty God.' They speak of it, as matter not of argument, but of knowledge, as simply and as naturally.

The witnesses are no ordinary witnesses. In the first half of the second century S. Justin, a convert from Platonism, in an Apology for the faith, publicly addressed to the Emperors, pleaded the belief in it, as held by Christians, as a ground for toleration. They who believed in it could not be alleged to be bad subjects [t].

S. Irenæus gives vividly his own early memories ('which grow on,' he says, 'with our soul and are a part of it'). He says, ' [u] I can even tell the place where the blessed Polycarp used to sit and converse; and his goings forth and comings in; and the manner of his life and form of his body; and discourses that he used to make to the people; and his intercourse with John, how he would tell of it, and that with the rest of those who had seen the Lord, and how he would recount their words: and concerning the Lord, what things they were, which he had heard from them, both as to His mighty works and His teaching, as Polycarp, having received them from the eyewitnesses of the Life of the Word, used to recount them, consonantly to the Scriptures. These things did I then too, by the mercy of God which was upon

---

[t] ab. p. 177.
[u] Fragment of the Epistle to Florinus n. 2. Works p. 540 Oxf. Tr.

me, hear diligently; noting them not on paper, but in my own heart, and ever by the grace of God do I ruminate them aright.' Such having been his early youth, he succeeded Pothinus as Bishop of Lyons A.D. 167. He was then personally acquainted with East and West. Yet, giving an account of the Creed [v], as held by many nations of Barbarians too—diligently holding the old Tradition, in his paraphrase of the Creed, he mentions the 'eternal fire.'

When the Creed was explained, 'eternal death' was an article mentioned, as contained in it, by minds as different, as S. Cyril of Jerusalem, or Ruffinus, or S. Maximus with S. Peter Chrysologus. The heathen acknowledged it to be the Christian belief; some, as Celsus, said that their own philosophers taught it as well; others, as those mentioned by Arnobius, ridiculed it, but both attested that it was a part of the Christian faith. It was held in common by those who defended or impugned other faith. S. Athanasius [w] and S. Hilary [x] or the Ebionite [y] author of the Clementines; Eusebius [z], Arians [z], semi-Arians [z], or the worst Arians, but learned men, as Acacius [a]. It was held equally by S. Augustine [b] and Pelagius [c] and semi-Pelagians [d], as Faustus of Riez [e]: by Cassian [f] or by S. Prosper [g] who wrote in detail against one of his works; it was held by those otherwise in active conflict with one another, as S. Jerome [h] and Ruffinus [i]; or again by S. Cyril of Alexandria [k] and

[v] see ab. p. 182.   [w] ab. p. 204.   [x] ab. p. 208.   [y] ab. p. 197.
[z] ab. p. 206.   [a] ab. p. 207.   [b] ab. pp. 245—249.   [c] ab. p. 269.
[d] ab. p. 273.   [e] ab. p. 281.   [f] ab. p. 273.   [g] ab. p. 280.
[h] ab. pp. 238—242.   [i] ab. pp. 243, 244.   [k] ab. p. 270.

Theodoret[1]. Why but because it was part of the Faith written by God's hand upon the soul, the last hold, which God has upon the soul, that it may not finally part with Him; a faith of which such minds as Diderot and Voltaire [m] could not rid themselves?

[1] ab. p. 272.

[m] Quoted in my Sermon 'The Responsibility of intellect in matters of faith' p. 6. The dialogue between Diderot and his soul is so vivid and true to nature, and Voltaire's sarcastic non-acceptance of his correspondent's profession of certainty, so characteristic of his scepticism even as to others' scepticism and his inability to shake off his old faith, that it may be well to repeat them.

Diderot, to his soul. 'If you abuse your reason, you will be unhappy not only in this life, but, after death, in hell.' *Soul.* 'And who told you that there is a hell?' *Diderot.* 'If you have but a doubt, you ought to act as if there were one.' *Soul.* 'And if I am *sure* that there is none?' *Diderot.* 'I defy you to it.'

Voltaire's correspondent. 'I believe, at last, that I have discovered the certainty of the non-existence of hell.' *Voltaire.* 'Most happy are you! I am far from having arrived at it!' The passages are given by Nicolas, 'Études Philosophiques' c. 8, t. 11. 462.

www.ingramcontent.com/pod-product-compliance
Lightning Source LLC
Chambersburg PA
CBHW062001220426
43662CB00010B/1193